THE ARIZONA GUN OWNER'S *Guide*

Who can bear arms?

Where are guns forbidden?

When can you shoot?

by *Alan Korwin*

illustrations by Gregg Myers and Ralph Richardson

BLOOMFIELD PRESS

Scottsdale, AZ

BLOOMFIELD PRESS

4848 E. Cactus #505-440
Scottsdale, AZ 85254
(602) 996-4020 Office
(602) 494-0679 Fax
1-800-707-4020 Order Hotline

gunlaws.com

ISBN-13: 978-1-889632-40-7
Get this as an eBook on Amazon or at GunLaws.com

Photograph of the author by Jeremy Voas

ATTENTION
Clubs, Organizations, Libraries, **Firearms Training Instructors**,
Schools, Educators and all interested parties:
Contact the publisher for wholesale prices!

Every gun owner needs this book—
"It doesn't make sense to own a gun and not know the rules."

NOTE: Was a new law passed yesterday?
Send us a stamped, self-addressed envelope for update information when it becomes available—or just visit our website!

Printed and bound in the United States of America
at United Graphics, LLC, Mattoon, Illinois

26th Edition

TABLE OF CONTENTS

ILLUSTRATIONS

ACKNOWLEDGMENTS

This book is really the result of all the help I received, great and small, from the good people who shared their thoughts and resources with me in 1988 when I got started. Thank you.

Landis Aden, Legislative Liaison,
    Arizona State Rifle and Pistol Association
Terry Allison, President,
    Arizona State Rifle and Pistol Association
Ben Avery, *Arizona Republic* columnist,
    Co-author of Arizona's gun laws
Mark Barnett, Community Relations Officer, Scottsdale Police
Bob Cecil, Protection and Compliance Manager,
    Arizona State Land Department
Bob Corbin, Attorney General, State of Arizona
Nelson E. Ford, Owner, The Gunsmith, Inc.
Howard Gillmore, Assistant Director/Field Services,
    Parks and Recreation
Lt. Colonel Michael Haran, Staff Judge Advocate,
    Arizona Army National Guard
Wayne J. Higgins, Criminal Investigator,
    Bureau of Indian Affairs, Phoenix
Don Jansen, Director, Arizona Legislative Council
Mark Jecker, Public Information Officer,
    Arizona Game and Fish Department
Wes Keys, Information Coordinator,
    Arizona Game and Fish Department
Tony Machukay, Executive Director,
    Arizona Commission on Indian Affairs
Marty Mandall, Owner, Mandall Shooting Supplies, Inc.
Jordan Meschkow, Registered Patent Attorney
Richard B. Oxford, Director, Contract and Records Division,
    Arizona State Land Department
Mary Peterson, NRA Representative
Ron Peterson, Inspector,
    Bureau of Alcohol, Tobacco and Firearms, Phoenix Branch
Ruth Peterson, Secretary to the Forest Supervisor,
    U.S. Forestry Service
Bob Reyes, Park Operations Specialist, National Park Service
Robert J. Spillman, Attorney at Law
Paul Stearns, Police Officer, Scottsdale Police Department

Deborah Stevens, Public Affairs Specialist,
    Bureau of Land Management
Russell Vanden Wolf, Inspector,
    Bureau of Alcohol, Tobacco and Firearms, Phoenix Branch
Ken Wagner, Chief of Operations Section, Arizona State Parks
Pete Weinel, Assistant Recreation/Wilderness Staff,
    U.S. Forest Service

This list would be incomplete without the friends who have been
supportive, informative, and whose time and thoughts made a real
difference: Harvey and Eileen Barish, Linda Brott, Steve Cascone,
Crosby!, Candice DeBarr, Adam Mohney, Gregg Myers, Bill Plummer,
Curt Prickett, Dan and Mary Sharayko, Pete Slater, Mary Westheimer
and Howard White.

The National Rifle Association Institute allowed the use of material in
their pamphlet, "Your State Firearms Laws."

For the first edition of this book, March 1989:
Illustrations by Gregg Myers
Book design by Ralph Richardson
Edited by Howard White
Proofread by Candice DeBarr
Typesetting by Mesa Graphics, Inc.
Digital disk transfers by Code Busters

For the re-plated eleventh edition of this book, June 1994:
Document scans and OCR by Directional Data, Inc.
Proofread by Toni Joyce
Typesetting, editing and updated design by the author
Legislative and update assistance by Landis Aden,
Michael P. Anthony, John Gilbert, Gwen Henson, Jim Norton,
Edward J. Owen, Ted Parod and Richard Twitchell

◆

Revised and Expanded 18th Edition, Sept. 1997
This is the 26th Edition, 2015

The people who have contributed to this book since it first appeared in
1989 (when the acknowledgments list was made) are too numerous to
mention. You know who you are. Thank you.
And thank you Arizona, you've been good to me.

PREFACE

Arizona has strict gun laws. You have to obey the laws.
There are serious penalties for breaking the rules.

Many gun owners don't know all the rules.
Some have the wrong idea of what the rules are.
It doesn't make sense to own a gun and not know the rules.

Here at last is a comprehensive book, in plain English,
about the laws and regulations concerning firearms in Arizona.

This book is published under the full protection of the
First Amendment with the expressed understanding that you,
not we, are completely responsible for your own actions.

The One-Glaring-Error theory says there's at least
one glaring error hidden in any complex piece of work.
This book is no different. Watch out for it.

"It will be of little avail to the people that the laws are made by men of their own choice, if the laws be so voluminous that they cannot be read, or so incoherent that they cannot be understood; if they be repealed or revised before they are promulgated, or undergo such incessant changes that no man who knows what the law is to-day can guess what it will be to-morrow." –James Madison, *The Federalist Papers, #62*

"Do you really think that we want those laws to be observed? We want them broken. We're after power and we mean it. There's no way to rule innocent men. The only power any government has is the power to crack down on criminals. Well, when there aren't enough criminals, one makes them. One declares so many things to be a crime that it becomes impossible for men to live without breaking laws. Who wants a nation of law-abiding citizens? What's there in that for anyone? But just pass the kind of laws that can neither be observed nor enforced nor objectively interpreted, and you create a nation of law breakers—and then you cash in on guilt." –Ayn Rand *(Atlas Shrugged)*

FOREWORD • WARNING! • DON'T MISS THIS!

This book is not "the law," and is not a substitute for the law. The law includes all the legal obligations imposed on you, a much greater volume of work than the mere firearms statutes contained in this book. You are fully accountable under the exact wording and current official interpretations of all applicable laws, regulations, court precedents, executive orders and more, when you deal with firearms under any circumstances.

Many people find laws hard to understand, and gathering all the relevant ones is a lot of work. This book helps you with these chores. Collected in one volume are copies, reporduced with great care, of the principal state laws controlling gun use in Arizona.

In addition, the laws and other regulations are expressed in regular conversational terms for your convenience, and cross referenced to the statutes. While great care has been taken to accomplish this with a high degree of accuracy, **no guarantee of accuracy is expressed or implied, and the explanatory sections of this book are not to be considered as legal advice or a restatement of law.** In explaining the general meanings of the laws, using plain English, differences inevitably arise, so **you must always check the actual laws**. Only edited pieces of the laws are included here. The author and publisher expressly disclaim any liability whatsoever arising out of reliance on information contained in this book. New laws and regulations may be enacted at any time by the authorities. **The author and publisher make no representation that this book includes all requirements and prohibitions that may exist**. Local ordinances, rules, regulations and policies are not covered.

This book concerns the gun laws as they apply to law-abiding private residents in the state of Arizona only. It is not intended to and does not describe most situations relating to licensed gun dealers, museums or educational institutions, local or federal military personnel, American Indians, foreign nationals, the police or other peace officers, any person summoned by a peace officer to help in the performance of official duties, persons with special licenses (including collectors), posse members, non-residents, persons with special authorizations or permits, bequests or intestate succession, persons under indictment, felons, prisoners, escapees, dangerous or repetitive offenders, criminal street gang members, delinquent, incorrigible or unsupervised juveniles, judicial officers, government employees, or any other people restricted or prohibited from firearm possession.

While this book discusses possible criminal consequences of improper gun use, it avoids most issues related to deliberate gun crimes. This means certain laws are excluded, or not explained in the text. Some examples are: 1st degree murder; 2nd degree murder; homicide; manslaughter; gun theft; gun running; concealment of stolen firearms; enhanced penalties for commission of crimes with firearms, including armed robbery, burglary, theft, kidnapping, drug offenses, assault and priors; smuggling firearms into public aircraft; threatening flight attendants with firearms; possession of contraband; gun shoplifting, possession of a firearm in a prison by a prisoner; false application for a firearm; shooting at a building as part of a criminal street gang; removal of a body after a shooting; drive by shootings; retaliation; and this is only a partial list.

The main relevant parts of Arizona statutes that relate to guns are reproduced in Appendix D. These are formally known as *Arizona Revised Statutes,* and are mostly found in *Title 13, Criminal Code.* Other state laws that may apply in some cases, and official agency regulations, are discussed but may not be reproduced. Key federal laws are discussed, but the laws themselves are *not* reproduced. Case law decisions, which affect the interpretation of the statutes, are generally *not* included.

FIREARMS LAWS ARE SUBJECT TO CHANGE WITHOUT NOTICE. You are strongly urged to consult with a qualified attorney and local authorities to determine the current status and applicability of the law to specific situations you may encounter. A list of the proper authorities appears in Appendix C.

Guns are deadly serious business and require the highest level of responsibility from you. Firearm ownership, possession and use are rights that carry awesome responsibility. Unfortunately, **what the law says and what the authorities and courts do aren't always an exact match.** You must remember that each legal case is different and may lack prior court precedents. A decision to prosecute a case and the charges brought may involve a degree of discretion from the authorities involved. Sometimes, there just isn't a plain, clear-cut answer you can rely upon. Abuses, ignorance, carelessness, human frailties and plain fate subject you to legal risks, which can be exacerbated when firearms are involved. Take nothing for granted, recognize that legal risk is attached to everything you do, and **ALWAYS ERR ON THE SIDE OF SAFETY.**

Special Note on Pending Legislation

Many new bills have been proposed by legislators who would:
- Outlaw specific or classes of firearms by price range, melting point, operating characteristics, accuracy, type of safety mechanism, type of sights, point of origin, appearance, caliber and by name.
- Restrict the amount of ammunition a gun can hold, devices for feeding ammunition, allowable types of ammunition, or reduce ammo shelf life
- Restrict the number of firearms and the amount of ammunition a person may buy or own, and implement burdensome storage requirements
- Require proficiency testing and periodic licensing with expiration dates
- Register firearms and owners nationally
- Use taxation as a way to limit firearm and ammunition ownership
- Create new liabilities for firearm owners, manufacturers, dealers, parents and persons involved in firearms accidents
- Require firearms to be unloaded, locked away or otherwise inoperable
- Censor classified ads for firearms, eliminate firearms publications and outlaw any dangerous speech or publication
- Melt down firearms that are confiscated by police
- Prohibit gun shows and abolish hunting
- Deny or criminalize civil rights for government-promised security
- Adopt standards from countries that don't recognize the right to arms
- Require technologies that don't exist or cannot be economically used
- Repeal or flatly ignore the Second Amendment to the U.S. Constitution

In contrast, less attention has been paid to laws that would:
- Mandate public-school-based safety training
- Provide general self-defense awareness and training
- Encourage personal responsibility in resisting crime
- Protect and honor citizens who stand up and act against crime
- Guarantee people's right to travel legally armed for personal safety
- Fix the conditions that generate hard-core criminals
- Assure sentencing of serious criminals, increase the percentage of sentences that are actually served, provide more prison space and permanently remove habitual criminals from society
- Improve rehabilitation and reduce repeat offenses
- Reduce plea bargaining and parole abuses
- Close legal loopholes and reform criminal justice malpractice
- Reform the juvenile justice system
- Improve law enforcement quality and efficiency
- Establish and strengthen victims' rights and protection
- Hold the rights of all American citizens in unassailable esteem
- Provide for the common defense and buttress the Constitution

Some experts believe that easy-to-enact but ineffectual "feel good" laws are being pursued instead of the much tougher course of laws and social changes that would reduce crime and its root causes. Many laws aim at disarming citizens while ignoring the fact that gun possession by criminals is already strictly illegal and largely unenforced. Increasing attacks on the Constitution and civil liberties are threatening freedoms Americans have always had. You are advised to become aware of any new laws that may be enacted. Contact your legislators to express your views on proposed legislation.

To my wife Cheryl,
my daughter Tyler,
my brother Richard,
and my parents.

THE RIGHT TO KEEP AND BEAR ARMS 1

In the United States of America, people have always had the right to keep arms, and the right to bear arms. The Second Amendment to the United States Constitution is the national guarantee for this preexisting human right to have and use arms. The Second Amendment protects The Right To Keep And Bear Arms. This is what it says:

> "A well regulated Militia, being necessary to the security of a free State, the right of the people to keep and bear Arms, shall not be infringed."

The intentions of the revolutionaries who drafted the Constitution were clear at the time. It was this right to arms that allowed those citizens 200 years ago to break away from British rule. An armed populace was a necessity for the right of self defense and was a precondition for freedom and independence from oppressive government. The founders of our nation were unambiguous and unequivocal in their intent:

No free man shall be debarred the use of arms.
–Thomas Jefferson

The Constitution shall never be construed to authorize Congress to prevent the people of the United States, who are peaceable citizens, from keeping their own arms.
–Samuel Adams

Little more can reasonably be aimed at with respect to the people at large than to have them properly armed.
–Alexander Hamilton

Americans have the right and advantage of being armed.
–James Madison

The great object is that every man be armed.
Everyone who is able may have a gun.
–Patrick Henry

Today the issue is controversial and emotionally charged. There are
powerful and vocal groups on all sides of the topic of guns. Some
people who would like to see the American public disarmed have
called for repeal of the Second Amendment, and claim it is outdated.
The U.S. Supreme Court has heard more than 100 gun-related cases,
and contrary to "news" reports, has recognized an individual right to
arms consistently for two centuries. The 2008 landmark *D.C. v. Heller*
decision unequivocally recognized it as a "specific enumerated right"
of individuals, on a par with the right to counsel and free speech. The
decision discarded the revisionist "collective rights" theory invented to
attack this fundamental liberty. The subsequent *McDonald v. Chicago*
case in 2010 made it clear that the states were obligated to obey the
Second Amendment, though some have been resisting that as hard as
they can. Importantly, all 50 states recognize an individual's right to
act in self defense, completely apart from firearms debates.

The Second Amendment of course means what it always used to
mean, which explains the armed populace we observe today. This is
also seen in the fact that 43 states have the right to keep arms and the
right to bear arms imbedded in their own Constitutions, often in terms
more direct than the wording in the Bill of Rights itself. If our Second
Amendment guarantee was ever torn asunder, the state Constitutions
would remain. Arizona has this to say (we became a state in 1912):

Excerpt from the Constitution of the State of Arizona
Section 26. Bearing Arms.

"The right of the individual citizen to bear arms in defense
of himself or the state shall not be impaired, but nothing in
this section shall be construed as authorizing individuals or
corporations to organize, maintain, or employ an armed
body of men."

Nothing in Arizona law may conflict with the U.S. Constitution, and so
the right to keep and bear arms is guarded for Arizonans, as it should
be for the people of all the states in the union. The states, however,
exercising their police powers, have passed laws that regulate the arms
people bear within their borders. That's what this book is about.

WELCOME TO THE STATE GUN LAWS

The majority of the Arizona "gun laws" (they are never actually called that) are in a book called, *Arizona Revised Statutes, Title 13, Criminal Code.* Widely available in libraries and online, a complete printed copy is also available from Lexis Nexis at 1-800-223-1940. You'll find the main relevant sections of the state gun laws printed in *The Arizona Gun Owner's Guide* in Appendix D. Many of the fine details about guns come from other sources, listed in Appendix C. Though people may tend to focus on Title 13, Arizona has gun laws in at least 15 other titles of state code, and all are covered in this book:

Title 4	Alcoholic Beverages
Title 8	Children
Title 9	Cities and Towns
Title 11	Counties
Title 12	Courts and Civil Proceedings
Title 13	Criminal Code
Title 15	Education
Title 17	Game and Fish
Title 26	Military Affairs & Emergency Mgmt.
Title 28	Transportation
Title 32	Professions and Occupations
Title 33	Property
Title 36	Public Safety
Title 38	Public Officers and Employees
Title 41	State Government

It's important to remember that "the law" includes many things that are not statutes passed by the legislature, and may not be covered in detail in this book. The law is also found in court decisions, official regulations, common law, civil law, bureaucratic policies at state and federal levels and more. *Guns have become so heavily regulated that it strains the ability of an average person to know all the requirements.*

A Word About Federal Law

The Arizona Gun Owner's Guide covers federal laws that are directly related to your right to keep and bear arms. This is only a small portion of the more than 94,000 words of federal gun law. For an unabridged edition of federal firearms statutes, with plain English summaries of each law, get *Gun Laws of America,* listed in the back of this book.

Federal law generally does not control day-to-day details of carrying a firearm in a state, or the rules for self defense and crime resistance, or where you can target practice. The several states control these things. Federal law focuses on commercial aspects, interstate transportation, prohibited weapons, people prohibited from bearing arms, arming the "proper authorities," regulating the dealer network, crimes against the nation, armed federal forces and other specifically defined areas.

Many people think federal laws are "higher" than state laws, or they come first. In fact, federal and state laws control different things. This is guaranteed by the 10th Amendment to the U.S. Constitution: "The powers not delegated to the United States by the Constitution, nor prohibited by it to the States, are reserved to the States respectively, or to the people." That's complicated by the apparent discrepancy with Article VI of the Constitution, in the so-called supremacy clause: "This Constitution, and the Laws of the United States... shall be the supreme law of the land."). Frequent disagreement plagues where the lines are.

The Dreaded "§" Section Symbol:
Arizona Revised Statutes § 13-3102

The character "§" means "section." You read it aloud (or to yourself) as "section" whenever it appears. Practically every chunk of law in America is called a section and has a section number, so you see this symbol a lot. It's an integral part of the written name for every statute on the books. A section may be just a few words or extremely long, and it may be amended by new laws. Criminal Code section thirteen thirty one oh two (§13-3102) is one of Arizona's main gun laws.

The section "§" symbol intimidates many people and as such, is valuable for keeping the law mysterious and somehow unknowable to the general public. Don't let it scare you. Just think "section" whenever you see "§." To write a section symbol, make a capital "S" on top of another capital "S." Each section of Arizona gun law noted in the text is in Appendix D in numerical order.

To make a "section" symbol
draw an "S" over another "S"

REASONS FOR ARIZONA'S GUN LAWS

Arizona criminal law begins with a list of reasons for its existence (§13-101 et seq.), all of which impact gun ownership and use:

1–To prohibit conduct that might harm people;

2–To give fair warning of conduct that is against the law and the penalties involved;

3–To define the acts that are crimes and to limit condemnation of behavior that isn't criminal;

4–To organize crimes by how bad they are, and to match the penalty to the crime;

5–To discourage crime by authorizing punishment;

6–To mete out punishment;

7–To promote truth and accountability in sentencing;

8–To identify and remove from society people whose conduct repeatedly threatens public safety.

WHAT IS A FIREARM?

In Arizona, a firearm is generally defined as a *deadly weapon,* a term that includes anything designed for lethal use. Specifically, §13-3101 of state law says *firearm* means:

> "...any loaded or unloaded handgun, pistol, revolver, rifle, shotgun or other weapon that will expel, is designed to expel or may readily be converted to expel a projectile by the action of an explosive. Firearm does not include a firearm in permanently inoperable condition."

This definition is used in connection with Chapter 31, Weapons and Explosives, in Arizona's criminal code, where the CCW and other main gun laws reside. The *permanently inoperable* phrase applies primarily to antique or collectible guns that have been thoroughly disabled and are only for show. Questions about how to make a specific gun unserviceable can be directed to the Firearms Technology Branch of the Bureau of Alcohol, Tobacco, Firearms and Explosives.

Federal law excludes a long list of curio and relic guns, antiques made in or before 1898, and modern replicas of them, from its general definition of guns. Arizona law however is more restrictive, and all antique, replica, curio, relic and similar firearms capable of firing (or that can be modified to fire) are treated as ordinary guns here.

The phrase *action of an explosive* is commonly understood to mean "gunpowder" of some sort, which these days is typically a non-explosive smokeless powder propellant, contained in a cartridge of ammunition, for most modern arms. In a notable paradox in state law, the official definition of *explosive* used in this section specifically excludes all components of ammunition (so ammunition does not get lumped together with explosives laws). The very thing that defines a firearm is excluded from the definition. Yes, it's confusing.

Black powder guns and muzzle loaders in general do use the explosive that used to be called gunpowder, namely black powder (or modern-day equivalent powders), which have their own specific storage, transportation, handling, fire code and other requirements.

In this book, the words *gun* and *firearm* are used interchangeably, and include handguns, aka sidearms (pistols and revolvers), and long guns (rifles and shotguns) as defined under §13-3101 (it expels the projectile by "the action of an explosive"). When you see the terms *handgun, rifle, shotgun, long gun, semi-automatic pistol* or *semiauto,* or *revolver,* the reference is to that specific type of firearm only. *Arms,* the word used in the Second Amendment, is the most inclusive term, including edged weapons and more.

For purposes other than Weapons and Explosives laws in Chapter 31 of the Criminal Code, §13-105 says *firearm* means:

> "...any loaded or unloaded pistol, revolver, rifle, shotgun or other weapon which will or is designed to or may readily be converted to expel a projectile by the action of expanding gases, except that it does not include a firearm in permanently inoperable condition."

The key difference is the phrase *action of expanding gases.* This describes air pressure mechanisms or compressed carbon dioxide, as used in a wide category of "nearly" guns, and distinct from the "action of an explosive." It includes many *BB, pellet* or *dart guns,* some of which are powerful enough for hunting, or accurate enough for international competitions.

In a notable paradox in state law, the phrase *action of expanding gases* can also be understood to include the action of gunpowder or its more common propellant substitutes, or even explosives. At some point the legislature will have to step in and make sure the rules are clear and uniformly understood.

The Official State Firearm

In 2011, following the example set by Utah, which declared the John M. Browning-designed classic M1911-model .45-caliber sidearm as its official state firearm, Arizona established the Colt Single-Action Army Revolver as our official state firearm, in a new statute, §41-860.02. This was a tougher legislative battle than anyone expected, but it found a place of honor in our laws for a firearm that won the West.

"Nearly" Guns—BB, Airsoft, Paintball and Similar

BB-type guns are not firearms for the purposes of the misconduct-with-weapons laws, because the projectile is not propelled by an explosive (§13-3101), but can be treated as firearms under other laws, e.g., in, assault, disorderly conduct, aggravation, etc., since the projectile is powered by the action of expanding gasses (§13-105). Basic safety requires that you give the various "nearly" guns the care and respect you would for regular firearms. Unscrupulous prosecutors could use this confusion in the law to selectively harm people and it needs a fix.

A step down from BB-type guns is the category of *toy gaming guns*, often used for playing "tag." These include paintball and airsoft guns, using compressed CO_2, or battery or hand-powered piston action to compress air. They are not traditionally viewed as firearms, but are serious toys and should be used with care and safety precautions such as goggles and protective clothing. Adult supervision is required (§13-3107) for all use of "air or carbon dioxide gas operated" guns within city limits.

The offense of discharge of a firearm within city limits "does not apply if the firearm is discharged...On a properly supervised range...For the purposes of this section...'Properly supervised range' means a range that is...Operated with adult supervision for shooting air or carbon dioxide gas operated guns, or for shooting in underground ranges on private or public property" (§13-3107), and "officials" have been known to ignore or bend this rule if they think behavior should cease.

The nearly-gun issue continues to grow, with the introduction of the TASER-brand electronic-control device. Regulated in 2005 under §13-3117 as an *authorized remote stun gun* (ARSG) they are now available for sale to the public in Arizona and some other states, and to officials in 107 countries. The stringent requirements enacted for such products can be found in Chapter 3. Rumors that a Class 3 Officer's Phaser will be on the market soon are unsubstantiated.

Airsoft and other designs are often precise replicas of popular firearms and virtually identical at a quick glance, so care must be taken to avoid giving the impression they are real. Don't panic the neighbors. And remember, people have been shot for brandishing nearly guns.

Toy Guns

Cap guns are regulated under fireworks laws (§36-1601 et. seq.), may not exceed one-quarter grain of explosive compound, and must be designed so a hand cannot come into contact with the cap when it is positioned for explosion.

Federal toy-gun laws since 1988 have required a blaze orange plug of at least 6mm in the muzzle of certain toys, except for theater, movie and TV use, or as modified by the Secretary of Commerce. Toy, look-alike and imitation guns, including water guns as federally defined (yes, the feds define water guns), specifically exclude traditional BB, paintball or pellet air guns. The sale of BB-type air guns or certain non-firing replicas have federal protection that even real firearms do not presently enjoy—states are specifically prohibited from banning sales, under 15 USC §5001. The government is authorized to study the criminal misuse of toy guns and the effectiveness of the marking systems in police combat situations. The initial study was due in 1989.

Non-Guns

No consistent legal status for non-guns has surfaced in the state. These include gun drawings, pointed-finger guns, gun-t-shirts, gun bumper stickers and slogans, twig guns, gun speech and the notorious brandished chicken leg. These are used primarily by schools to threaten, harass and intimidate students, for expulsions, suspensions, reprimands, demerits, derision, scorn, and reportedly in some cases, anti-rights bigotry directed at the public, and letters to parents.

Up until the 1970s, many high schools had shooting ranges on campus and kids brought guns to school for competition, got varsity letters in marksmanship, went to ROTC or hunting after class, and even brought guns and ammo for show and tell. Today we find a system that has vilified these vital exemplars of freedom out of the school experience. We remind readers, or anyone who might be tempted to ban a person from speech about the "specific enumerated right" to arms, that denial of a person's civil rights under color of law is a federal felony, under 18 USC §241 et.seq., and carries prison time and a fine.

Fireworks

Many fireworks (listed in §36-1601) that use small amounts of explosive compounds, are no longer banned for the public as of 2011, with permits available for large public displays. Fireworks are a gunpowder-type toy, tangentially attached to the broad right to arms. Some people have been known to enjoy the dangerous art and science of making their own fireworks, cautious to not run afoul of bomb-making law and properly managing the very serious risks involved, using commercially available powders and other supplies.

By repealing the ban on sale of consumer fireworks, the state created jobs, sales-tax revenue, economic stimulus, and colorful sales outlets statewide. However, to pass the law, it had to allow cities and towns to ban the use on basically fire-hazard grounds, and most cities chose to do so. Fireworks can only be sold within 30 days of two holidays, and by and large, the ban on use (a class 3 misdemeanor and possible fines), is ignored around July Fourth and New Year's, as your ears and one sniff of air will tell you. Public lands are banned as well, often under federal jurisdiction. *The fire hazard and need for caution is very real especially here in Arizona.* Causing damage creates serious liability for you. Using fireworks gives people experience in dealing with things that are dangerous, a useful skill to develop, and one that is becoming more rare.

Industry standards specify what types are legal, and in plain English include: Snappers, snap caps, party poppers, glow worms, snakes, toy smoke devices, ground and handheld sparkling devices, cylindrical fountains, cone fountains, illuminating torches, wheels, ground spinners, flitter sparklers, toy smoke devices, wire sparklers or dipped sticks, multiple tube fireworks devices and pyrotechnic articles.

Classic exploding noisemakers like firecrackers, ash cans, M80s and cherry bombs, or anything that is designed to rise into the air and explode or to fly above the ground, including bottle rockets, sky rockets, missile-type rockets, helicopters, torpedoes, roman candles, jumping jacks and similar are banned. Dealers only get deliveries of legal-for-sale items, so don't worry.

Knives

The Second Amendment protects *arms*, which include things with blades—a cavalry sword in revolutionary times was crucial because it didn't need reloading. State law addresses knives designed for lethal use (e.g., a bayonet), the same as other *deadly weapons*. Other knives are treated as *dangerous instruments* (e.g. a baseball bat or kitchen knife) that can be used lethally but aren't designed for such use.

Pocket knives per se are excluded from the main weapon laws, are not defined beyond the common meaning of the term, and no blade length is specified (though federal facilities have a 2-1/2-inch blade limit). For a more complete discussion, including switchblades, see the federal rules found in Chapter 7. Arizona became the first state in the union to enact a knife preemption law, §13-3120, that protects people by stopping local authorities from passing their own knife rules.

As of 2010, only the state can make laws about transport, possession, carry, sale, transfer, purchase, gift, devise, licensing, registration or use of knives or knife-making components, and any existing local rules are voided (which some local LEOs may not be aware of at first). Officials below the state level can make knife rules for their employees, but only consistent with state law, and any excess is null and void.

Arizona also breaks new ground by defining a knife comprehensively and simply, a model other states are looking at: "a cutting instrument and includes a sharpened or pointed blade." Constitutional Carry protects knife possession the same as it does for firearms. Arizona does not ban ownership, possession or legal use of any bladed instruments, including knives that can be opened with one hand.

WHO CAN BEAR ARMS IN ARIZONA?

An adult resident of Arizona is free to have guns unless:

1–You have been found to be dangerous to yourself or other people by a court of law, unless the courts have restored your rights;

2–You have been convicted of a felony or judged a delinquent, and your civil rights have not been fully restored, for out-of-state convictions see §13-105;

3–You are serving a term of imprisonment in any correctional or detention facility;

4–You are on probation for a domestic violence or felony conviction, parole, community supervision, work furlough, home arrest, or other form of early release program;

5–You are an "undocumented alien" or a "nonimmigrant alien" traveling under specified conditions, with exceptions for specified sporting pursuits and for diplomats.

Arizona law calls these people *prohibited possessors*, with precise definitions in §13-3101. Knowingly selling or transferring a deadly weapon or ammunition to a prohibited possessor is a class 6 felony. Having a deadly weapon or ammo if you are a prohibited possessor is a class 4 felony. Providing a deadly weapon for use in a felony, or having or using one in terrorism is a class 2 felony. See §13-3102 for the letter of the law. While you are a defendant under a court order of protection in a domestic violence case a court can suspend your right to arms (see §13-3602).

Local authorities can appoint police aides and private contractors with authority for vehicle parking violations, traffic investigations and to serve certain legal papers. Under §28-627, these individuals must be unarmed while on duty. No such blanket infringement of rights, based on job description, is known to exist anywhere else in the law. Employers sometimes require people to relinquish the right to arms while at work, as a condition of employment. Authority for denying your rights in this manner is unclear. In 2001, the state's referral system for child-care home providers was modified to allow exclusion of providers who don't store firearms and ammunition separately and under a key or combination lock. In 2002, weapons were banned for terrorists (§13-3102). In 2009, a law barred employers from banning guns in their parking lots, if in locked vehicles, with exceptions, see *Guns in Cars*).

The Federal Prohibited Possessors List

In addition to state requirements, you may also be prohibited from firearm possession under federal laws designed to keep weapons out of the hands of criminals and certain others (18 USC §922(g)). These overriding restrictions are listed in Section 8 of the Firearm Transaction Record, form 4473, which must be completed when you buy a gun at retail from a federally licensed dealer. Federal law prohibits having, shipping, transporting or receiving a gun by anyone who:

- Is charged with or has been convicted of a crime that carries more than a one-year sentence (except for state misdemeanors with up to a two-year sentence);
- Is a fugitive from justice;
- Unlawfully uses or is addicted to marijuana, a depressant, a stimulant or a narcotic drug;
- Is mentally defective;
- Is mentally incompetent;
- Is committed to a mental institution;
- Has been dishonorably discharged from the armed forces;
- Has renounced U.S. citizenship;
- Is an illegal alien;
- Is here under a nonimmigrant visa, with exceptions for certain hunting, sporting, diplomatic and official purposes (§922(y)(2)
- Is under a court order restraining harassment, stalking or threatening of an intimate partner or partner's child;
- Has been convicted of a domestic-violence misdemeanor as described by federal law (for more on this 1996 addition to federal law see Chapter 7).

When filling out a Firearm Transaction Record form, you must state that you are not in these categories. Making false statements on the form is a five-year federal felony, and it's illegal to knowingly provide firearms to a prohibited possessor.

Keep in mind that the right to bear firearms isn't the right to bear anything, anywhere, at any time. Nor is it the right to organize a body of armed individuals.

Domestic Violence Cases

Under state law, domestic violence refers basically to crimes against children, or disorderly conduct, criminal damage, kidnap, trespass, assault or aggravated harassment among family members, as described in §13-3601. In 2009 this was expanded to include people in a loosely defined romantic or sexual relationship. If domestic violence involves shooting, using or the threatening display of a deadly weapon, the police are obliged to make an arrest.

As of 1996, in a domestic-violence case, if a peace officer learns, by asking or observing, that a firearm is present, the officer may seize the weapon if it's in plain sight or was found with a consent to search. The officer must also reasonably believe that the firearm poses a serious risk to the victim or another household member. A firearm owned or possessed by the victim may not be seized unless there is probable cause to believe that both parties committed domestic violence.

When seized, the peace officer must provide a detailed receipt, identifying each firearm taken. All such guns must be held by the agency that took them for at least 72 hours. Before a firearm may be released, the victim must be notified by a peace officer. If there's reason to believe that returning a firearm would endanger the victim, the person who reported the threat, or another household member, the prosecutor must file a court order to retain the firearm for up to six months. §13-3601 describes how to appeal an order, and if successful, the firearms must be returned. Under §13-3602, a court protection order can require confiscating all guns from a defendant, and prohibit any gun purchases or possession while the order is in effect. This was made mandatory in 1998, if the court decides the defendant poses a credible threat to the safety of people named in the order. A court-issued emergency order of protection (§13-3624) may prohibit a person from purchasing or possessing a gun for the order's duration.

Following the passage of Arizona's domestic violence laws, the federal government enacted *ex post facto* (retroactive) domestic violence measures, described in Chapter 7.

Security Guards

Anyone acting as a security guard or operating a security guard agency must first obtain a registration certificate from the Dept. of Public Safety. Applicants must be citizens or legal residents of the United

States, with clean criminal records, and other requirements spelled out beginning in §32-2422. Any felony conviction, a misdemeanor conviction for misconduct with weapons in the past five years, or a conviction for impersonating an armed guard are grounds for disqualification. The authorization lasts for three years.

Guard agencies must provide training to their guards, and a minimum of 16 hours of firearms training are required for any guards who will be armed in the course of their work. The training must be conducted by a DPS-certified instructor under DPS rules, and must be successfully completed before the guard may be armed. The person must also be registered as an armed guard, authorized by the employer to be armed, and visibly display an official ID card while on duty. (§32-2624)

Security guards are not law enforcement officers, and may not act in ways, carry badges, wear uniforms or have insignias that could deceive the public into thinking they are law enforcement officers or connected with a government agency (though approved uniforms and accessories are allowed). Any duties performed by a security guard are performed in the capacity of a private citizen. A violation of the security guard statutes, which includes giving the impression you are one if you're not (§13-2611), is a class 1 misdemeanor. (§32-2637)

A company that has armed guards exclusively for its own use is exempt from most of these requirements as long as the guards receive an initial 16 hours of training and an 8-hour annual refresher (§32-2606). Also exempt from the security-guard laws are Arizona Rangers on duty for 501(c)(3) non-profit organizations. (§32-2606)

Active-duty, off-duty and retired law enforcement officers were granted the ability to bear arms nationwide, with restrictions, under a federal law in 2004, 18 USC §926B and C, known as LEOSA, giving police Second Amendment rights the public is supposed to have but does not.

Armed Nuclear Security Guards

A new guard category was added in 2005 for Nuclear Regulatory Commission certified armed guards for nuclear generating stations. These guards have different standards for use of deadly force, spelled out in §§13-4901 to 13-4904, which allows them more latitude to use deadly force to defend the plant if they "reasonably believe" it is necessary to prevent commission of a long list of serious felonies. The guards also have expanded powers of detention, and immunity from certain liabilities if they are acting within the scope of their duties.

Specified Court Officers

Certain court officers may carry firearms in court facilities where they work, if they've shown competence with a firearm as described in the CCW law, and they comply, while in the facility, with any rule or policy of the presiding judge of the Superior Court. This literally gave some gun-law-making capacity to presiding judges in 2014, for people under their command, without legislative oversight, a dangerous new power completely without precedent. (§13 3102)

Private Armies

It's a class 5 felony for any person, partnership or corporation to maintain armed troops, but a business, plant or firm can maintain armed guards for protection of their property from damage or loss. This law also allows forming a state police or highway patrol, or the existence of county and municipal police forces and sheriff's posses.

POSSESSION OF FIREARMS BY MINORS

The first law for parents to remember nowadays is, any time your child goes shooting with you or without you, the child must carry written permission from you. Even if you're right there with your child. That's the net effect of a Clinton-era federal gun law (18 USC §922x) that regulates children.

In Arizona, since 1994, a minor generally can only have or use a firearm if accompanied by a parent, grandparent or guardian. Detailed exceptions are listed below and under *Hunting Regulations* in Chapter 6. Prior to 1994, minors were banned from purchasing firearms, but were basically unregulated concerning possession in Arizona as long as criminal activity wasn't involved. Many people fondly remember getting their first .22 rifle by age ten. That approach broke down with the national rise of hard-core gangs, and ruthless children committing brazen acts of violence, in defiance of every law ever enacted.

Giving or selling a gun, ammunition, or even a toy gun that can expel dangerous and explosive substances to a minor, without written consent from the minor's parent or legal guardian, is a class 6 felony. With consent from a parent or guardian, minors are free to accept temporary transfer of firearms and ammunition by instructors, coaches or their assistants, for competition, courses or training, along with temporary transfer by adults accompanying minors for hunting or target practice. See §13-3109 for the letter of the law.

The following rules from §13-3111 had been invalidated by the courts (because they only applied in Pima and Maricopa counties) but were reinstated in 2006 by applying the law statewide. For this law, people under 18 who are unemancipated are minors. Minors can knowingly carry or possess firearms on themselves, or within their immediate control, or in a means of transportation, in any public place, street or private property, *only* if the minor is with a certified instructor, parent, grandparent, guardian or acting with a parent or guardian's permission.

The minor can also knowingly carry or possess on private property owned or leased by the minor, the minor's parent, grandparent or guardian. Violation by a minor is a class 6 felony. This restriction does not apply to people 14 to 17 who are:

• Legally hunting, or

• Transporting an unloaded gun to legally hunt, or

• At a shooting event or marksmanship practice at an established shooting range or at other areas where shooting is not prohibited, or transporting an unloaded gun to such places between 5 a.m. and 10 p.m., or

• In need of a firearm related to the production of crops, livestock, poultry, ratites (ostrich-like birds), or similar agricultural pursuits.

Minors violating these rules are subject to sanctions:

• A peace officer must immediately seize a firearm found in violation of this law, and it must be held by the agency that seized it until the charges have been duly settled. If the minor is found guilty, the firearm is forfeited, but if the authorities can identify the lawful owner of the firearm, it must be returned to that person. Minors who are judged delinquent for violating this law:

  – May have their driver's license suspended or revoked at court discretion, until they are 18, or if they don't have a license, the court may prohibit issuing a license until the person is 18, and

  – May be fined up to $250 for an unloaded gun, and up to $500 for a loaded gun.

• If the offense involves possession of a loaded or unloaded firearm in a motor vehicle, the fine is up to $500 and the court must revoke or suspend the person's driver's license, or if the person doesn't have one, prohibit issuing one until the person is 18 years old. The court may allow driving privileges limited to between home, school and work, specified to match the person's schedule, if no other means of transportation is available.

Under §13-3102, people under 21 commit a class 1 misdemeanor by knowingly carrying a deadly weapon except a pocket knife concealed on themselves or concealed within their immediate control in a means of transportation, unless the firearm is carried so any portion of the firearm or holster it's in is *visible*, a term subject to some discretion. The firearm may also be in a scabbard or case designed for carrying weapons that is wholly or partially visible, or in luggage, a case, holster, scabbard, pack or luggage within a means of transportation or within a storage compartment, map pocket, or the trunk or glove compartment of a means of transportation.

When you combine §13-3102 with §13-3111. people under 18 must be accompanied and meet the other listed requirements above; people between 18 and 21 don't require accompaniment (or permission slips from parents) but must carry only as specified above; and people over 21 are treated as adults. Under 18, written permission must come first.

Under preemption, §13-3108, localities in Arizona may adopt essentially redundant rules concerning juveniles, so as long as you're in compliance with the state rules you should be in compliance with county, city or other ordinances on the same topic (though you could be charged or prosecuted in different jurisdictions).

A separate education statute (§15-841) says that possession, display or use of a firearm by a pupil is grounds for expulsion from school at the discretion of the authorities on a case-by-case basis. Minors are also affected by gun rules educational institutions must make. (§13-2911)

A youth found to be delinquent for a crime, which would be a felony for an adult, becomes a prohibited possessor (§13-904 and §13-3101), and carry, possession or use of a firearm for ten years afterwards is at least a class 5 felony (§13-3113). A youth found to be delinquent for a crime that would be a misdemeanor for an adult may be banned from carrying or possessing a firearm while under jurisdiction of the juvenile court or the Dept. of Juvenile Corrections. (§8-341)

Under §13-501, minors between the ages of 15 and 18 may now be criminally charged as adults in violations that are class 3 through 6 felonies involving firearms.

If you knew, or reasonably should have known, that your minor child was violating the law and you made no effort to stop it, you can be held responsible for the fines or actual civil damages resulting from illegal use of the firearm. This law is in addition to any other laws concerning the use or exhibition of a deadly weapon, and a minor guilty of breaking this law may also be prosecuted and convicted on other charges.

Federal rules below for minors, from the 1994 Violent Crime Control and Law Enforcement Act, are in addition to state laws.

Federal Regulation of Juveniles

Derived from Arizona law, federal law 18 USC §922(x) generally prohibits people under 18 from having handguns or matching ammunition, or providing the same to juveniles, with some exceptions and requirements:

While carrying written consent from parent or guardian (who isn't a prohibited possessor), minors may have a handgun:

1–in the course of employment;
2–in legitimate ranching or farming;
3–for target practice;
4–for hunting;
5–for a class in the safe and lawful use of a handgun; and
6–for transport, unloaded in a locked case, directly to and from such activities.

An exception exists for minors who use a handgun against an intruder, at home or in another home where the minor is an invited guest.

If a handgun or ammo is legally transferred to a minor, who then commits an offense with the firearm, the firearm must be returned to its lawful owner after due process. Minors may inherit title (but not possession) of a handgun. Violation of this law carries fines and a one-year jail term.

HOW DO YOU OBTAIN FIREARMS?

Guns and ammunition may be bought or sold between private residents of this state under the same conditions as any other private sale of merchandise, provided you comply with all other laws (no sales to prohibited possessors, minors, etc.). Sale *and delivery* of firearms by a private resident to a non-resident is prohibited by federal law. Such sales are OK but must take place through licensed dealers in the two people's states, described later under *Transport and Shipping*.

Arizona honors the basic freedom of law-abiding adults to own and possess firearms without government interference, resulting in no registration systems or paperwork beyond what the feds require of dealers. There are no central filing points or similar encumbrances on the right to privately keep and bear arms in this state.

Some people, unfamiliar with this level of freedom, feel we might be safer somehow if state authorities kept a list, without realizing that a list of innocent people has no crime-fighting component. But at least it would be expensive, labor and time intensive and, even under the best conditions, error laden. States that keep lists, such as New York and California, suffer enormous crime problems despite the controversial practice, and scarce resources that could go into crime fighting are diverted to record and track people who haven't done anything.

History has also repeatedly shown that gun-registration schemes precede confiscations, genocides and atrocities, against publics disarmed based on the lists. It is a very bad idea in a free society. Remarkably, criminals or other prohibited possessors are banned from being listed, because it would require self incrimination, forbidden by the Fifth Amendment. It's unclear why that never makes the "news."

As long as all other laws are complied with, a non-resident may temporarily borrow or rent a firearm for lawful sporting purposes from a dealer or a resident. You are free to own any number of firearms and any amount of ammunition, the same as any other private property.

If you are going to deal in guns (or for that matter, import, manufacture or ship firearms in interstate or foreign commerce), you need a Federal Firearms License (FFL) from the Bureau of Alcohol, Tobacco, Firearms and Explosives. Federal and state authorities may exercise a degree of judgment in determining when multiple firearm sales by a private individual constitute "dealing" in firearms, which is a felony without the license. Federal regulations provide some guidance on the matter. A dealer is:

> "A person who devotes time, attention, and labor to dealing in firearms as a regular course of trade or business with the principle objective of livelihood and profit through the repetitive purchase and resale of firearms, but such a term shall not include a person who makes occasional sales, exchanges, or purchases of firearms for the enhancement of a personal collection or for a hobby, or who sells all or part of his personal collection of firearms." (CFR §178.11)

The NICS National Background Check

All retail firearm purchases from licensed dealers must now go through the FBI's National Instant Criminal Background Check system (dubbed "NICS"), required since 1994 by the Brady handgun law. In 1998, to the surprise of many observers, an obscure five-year delay clause in Brady added all long guns to NICS, effectively federalizing all retail gun sales in the country. From 1994 to 2002, Arizona dealers called the local Firearms Clearance Center, run by DPS, who would contact the FBI and help handle any problems. The Center was closed after its enabling law, §13-3114, was repealed. Today, dealers call the FBI NICS "call center" directly. Fax and online clearance systems have been developed too.

From inception on 11/30/98 through 12/31/04, NICS handled over 53 million background checks, issuing more than 406,000 denials, with a denial rate that decreased to 1.4%. At the end of 2004, the NICS Index had 3,664,827 records, triple what it began with, growing to 5.6 million by May 2009. Illegal aliens were 74% of the total, felons 3.8%, fugitives 6.7%, mental cases 13.4% and other types below 1% each. Instant responses in 2004 were about 92%, system uptime was at 99%, and NICS referred more than 7,200 firearm retrieval cases to BATFE. Total NICS checks through June 2009 was 103,019,294, which by July 2011 had grown to 132,630,806. About 31 million of those were for permit background checks. Since some checks are for multiple sales and others for sales that don't take place, it implies roughly 100 million guns were sold in just the past 13 years. NICS did 197,081,761 checks by Oct. 2014, roughly 60 million not for sales.

In-State Purchase
Federally licensed firearms and ammunition dealers (FFLs) are spread across the state. Residents need no special license or permit to walk in and buy a regular firearm from a regular dealer. Firearms may be paid for in the same ways as any other retail merchandise. You may sell guns you own to any Arizona FFLs willing to buy them from you.

To purchase a handgun and matching ammunition you must be at least 21 years old. Your request to purchase a handgun from a dealer, if you don't have a concealed-weapon permit, is sent by the dealer to the FBI by phone, fax or web. (Because permit holders are already filed in the DPS database, there is no need to check them for each purchase. The NICS-free aspect of the CCW permit is a valued feature to many people, even though permanent registration is its price.)

The FBI then conducts the instant criminal-history background check required by state and federal law. Though most checks are completed while you are in the store, a waiting period of up to three business days may apply if the FBI decides it needs more time to make a determination (see Chapter 7 for more on the Brady law). Once issued, the federal NICS approval is good for 30 days, but only for a single business transaction, which may include more than one firearm. For another transaction (that is, to make another purchase at another time), another check is required. The NICS check became effective Nov. 30, 1998. Additional rules in the Brady law are described in Chapter 7.

To purchase a rifle or shotgun and matching ammunition you must be at least 18 years old, and the same NICS process applies. Some ammunition may be used in either a handgun or a rifle. This type of ammo can only be sold to a person between the ages of 18 and 21 if the dealer is satisfied that it will be used only in a rifle.

Government-issued photo ID with your name, address, date of birth and signature must be shown to the dealer. A driver's license (or state ID card issued in place of a driver's license) is the usual form of ID expected by most dealers.

When you buy firearms from a licensed dealer you must fill out a federal Firearms Transaction Record, form 4473. There are no duplicate copies made of this form, and the original is permanently filed by the dealer. The form requires personal identification information, identification of the gun and its serial number, and your signature, stating that you are not ineligible to obtain firearms under federal or state law. Dealers keep copies of this form available.

The purchase of more than one handgun from the same dealer in a five-day period is reported to BATFE and, under the Brady law, to local authorities as well, before the close of business on the day of the sale.

Officials and agencies are immune from liability for allowing a person to get a gun who should be prohibited, or preventing a person from getting a gun who is not prohibited, under §12-820.02, unless they intended to cause injury or were grossly negligent.

Out-of-State Purchase

Residents of this state, including businesses and corporations, are specifically granted permission in the state statutes (§13-3106) to buy guns anywhere in the United States. Such purchases must conform to the local laws at the place of purchase. However, the overlapping local, state and federal gun laws in the U.S. are frequently incompatible, and can sometimes make this difficult.

When you buy a long gun in person from a licensed dealer out of state, you may take possession right then and there (assuming this is not prohibited under the other state's law, and that you pass the background check), and such a purchase may be shipped directly to your home (one of the rare times when direct interstate shipments are permissible). Federal law requires that handguns you want to get from out of state must be shipped to you from an FFL there to an FFL in your home state—you cannot take possession of the gun over the counter.

Some dealers, concerned with overlapping, confusing and often conflicting state and federal gun laws, and reluctant to jeopardize their licenses, have been known to refuse sales to residents of other states, even when those sales would be perfectly legal.

In any case, to purchase a firearm from an out-of-state dealer, you can always have that dealer transfer the firearm (handgun or long gun) to an Arizona dealer, from whom you can legally make the purchase and take possession with few concerns about the "plethora of perplexing proprieties" (red tape) for interstate shopping.

Gun Shows

Gun shows are periodically sponsored by national, state and local organizations devoted to the collecting, competition, sporting and other legal uses of firearms. You may purchase firearms from in-state dealers at a gun show the same as you could on their regular retail premises. Out-of-state dealers can display their wares and take orders, but cannot make deliveries at the show. Purchases made from an out-of-state dealer must be shipped to a licensee within this state, from the out-of-state dealer's licensed premises.

Transport and Shipping

You may ship and transport firearms around the country, but it's illegal to use the U.S. Postal Service to ship handguns, under one of the oldest federal firearms statutes on the books, enacted on Feb. 8, 1927. (The oldest federal law still in effect—except for constitutional provisions—appears to be a firearm forfeiture law for illegal hunting in Yellowstone National Park, passed on May 7, 1894. It's interesting to note that no federal gun laws from the country's first 128 years are still on the books. The very first federal gun laws, in the late 1700s, actually *required* gun possession.) The Post Office says to use registered mail and not identify the package as containing a firearm (long gun). Check with your local Post Office yourself before shipment.

You may have a weapon shipped to a licensed dealer, manufacturer or repair shop and back. However, depending upon the reason for the shipment and the shipper being used, the weapon may have to be shipped from and back to someone with a federal firearms license. You should check with the intended recipient and you must inform the shipping agent in writing before shipping firearms or ammunition.

Any handgun obtained outside Arizona, if shipped to you in Arizona, must go from a licensed dealer where you bought it to a licensed dealer here. Many dealers in the state will act as a "receiving station" for a weapon you obtain elsewhere, sometimes for a fee. Taking *any* gun with you, from a *private transfer out of state*, if it's coming back to your home state, is generally prohibited by federal law, and must be transferred between licensed dealers.

The only times when you may directly receive an interstate shipment of a gun are:

1– the return of a gun that you sent for repairs, modification or replacement to a licensee in another state, and,

2– a long gun legally obtained in person from an out-of-state dealer.

Interstate Travel

Personal possession of firearms in other states is subject to the laws of each state you are in. The authorities have been known to hassle, detain or even arrest people who are legally traveling with weapons, due to confusion, ignorance, personal bias and for other reasons, even when those reasons are strictly illegal.

Federal law guarantees the right to transport (not the same as carry) a gun in a private vehicle, if you are entitled to have the gun in your home state and at your destination. The gun must be unloaded and locked in the trunk, or in a locked compartment other than the glove compartment or the console, if the vehicle has no trunk. Some states have openly challenged or defied this law, creating a risk for anyone transporting a firearm interstate. Carrying a firearm (armed and ready) is practically impossible unless you're willing to face misdemeanor or felony criminal charges as you pass through each state. A helpful book, *The Traveler's Guide to the Firearm Laws of the Fifty States*, summarizes the requirements and restrictions on keeping a gun with you on the road, and is listed in the back of this book. Another book, *The Traveler's Gun and Knife Law Book* covers similar ground.

Article IV of the U.S. Constitution requires the states to respect the laws of all other states. In addition, the 14th Amendment to the Constitution forbids the states from denying any rights that you have as an American citizen, and 18 USC §241 et seq. makes it a federal crime to deny a person's civil rights. These requirements are unfortunately frequently ignored by some states. Your constitutional guarantees may be little comfort if a state trooper has you spread eagled for possession of a firearm that was perfectly legal when you were at home.

The bottom line is that the civil right and historical record of law-abiding American citizens traveling with firearms for their own safety has evaporated due to laws and policies at the state level.

People often have no idea what the gun laws are in any state but their own (and rarely enough that), a complete set of the relevant laws is hard to get, understanding the statutes ranges from difficult to nearly impossible, and you can be arrested for making a simple mistake.

The legal risk created by our own government for a family traveling interstate with a personal firearm may be greater than the actual risk of a criminal confrontation. Because of this, the days of traveling armed

and being responsible for your own safety and protection have all but ended in the United States for people who leave their home state. The "proper authorities" are generally exempt from these restrictions. A system of "reciprocity" for people with government-issued carry permits provided some relief, described in Chapter 2.

The chilling conclusion is that the Constitution no longer constrains law making as it used to, and government agents have rights to travel that the people do not.

You don't fix a major national problem like this by writing a book. You fix it by restoring the Lost National Right to Carry, also known as the Second Amendment, to the position it always held in America until the last few decades, during which its erosion has been nearly total for interstate travelers.

Those readers who purchased this book hoping it would somehow enable or empower them to legally travel interstate with a loaded personal firearm must contact their elected representatives and begin to ask about the Lost National Right to Carry. It has quietly disappeared through incremental attrition at the local level.

Common or Contract Carriers

You may transport firearms and ammunition interstate by "common carriers" (scheduled and chartered airlines, buses, trains, ships, etc.), but you must notify them in writing and comply with their requirements. It must also be legal for you to possess the firearms and ammunition at your destination.

Although federal law requires written notice from you and a signed receipt from the carrier when you pick up the firearm, verbal communication is often accepted. Call in advance and get details and the names of the people you speak with—you wouldn't be the first traveler to miss a departure because of unforeseen technicalities and bureaucratic runarounds.

For air travel, firearms must be unloaded, cased in a way deemed appropriate by the airline, and may not be possessed by or accessible to you in the "sterile" area anywhere on the gate side of the passenger security checkpoint, including on the aircraft. Your firearms may be shipped as baggage, which is the usual method, and it is also legal to give custody of them to the pilot, captain, conductor or operator for the duration of the trip (though they're not required to take custody and generally will not). It is an interesting anomaly that statute permits pilots to legally take possession of your arms (though they no longer do), but have been stonewalled and red taped when trying to arm themselves against terrorist attack, by our government bureaucrats.

Airlines are required to comply with firearms rules found primarily in the Code of Federal Regulations, Title 14, Sections 107 and 108, and, along with other carriers, with the United States Code, Title 18, section 922, and Title 49. A little known provision of the Brady law prohibits carriers from identifying the outside of your baggage to indicate that it contains a firearm, a prime cause for theft in the past. In 2008, state law (§28-8429) made it explicit that the public cannot carry or possess arms in the sterile security areas of airports, but that carry in other areas in general is lawful.

New rules posted on the Internet by the Transportation Security Administration say that when in airport sterile areas, or onboard an aircraft for which screening is conducted, passengers may not carry these items as accessible property or on their person: BB guns, compressed air guns, guns and firearms, flare pistols, gun lighters, parts of guns and firearms, pellet guns, realistic replicas of firearms, spear guns, starter pistols, stun guns/cattle prods/shocking devices. The rules for private aircraft that are not subject to screening are ambiguous.

PREEMPTION

Historical note: For decades, gun law in Arizona was made at the state level only. Known as *preemption*, this was put in place because, as the legislature has said, "Firearms regulation is of statewide concern." The infringement of rights, and confusion that numerous local ordinances would create was unacceptable. If a rule was needed at all, it should apply equally across the state, and citizens shouldn't be subject to unknowable rules every time they crossed a county or city line.

However, the city of Tucson, in defiance of this tradition, knowingly decided to ignore state law and issue its own gun rules, in particular, an ordinance banning guns from innocent people in parks (criminals were already totally banned). In a now-famous case they arrested and convicted a prominent civil-rights activist who challenged the law in a carefully orchestrated arrest at Himmel Park, for simple possession of private property, namely, a personal firearm. The city court easily dismissed the charges, stating the obvious, that Tucson had no power to enact such a law in the first place, in violation of long-standing state law. The city however, was able to find an activist appeals judge willing to re-interpret preemption, and basically declare that the city could do whatever it pleased, sealing the arrest victim's fate, and rewriting, from the bench, the protection of the traditional preemption legislation.

This led to a rancorous battle between our local bureaucrats, the state legislature, and gun-rights activists statewide, yielding a complex new preemption law in 2000 (with 1,095 words), instead of the simple one (57 words) that had no value after Tucson found a way to ignore it.

The complicated new preemption law was the subject of confusion and heated debate, numerous apparent violations by local "authorities," and re-appeared in the legislature often. Below are the statutory conditions as they currently stand, but you would be wise to anticipate local officials who repeatedly play fast and loose with your rights and their restricted powers under this law. Additional language was added in 2003, then again in 2005, 2006, 2010, and 2011 to help restrain Tucson and others from trying to push the envelope The new preemption law clearly limits local government to only those powers specifically delegated in the statute, which are few in number, and no others.

Preemption In General

No government entity in Arizona can pass any ordinance, rule or tax relating to transportation, possession, carrying, sale, transfer, purchase, acquisition, gift, devise, storage, licensing, registration, discharge or use of firearms, ammunition, or firearms or ammo components, or related accessories, that is more restrictive or carries greater penalties than state law, with exceptions described below (§13-3108). Only the legislature can change firearm secure-storage and access requirements for people attending public establishments or events. (§13-3118)

No government entity in Arizona can require any licensing or registra- tion of firearms, ammunition, or firearms or ammunition components.

No government entity in Arizona can prohibit the ownership, purchase, sale or transfer of firearms, ammunition, or firearms or ammunition components.

Exceptions to Preemption

Local authorities can apply taxes to firearms, ammunition or their components, that apply generally to other tangible personal property (in other words, preemption doesn't exempt firearms, ammo and parts from the same taxes that normally apply on other goods).

Local authorities can make zoning types of rules concerning firearms, ammunition or their components, or firing ranges, in the same manner as other commercial businesses.

Local authorities can regulate their employees or contractors with respect to firearms, ammunition and their components, and knives, within the course of their work.

Minors and Preemption

A minor who is not with a parent, grandparent, guardian, or properly authorized firearms safety instructor or hunting safety instructor can be banned by local authorities from having a firearm on themselves, near them, or in a vehicle, on any street or highway, or in any place open to the public, or on private property, unless the private property is owned or leased by the minor's parent, grandparent or guardian. Those authorities cannot make any such rules for minors who are 14 to 17 years old who are:

- Legally hunting, at shooting events, or at marksmanship practice at established ranges or areas where shooting is not prohibited;
- Legally transporting unloaded firearms to legally go hunting;
- Legally transporting unloaded firearms between 5 a.m. and 10 p.m. to go to a shooting event or marksmanship practice at an established range or areas where shooting is not prohibited;
- Engaged in producing crops, livestock or poultry or related products, ratites (flightless birds such as ostrich or emu), or storage of agricultural products.

Parks and Preserves

Firearm bans in state parks and preserves were repealed in 2010, and the power of cities or any authority other than the state to implement bans was removed. The make-believe gun-free zones in parks are now gone, replaced by the right to keep and bears arms. Dire concerns expressed on reinstating the right to arms have proven to be baseless.

Shooting In Parks and Preserves

Local authorities cannot prohibit shooting in parks or preserves:

- In cases of legal justification, such as self defense;
- On a properly supervised range;
- On properly approved and posted hunting areas;
- To control nuisance wildlife with a proper permit;
- With a special permit by the local chief law enforcement officer;
- By an animal control officer performing official duties;
- In self-defense or defense of another person against an animal attack if a reasonable person would believe that deadly physical force against the animal is immediately necessary and reasonable under the circumstances to protect yourself or the other person.

Gun Lockers and Checking

If people running a government establishment or government-licensed temporary event don't want you to enter with a firearm, they must check it (take custody at the site temporarily) for you. Preemption prevents them from making up their own rules, and checking is their only option—if they refuse to check it they cannot keep you out—there is no charge to bring against you for entering. If they require you to check it, you cannot legally go in unless you do (it's a class 1 misdemeanor under §13-3102).

Some localities had tried to make people wait out in the open while police officers were summoned, the officers took your property to the police station, and you were required to go there during business hours to retrieve your piece later. It was pure harassment, and is now banned. Sometimes serial numbers or other information was recorded creating an illegal registry, now also specifically banned (as of 2010 and 2013). Authorities running lockers may however require valid ID when you're checking, place the ID with the firearm, and return it immediately when you leave, *without keeping any records* from this process (§13-3108). A background check before returning your private property had even been proposed by the most repressive officials, but is now completely banned.

These abusive affronts to law-abiding citizens were contrary to the spirit and letter of the law, and are now fully prohibited. None of this, you may have noticed, deals with criminals. It's not about gun control, it's about control. It's not even about safety, since several safety issues arise from all the gun handling and disarming. It's about fear by the fearful, without rationale.

Some remedies came in 2006 when §13-3102.01 passed requiring any gun check to be secure and "readily accessible on entry into the establishment or event and allow for immediate retrieval on exit." Also added was §13-3118, which specifically forbids any localities from changing the possession or secure storage "checking" requirements.

Violation by the public of any lawful *local* ordinance enacted under preemption is a class 2 misdemeanor, or less at the locality's option. Violation of the preemption law's *protections*, by the authorities, carries no punishment at present, a serious oversight. We have seen many attempts by local "authorities" to circumvent these laws.

It's important to remember that localities are *not required* to ban your rights, nor are they required to check legally possessed weapons in the hands of the innocent. They are granted this *option*. In these difficult times, many people recognize the value in keeping the public armed, and have decided to simply let people come and go in peace.

RELATED SUBJECTS

No-Guns-Allowed Signs

• Little currently prevents **private places** from having a no-guns policy or posting no-guns-allowed signs. Property owners have clear rights and control many of the terms by which you may enter their private places. But can a place that's open to the public (quite different from your private home) discriminate against people based on creed—people who bear arms or exercise other constitutional guarantees? Does a place that restricts your defense take on a life-and-death liability? These are unsettled questions of law. A *gun-free-zone liability law* has been introduced here but not enacted—it would stipulate liability if a "pretend" gun-free zone caused harm.

Deliberately ignoring **private signs** (or especially a *direct request*), opens you to a possible charge of criminal trespass (§13-1502) if the place wants to make it an issue instead of the usual, just asking you to leave. The exposure is obviously greater for a person carrying openly than for a person carrying discreetly. Signs at *parking lots* came under a new law in 2009, covered in Chapter 2 under *Guns In Cars*.

• Under §13-3102 you must check your guns (relinquish custody while on the premises) if asked at a **public establishment** or **public event** (defined as government places and events), but only if secure, readily accessible storage is provided. This is often called the *gun-locker law*. A properly worded sign counts as asking, but doesn't give complete proof you saw it (i.e., "constructive notice").

They are not compelled to check guns you may have, but if they do require it (and have suitable storage) you must comply or leave. If a public establishment or event will not check guns they have little grounds for keeping you out, but don't be surprised if they try.

• In contrast to *private* or *public* signs, **official signs** may legitimately warn you against entering an area prohibited by law, where misdemeanor or felony charges could be brought for possession of a firearm (e.g., nuclear power stations, court houses, airports, etc.). The validity of a posted sign is not always perfectly clear.

• In 2009, CCW permitees (and certain officials) were granted access to **places licensed to serve alcohol**, as long as they do not drink alcohol while there. However, official *no-guns-allowed signs* were established for licensees who choose on their own to ban CCW.

With a red circle-and-slash over a drawing of a fictitious gun, the words "No firearms allowed" and reference to the law (§4-229), these signs legally deny CCW carry in such places.

If a licensee decides to ban CCW, the sign must be conspicuous to the public, next to the liquor license, and must be an official sign provided by the liquor department at no charge (or an exact duplicate), with lettering, paper, wording, size, color, imagery and text as set out by law. It's ironic—our tax dollars finance the signs that deny our rights.

If you are charged with violating this law, you can claim exemption if: a) you weren't informed of the notice; b) the sign had fallen down; c) you weren't a state resident at the time or d) the sign had been posted not more than 30 days beforehand. A person with a CCW permit is allowed to enter for a limited time to seek emergency aid, or to see if a sign is legally posted. A violation is a class 3 misdemeanor.

The Arizona Gun Safety Program

In 2005, the state enacted The Arizona Gun Safety Program, §15-714.01. This is an elective one-credit, one-semester class that can be offered at any school district or charter school in the state, the first program of its kind in the nation. Students must safely discharge a real firearm at one or more targets to complete the course. The curriculum is jointly developed by The Arizona Game and Fish Commission, The Dept. of Public Safety and private firearms organizations, and may include materials from private youth groups.

As of 2010, a person who is currently certified as a firearms safety instructor by the Arizona Game and Fish Dept., the National Rifle Association, a federal, state or local law enforcement agency, a branch of the United States military, a federal agency, the Reserve Officer Training Corps, the Junior Reserve Officer Training Corps or the Civilian Marksmanship Program is qualified to teach the course. School districts and charter schools must arrange for use of shooting ranges by pupils in the program, at any established ranges. Pupils who satisfactorily complete the course get a certificate of accomplishment. The program must include at least:

1–The rules of firearm safety.
2–The basic operation of firearms.
3–The history of firearms and marksmanship.
4–The role of firearms in preserving peace and freedom.
5–The constitutional roots of the right to keep and bear arms.
6–The use of clay targets.
7–Practice time at a shooting range.

Frivolous Lawsuits

Arizona attempted to restrict serious criminals from suing their victims or the police, for harm the criminal suffered while committing a felony. You might think that goes without saying, but levels of legal abuse had risen to the point where, in 2006, the state enacted §12-716. Less than perfectly worded, it attempts to say that if a plaintiff in a lawsuit was harmed while committing a felony, the person doing the harm was acting reasonably (and hence plaintiff's claim is weakened or eliminated) if any of the following apply: the victim or police officer threatened or used physical or deadly physical force to either protect themselves against the plaintiff's illegal use of such force, or to arrest, prevent or assist in preventing the plaintiff's escape.

Additional protections are provided for peace officers and a "police tool product" (any weapon or product they use) that causes physical harm. It is presumed to not be defective, and its manufacturer not negligent, if it conforms to the generally recognized state of the art at the time it was designed, made, packaged and labeled, and complies with any relevant rules of the feds or the state.

Passed at the same time, §13-420 puts teeth in these protections: the defendant collects attorney fees, costs, compensation for lost income and all defense expenses if the defendant prevails. This deters suits. To further strengthen it all, Prop 114 was passed in 2012 with an 80% majority, amending the state Constitution to make it pretty airtight and not limit damages. (See Art. 2, §31 and Art. 18, §6)

Nationally, in an effort to disarm the public, various groups, including in some cases tax-funded government officials, have initiated enormously expensive junk lawsuits against gun manufacturers, distributors and related businesses—for the non-criminal manufacture and sale of firearms. Destroying the domestic firearms industry is a clever tactic, and would have a devastating impact on the civil right of gun ownership. The Defense Dept. testified to Congress on the severe national security threat a weakened or eliminated gun-making industry would have on the nation as a whole. Arizona has enacted a statute forbidding such suits by political subdivisions of this state, saying:

"The citizens of this state have the right, under the Second Amendment to the United States Constitution and article 2, section 26 of the Arizona Constitution, to keep and bear arms."

"Businesses in the United States that are engaged in the lawful sale to the public of firearms or ammunition are not, and should not be liable for the harm caused by those who unlawfully misuse firearms or ammunition."

"The possibility of imposing liability on an entire industry for harm that is the sole responsibility of others is an abuse of the legal system, threatens the diminution of a basic constitutional right and constitutes an unreasonable burden on the free enterprise system."

"The liability actions commenced by political subdivisions are based on theories without foundation in the common law and American jurisprudence. Such an expansion of liability would constitute a deprivation of the rights, privileges and immunities guaranteed to citizens of this state under both the Constitution of Arizona and the United States Constitution." See (§12-714) for complete details.

Federal law was amended in 2005 (Public Law 109-92), to prohibit frivolous lawsuits, and Congress noted among many things:

"The Second Amendment to the United States Constitution protects the rights of individuals, including those who are not members of a militia or engaged in military service or training, to keep and bear arms." They refer to it as, "a basic constitutional right and civil liberty," and that they are enacting this law, "To preserve a citizen's access to a supply of firearms and ammunition for all lawful purposes, including hunting, self-defense, collecting, and competitive or recreational shooting."

Congress notes that the lawsuits are, "an abuse of the legal system," and, "based on theories without foundation in hundreds of years of the common law and jurisprudence of the United States," and an, "attempt to use the judicial system to circumvent the Legislative branch of government." And finally, they are enacting this law, "To guarantee a citizen's rights, privileges, and immunities, as applied to the States, under the Fourteenth Amendment to the United States Constitution, pursuant to section 5 of that Amendment."

The U.S. Congress has now addressed the applicability of the Second Amendment in enacted legislation six times, and in every case it has specifically recognized it as an individual right:

The Freedman's Bureau Act of 1866
The Property Requisition Act of 1941
The Firearm Owner's Protection Act of 1986
The Protection of Lawful Commerce in Arms Act of 2005
Disaster Recovery Personal Protection Act of 2006
Protecting Americans From Violent Crime (P.L. 111-24, Sec. 512) 2009

Congress also required dealers to provide locks with every gun sold, and included immunity for anyone who uses them, from a "qualified civil liability action." They used the same name for this immunity as for the industry immunity, even though they are quite different. If your gun is locked up and useless you are protected from a certain type of liability, from a thief who steals it and criminally misuses it. If your gun is not locked up and is available for immediate use, you have whatever protections you had before the law passed, from a thief's victims. Language was also added to help prevent courts from creatively "finding" any new liabilities.

Governor's Emergency Powers

In the aftermath of hurricane Katrina in 2005, authorities in Louisiana took it upon themselves to confiscate firearms from innocent residents. In 2007, Arizona's governor was prohibited from using emergency powers (under §26-303) to attempt any similar abuse. The rewritten statute allows the governor to "commandeer and utilize any property, except for firearms or ammunition or firearms or ammunition components." In addition the governor cannot act in an emergency to impose any "additional restrictions on the lawful possession, transfer, sale, transportation, carrying, storage, display or use of firearms or ammunition or firearms or ammunition components," with an exception for the reasonable movement of stores of ammunition out of the way of dangerous conditions (such as wild fires).

Firearms Freedom Act of 2010

Arizona joined a national effort to end federal abuse of the Commerce Clause, using one of the few constitutionally guaranteed pieces of property Americans can own—firearms. This act is a test of government power, not a free license to start making your own guns, despite hysterical "news" reports and flying rumors on the subject. Anyone who attempts to use this law for their own gun making risks arrest, confiscations, loss of rights, and could set precedents that will seriously hurt everyone in the state.

Arizona declares (under §13-3114, if it survives legal challenges), that a personal firearm, firearm accessory or ammunition manufactured commercially or privately in this state, which remains within the borders of this state, is not subject to federal law or federal regulation, including registration, under Congress' authority to regulate interstate commerce, and is not considered to have traveled in interstate commerce—the main ruse Congress has been using to regulate virtually anything.

The law applies to a firearm, a firearm accessory or ammunition that is manufactured in this state from basic materials and that can be manufactured without the inclusion of any significant parts imported from another state (to avoid the interstate commerce nexus).

Importing a firearm accessory, any generic or insignificant part that has other manufacturing or consumer product applications, or any basic materials, including unmachined steel and unshaped wood that is incorporated into, attached to or used in conjunction with a firearm, firearm accessory or ammunition manufactured in this state, does not subject those goods to federal regulation, Arizona says. Many other states are taking a similar position, to challenge federal overreach.

The law excludes crew-fired weapons, firearms with a bore larger than 1-1/2 inches that use smokeless powder, ammo with exploding projectiles, or a firearm discharging two or more projectiles with one trigger pull. That last condition was picked up from the model law, introduced in Montana, to keep machine guns out of the mix and not confuse the federalism issue. As written, it also excludes shotguns, not the original intent, and is something that might be changed later.

A firearm made and sold here must have the words "made in Arizona" clearly stamped on a central metal part such as the receiver or frame.

"Firearm accessory" is an item used in conjunction with or mounted on a firearm but that is not essential to the basic function, including telescopic or laser sights, magazines, flash suppressors, folding or aftermarket stocks and grips, speedloaders, ammunition carriers and lights for target illumination. A "generic or insignificant part" includes springs, screws, nuts and pins. "Manufactured" means that a firearm, a firearm accessory or ammunition has been created from basic materials, including forging, casting, machining or similar processes.

If the law survives challenge from the feds, who have already expressed intense dislike for the plan and have begun to attack the law with letters to FFLs in some states, Arizona itself is likely to add controls so that you can't just start making your own armory in your basement. Using this law for any purpose until the complex, carefully structured challenges have been resolved is very dangerous to your personal freedom. The legislative intent included with this act describes the law's reasoning, our rights under the 9th and 10th amendments to the U.S. Constitution, is included with the statute in Appendix D, and makes fascinating reading.

Trafficking

A new law in 2012 defines certain firearm transactions as *trafficking*. Under §13-3101, trafficking occurs when a person transfers a firearm (or explosives) to another person. *Transfer* is defined broadly, "to sell, transfer, distribute, dispense or otherwise dispose of," a weapon or explosives. Trafficking also occurs when a person receives or possesses a firearm or explosives with intent to transfer those to another person.

The kind of receiving or possessing is defined broadly to include "to buy, receive, possess or obtain control of," a weapon or explosive.

This broad definition is very troubling from a rights perspective, since no inherently criminal behavior is involved. *Trafficking* becomes a class 3 felony under a simultaneous change made to §13-3102, if a person engages in it, "for financial gain in order to assist, promote or further the interests of a criminal street gang, a criminal syndicate or a racketeering enterprise." For an average gun owner the law has no effect, but in the hands of a misguided or overzealous prosecutor or court system it could be very problematic since it reaches virtually all firearms activity, such as training and practice, and should be amended to unambiguously protect the innocent.

LOSS AND RESTORATION OF RIGHTS

Your right to keep and bear arms can be lost. The right to arms is forbidden to anyone who is or becomes a prohibited possessor under federal law, described earlier. Conviction of any felony suspends your civil right to possess firearms under §13-904, and the right to ship, transport, possess or receive firearms or ammunition under federal law (18 USC §922g). Also under §13-904 a minor found to be delinquent loses the right to carry or possess firearms.

As a condition of release from custody on bail, a judge can prohibit you from possessing firearms (§13-3967). Other court orders can prohibit bearing arms for the duration of the order. Illegal discharge of a firearm by a rental tenant is grounds for eviction. (§33-1368)

Surrender of Weapons

A *public place or event* can request custody of your guns—the "gun check" or gun-locker law. They must provide secure storage "readily accessible on entry into the establishment or event and allow for immediate retrieval on exit," (§13-3102.01), to make this request legal.

A public place used to mean places open to the public. Now, it is a structure, vehicle or craft owned, leased or operated by an Arizona governmental entity. A public event is a named or sponsored event of limited duration run by government, or run by a private entity with a permit or license from the government. It does not include an unsponsored gathering of people in public.

You are required to surrender any deadly weapons you possess if you are at a public place or event, and you are asked to do so by people in charge, but *only* if they provide proper secure storage. Failure to leave or give safe custody of your weapons to the people in charge is a class 1 misdemeanor. See §13-3102. The place is strictly banned from requiring or maintaining a record in any form, whether permanent or temporary, when you leave a weapon, but they can require a government-issued ID (or a reasonable copy) to establish ownership of the weapon, and return it when you retrieve the weapon. (§13-3108)

If a law enforcement officer (LEO) stops you on official business, which includes a lawful traffic stop, criminal investigation, arrest, detention or investigatory stop based on reasonable suspicion that an offense has been or is about to be committed, you must relinquish your weapon for the duration of the encounter, if asked. The officer is banned by law from recording information about the weapon except as part of a criminal investigation. Peace officers, military personnel, or other people specifically licensed or authorized, in performance of official duties, may be excluded from surrendering their weapons.

Forfeiture of Weapons

The authorities can take your weapons if they have just cause. Firearms may be seized by a peace officer during an arrest or search, or if the officer has probable cause to believe that a firearm is subject to seizure, under §13-4305. If you have, use or display a firearm in violation of any public-school rule, the firearm must be forfeited, sold, or otherwise disposed of, under §13-2911. A firearm in the possession of a minor, unless it meets certain narrow exceptions, is subject to seizure, under §13-3111. In domestic violence cases, all firearms may be seized, under §13-3601 and -3602.

If you are convicted of a felony or other specified violations involving one or more guns, you forfeit the weapons to the state, see §13-3105. The former must-destroy rule was repealed in 2010 but if the weapons cannot be legally owned, they are disposed of as ordered by a court.

Anyone making a lawful arrest may take weapons from the person arrested, and must turn the weapons over to the courts. See §13-3895 for the letter of the law.

Certain weapons are contraband if unregistered and are subject to seizure by the authorities. Included are weapons identified under the National Firearms Act as amended (see Chap. 3), or identified as prohibited weapons under state law. (§13-3101)

Personal property, including firearms and ammunition, may be seized by the Bureau of Alcohol, Tobacco, Firearms and Explosives when used or intended to be used or involved in violation of any U.S. laws that BATFE agents are empowered to enforce. Acquittal or dismissal of charges allows you to regain any confiscated property, in theory.

Property can be confiscated by court order from a person in sufficient debt, but certain personal items are exempt (§33-1125), including one rifle or shotgun or pistol, with a value of up to $500.

Sale of Firearms by State

In 2012, the state was required, under §12-945 to sell firearms that come into its possession to businesses authorized to buy and sell firearms to the public, if the firearms are legal for that purpose, within one year after forfeiture. If a law enforcement agency has the firearm, it may trade it to an FFL for firearms, ammo or other gear it can use for law enforcement purposes. Destruction is not an option.

Protection of Firearms in Official Custody

Property was redefined in 2013 to include any guns that might come into officials' possession for any reason. They must be safely kept, honestly valued and handled only as defined by law. If officials take a gun from you, they must give you a detailed receipt, including how to retrieve it. If a gun that is legal to own and worth more than $150 is found and the owner is not known, a description of it must be publicly posted or published. If it is unclaimed after 30 days, the gun can be sold to a licensed firearm dealer for resale to the public, or a law enforcement agency can trade it to a licensed dealer for anything it needs for its own work. In a sale, the money goes to the general fund. In a trade, the police get the goods. Either way, the firearms become available to the public through FBI background-checked sales. See §12-940 et seq. and §13-3108. Firearms acquired by various agencies, a public asset in the hands of our government servants, can no longer be destroyed, under this law amended to prevent ongoing abuse of constitutionally protected property.

Restoration of Rights

A person with a truly compelling reason and sufficient time, money and luck, can conceivably pursue relief from federal firearms prohibition through the federal courts, or with a presidential pardon. Successful examples of this are few. Federal law (18 USC §925) also provides a method for restoring a person's right to arms if it has been lost. This has been useful to people who are responsible community members and whose restrictions were based on decades-old errors of youth, or other circumstances that pose little threat.

The Justice Dept. is responsible for implementing this law. Congress however, since 1992, has refused to provide funding and the federal rights-restoration process ground to a halt for anyone whose disability is based on federal rules. The U.S. Supreme Court in 2002 denied restoration in a case that seemed it might break the deadlock (*Bean v. U.S.;* see *Supreme Court Gun Cases,* listed in the back of this book). BATFE points out that if you can get your legal status changed so you no longer meet the definition of a prohibited possessor you no longer are one, and would then only need to have the NICS Index updated.

Arizona courts have been more responsive in re-examining and mitigating domestic violence misdemeanors (that are sometimes little more than routine pleas in divorce cases) and easing the gun-rights disability when circumstances warrant. Arizona restoration of rights procedures are described in §13-905 thru §13-912.01. Ten-year and two-year delays apply after full completion of probation or sentences. As of 2009, certain persons who lost the right to keep and bear arms due to mental illness can apply for limited restoration of rights under §13-924. In 2011 the legal means for making that happen improved, in §12-2101, §13-925 and §13-4441.

Procedures for correcting erroneous NICS records, which would stop a person from completing a retail purchase from a dealer, are described in federal law (18 USC §922(t)). The book *Brady Denial* describes the process in plain English, walks you through the steps needed to get your records cleaned up if needed, and is available at gunlaws.com.

WHAT DO YOU NEED TO GET A FIREARM?

WHAT DO YOU NEED TO GET A FIREARM FROM A FEDERALLY LICENSED DEALER?

- You must be over 18 years old for a long gun, over 21 for a handgun and not be a "prohibited possessor" under state or federal law;

- You need a government-issued photo ID that establishes your name, address, date of birth and signature;

- You must fill out and give the dealer federal form 4473, identifying yourself, the firearm you are buying, and certifying you are not a prohibited possessor (dealers keep these forms available, and they can now be done electronically);

- You must wait while the dealer conducts an instant background check by phone, fax or online to the federal "NICS" centralized data clearinghouse run by the FBI;

- If there is a delay in the NICS check the FBI has up to three business days to clear it up, during which you must wait, but after which your sale can take place automatically;

- If you have a valid Arizona CCW permit you may present it and be excluded from the background check and possible delay;

- And if you are not an Arizona resident:

  –It must be legal for you to have the gun in your home state;

  –The transaction must comply with your state's laws;

  –You may take possession of a long gun over the counter if that's allowed in your home state;

  –You may not purchase and take possession of a handgun out of your home state (federal law since 1968) but you may have a licensed dealer ship a handgun to your home state for purchase there, if dealers in both states are willing to arrange such a transaction (they typically are); and

- You must be able to pay for your purchase.

WHAT DOES IT ALL MEAN?

Arizona law books don't use the word *crime*—they use the terms *felony, misdemeanor* and *petty offense*. Crimes are divided into these categories to match the punishment to the crime. Felonies are extremely serious, misdemeanors are serious and petty offenses can be serious.

Felonies and misdemeanors are also grouped into "classes." Felonies go from class 1 to class 6, and include fines and jail terms of six months or more. *Class 1* means the worst crime, and carries a possible death penalty. Generally, a felony conviction revokes your civil rights, including your right to keep and bear arms, to hold public office and to vote, and may include limits on your right to travel, work, associate with designated people and other conditions at court discretion.

Misdemeanors run from class 1 to class 3, and include fines and jail terms of six months or less. Petty offenses have no class, and include fines only. The statute of limitations differs with the type of crime.

See the Crime and Punishment Chart on the inside back cover for the basic penalties for each type of crime.

CARRYING FIREARMS 2

Constitutional Carry

Arizona has become a shining example of freedom for the nation, now that most restrictions and interference on either open or discreet carry of firearms have been removed. With passage of Constitutional Carry in 2010, just about any method of bearing arms here is legal. The main limits are in the lists of prohibited places, people banned from firearms altogether, rules for youth and certain illegal arms.

Arizona has respected uninfringed open-carry freedom since statehood in 1912. A law-abiding adult here, not just residents, could always carry a firearm wholly or partially visible, with no need for classes, government applications, recordkeeping, registries, taxes called "fees," paperwork, testing, fingerprinting, listing in online criminal databases, permission slips, photos, or other interference or red tape. This has a name you've heard—it's called freedom.

This freedom served the state well, though it got confusing around the late 1990s when some activist court cases questioned what "visible" means. Those problems have been eliminated by new law. Now, the same open-carry freedom this state has always enjoyed is available for people who carry discreetly, a somewhat more suitable method now that urbanization, increased population and a media-fueled cultural shift has made the open carrying of arms less unobtrusive. After 16 years of CCW permits (1994–2010) evidence was overwhelming that CCW registration schemes were costly and didn't make you safer.

Firearms may be carried either openly or discreetly in Arizona, loaded or unloaded, by any adult legally in the state, who is not banned from possessing arms. Special rules for youngsters, and places where guns may not be carried, are described later. We have in essence extended the Second Amendment right to bear arms to the entire planet.

Although the word "concealed" appears in the law, and the permit still refers to concealed carry, the preferred term here is *discreet carry*, so the negative inference of something to hide is eliminated. Courts have been inconsistent in defining *concealed,* and it's not defined in statute.

There is a certain pride that Arizona has always been an open-carry state—it reflects our pioneer sense of freedom. Indeed, many states have made it much harder to move a gun from point A to point B than it is here, where people are free to take their firearms around pretty much as they see fit.

But as anyone who has tried it knows, strapping on a six shooter in most metropolitan areas attracts so much attention that it can serve as a deterrent. When open carry was the only legal means for bearing arms (prior to the permit system effective on July 17, 1994) it actually limited the practicality of traveling armed, in a modern society where being inconspicuous is the civilized norm. Unless you were in costume or at a special event, many people just wouldn't wear a gun out and about.

This is less true however in smaller towns and rural areas, where finding people strolling around with sidearms is somehow less poignant, and certainly a more common sight. And increasingly, you do see people from time to time, statewide, going about their affairs, openly bearing arms. Some gun-rights activists believe respectful open carry is important for its "inoculation effect," demonstrating publicly that firearm possession is a normal, safe and routine facet of life in a free country. Others think open carry is polarizing, builds support for more gun control, and does indeed relinquish tactical advantage. It's been observed that if you can't or won't exercise a right, then you do not really have it. Working to protect rights, some civil-rights groups here have issued meeting notices with the line, "Tasteful open carry appreciated," and open-carry banquets and gatherings are a popular form of event.

The Arizona Citizens Defense League, azcdl.org, largely responsible for the Constitutional Carry law, makes this very salient observation:

"The heaviest thing about wearing a firearm is the responsibility that comes with it. Take that money that you save on permit and renewal fees and spend it on quality training as often as you can. Lead by example—the world is watching." The Arizona State Rifle and Pistol Association, asrpa.com, worked hand-in-hand with AzCDL to enact the robust, common-sense gun laws we enjoy in Arizona, and is a leader in firearms training and competitions in the state. They both deserve your support. For additional training opportunities, check out the statewide training network, TrainMeAZ.com, which is supported by the firearms industry here.

The main risks associated with deciding to carry a firearm may not be evident until after an incident occurs, and then you get a crash course in the workings of the legal system and how people are treated after a shooting, even if they believe they are totally innocent. For a stark look at those issues, read *After You Shoot: Your gun's hot. The perp's not. Now what?* shown in the back of this book.

Reveal and Relinquish

As of 2010, Arizona is officially a *shall reveal* and *shall relinquish* state, with rules that used to be enforced by custom and are now law. This applies only if and when a law enforcement officer (LEO) stops you on official business—a lawful traffic stop, criminal investigation, arrest, detention or investigatory stop based on reasonable suspicion that an offense has been or is about to be committed. If you are thus asked if you are armed, you are required by law to answer truthfully (§13-3102), though you do not have to volunteer the information on your own. Lying would be a class 1 misdemeanor. There is no need to volunteer the fact that you are or aren't armed in a casual encounter.

There is also no typical need to show a CCW to an officer, if you have one, since no permit is needed to carry. The only time you must show your permit is when required by law. That only occurs under §13-3112 when you're carrying discreetly in a liquor-serving place that doesn't have a gun-ban sign properly posted. Since you cannot carry openly in there, the chances of ever *needing* to show the permit are nil. People really *want* to show that permit though, if they got one, because plain old freedom to arms just somehow isn't enough.

If you are properly asked to hand over a weapon for the duration of a police encounter, you must comply, even if you have done nothing wrong. Many rights advocates see this as an illegal seizure, an unwarranted invasion of privacy, and it is obviously dangerous, but it is a class 1 misdemeanor to refuse (§13-3102). The officer must return the weapon to you as soon as the encounter ends if you are free to go, it is *strictly illegal* for the officer to make any record of the weapon or create any sort of registry with you and the tool identified. (§13-3108)

Guns in Cars

State law in Arizona leaves all law-abiding adults free to carry arms, loaded or unloaded, anywhere in a person's car or other means of transportation. (§13-3102)

Because Constitutional Carry eliminates the old need to keep weapons (of any sort) out in the open, confusion from the former laws—about glove compartments and other concealed-but-legal methods—is gone.

The statute however retains the list of *concealed-and-legal* ways to carry, which apply to people under 21, described in Chapter 1. An adult's concealed firearm in a vehicle, if not holstered or properly cased, etc., could potentially put a minor at risk for inadvertently violating the law.

It's a class 6 felony to carry a concealed weapon in any vehicle in furtherance of any felony. It is a class 3 misdemeanor for people under 21 years of age to have a concealed weapon on themselves, or to have one within their immediate control in a vehicle, except as described in the Chapter 1 section on rules for minors.

Parking lots

As of 2009, no property owner, tenant, employer or business (PTEB) can make a policy or rule to prevent a person from lawfully transporting or storing a firearm in a private motor vehicle if the firearm is not visible outside the vehicle, and the vehicle is locked or the firearm is in a locked compartment (including motorcycles). Any such rule is null, void and has no legal force or effect. (§12-781)

Exceptions include: a) firearms that are prohibited by state or federal law; b) situations where compliance would violate a federal or state law or regulation; c) nuclear generating stations with security and temporary secure firearm storage as defined; d) current Defense Dept. contractors whose property is at least partially on a U.S. military facility; e) vehicles owned or leased by an employer and used by an employee in the course of employment, at the employer's discretion; f) if the PTEB provides parking space that is secured by a fence or other physical barrier, limits access by a guard or other security measure and provides temporary monitored secured storage readily accessible on entry and exit from the premises; g) if the PTEB provides alternate parking space reasonably near the primary area without extra charge for people who seek to transport or store firearms in their vehicles; or h) the parking area is on an owner- or tenant-occupied single-family detached residence.

Firearms are frequently stolen from parked vehicles. Police generally do not recommend leaving firearms in vehicles. Firearms should also be removed when bringing vehicles in for service.

CONCEALED-WEAPON PERMITS

Until 1994 it was essentially illegal to discreetly bear arms in this state. The Carry a Concealed Weapon law (CCW) eased this infringement on the right to keep and bear arms, but with a convoluted and expensive government permitting process that went through nearly constant change. Editions 10 through 24 of this book documented the tinkering the CCW law went through, burdening the public with an almost unknowable set of turbulent conditions. Sixteen years later the need for the permit was dropped and our rights are much more easily exercised, but a permit is still available, and it does retain some value.

Notice that Arizonans are dropping the use of the word *concealed*, because it implies you're doing something wrong or have something to hide. *Discreet carry* is the preferred term and civilized norm, along with handbag carry, normal carry and Freedom to Carry (as opposed to so-called *right-to-carry*, which in reality is just a government licensing program that 97% of the public avoids), and *Constitutional Carry*.

The main values of the CCW permit, now that it's no longer required:

1–Other states recognize your permit to carry under "reciprocity," which means we honor their permits and many of them honor ours;
2–You can buy firearms at retail without going through a NICS background check each time, since you're permanently in the criminal database;
3–You can enter an establishment licensed to serve alcohol, as long as it isn't properly posted to ban CCW, and you don't drink alcohol;
4–You're immune from the federal gun-free school zone (Chapter 7);
5–You can whip out your permit and show it off to people—don't laugh—permitees love doing this even if it is hopelessly statist.

Statute still retains the former list of free-to-carry-discreetly places:

1–In your own dwelling;
2–On your business premises;
3–On real estate owned or leased by you.

Certain authorities may be permitted to carry weapons openly or discreetly by their agencies. About 1.5% of the public, 60,000 people, obtained Arizona carry permits in the first four years of the permission-slip program.

A permit to carry a concealed weapon (CCW) is available to any person who is qualified as described below. See §13-3112 for the letter of the law. You are only required to show the permit when you are in a place licensed to serve alcohol that is not posted to ban CCW entry, and you are armed, and you are asked by an LEO. If you don't have the permit you face a $300 fine, but you can remedy this with no repercussions later by showing the permit, that was valid at the time, in court. Your firearm cannot be confiscated under those circumstances (you still retain the right to bear under Constitutional Carry), but the LEO may take temporary custody of it under the relinquish rule (and you would have to leave the establishment).

The Department of Public Safety (DPS) maintains a computerized record system to confirm the validity of all CCW permits. If you are found without your permit while carrying discreetly in a place licensed to serve alcohol, DPS must be notified, and the permit will be immediately suspended. As soon as DPS is notified that you presented the permit, they must restore it.

If you are arrested or indicted for an offense that would disqualify you for a CCW permit after you get one, it is immediately suspended and is subject to seizure. If you are convicted of such an offense the permit will be revoked. If you are found not guilty, or if the charges are dropped or dismissed, you can get the permit restored by presenting documentation from the court or county attorney. Under DPS regulations, you must wait at least two years before reapplying for a permit that was revoked.

Possession of a valid Arizona CCW permit allows you to purchase a firearm from a dealer without any delay or the national background check otherwise required by the Brady law. Because permitees' records are already in the system it would be redundant. As of 2006, to protect privacy, records for applicants and permitees are only available to law-enforcement personnel or upon court order.

National Police Discreet Carry

Federal law enacted in 2004 (originally HR 218, P.L. 108-277, the Law Enforcement Officers Safety Act "LEOSA," now 18 USC §926B and C) paved the way for specified active duty and retired law-enforcement officers to carry discreetly nationwide, despite any state laws to the contrary. Arizona amended its own law (§13-3112) to implement this, by providing a "certificate of firearms proficiency" to retired LEOs who qualify (they need to have this to get the law's benefit).

Arizonans who can bear arms nationwide under these provisions must qualify periodically (under state AZPOST rules) and meet some other requirements, check with your department for details, and know the rules for states you visit. In 2007, §38-1102 clarified where police can and cannot carry in this state. LEOs now have rights nationally that the public is supposed to have, but doesn't. When the struggle to enact this common-sense self-defense law was underway, the public was assured that after officials got this right in place, we the people would be next. That hasn't happened. Why are we not surprised.

CCW Application

DPS is required by law to issue your CCW permit if you:

1–Are a resident of Arizona or a United States citizen as defined by law (non-citizen "green-card" residents should check with DPS) and are not a prohibited possessor under state or federal law;

2–Are at least 21 years of age, lowered in 2014 to 19 for anyone currently in or honorably discharged from U.S. Armed Services, Reserves or State National Guards;

3–Are not under indictment for or have not been convicted of a felony anywhere (unless the felony has been vacated, expunged or set aside and you are not a state or federal prohibited possessor);

4–Do not suffer from mental illness and have not been adjudicated mentally incompetent or committed to a mental institution;

5–Are not an illegal alien; and

6–You can provide adequate documentation of having ever demonstrated competence with a firearm in any state or political subdivision in the United States, which includes:

- A valid current or expired CCW permit from DPS, or

- A valid current or expired concealed weapon, firearm or handgun permit or license from any U.S. state or political subdivision of any state that required training or testing when initially issued, or

- An original or copy of honorable or general discharge papers from the Dept. of Defense, or a certificate of completion of basic training or proof of current or former armed-forces service, or

- An original or copy of a card, certificate or document, or an affidavit from the instructor, school, club or organization, that shows you have ever completed:

–Any firearms safety or training course or class available to the general public, offered by a law-enforcement agency, a junior college, a college or a private or public institution, academy, organization or firearms-training school and that is approved by DPS or that uses instructors who are certified by the NRA;

–Completion of any hunter-education or hunter-safety course approved by the Arizona Game and Fish Dept. or a similar agency of another state;

–Completion of any NRA firearms safety or training course;

–Completion of any law-enforcement firearms safety or training
    course or class offered for security guards, investigators, special
    deputies or other divisions or subdivisions of law enforcement or
    security enforcement and that is approved by DPS;

–Evidence of current military service or proof of honorable
    discharge or general discharge under honorable conditions from
    the U.S. armed forces.

–Completion of any governmental police agency firearms-training
    course and qualification to carry a firearm in the course of
    normal police duties;

–Completion of any other firearms safety or training course or class
    that is conducted by a DPS-approved or National Rifle
    Association-certified firearms instructor.

The previously required elements of an official CCW course (prior to
2010) are still a valuable guide for your own study, including: safe
handling and storage of weapons, weapon care and maintenance,
legal issues relating to the use of deadly force, mental conditioning for
the use of deadly force, marksmanship, and judgmental shooting. This
book retains a Q&A section in Chapter 8 for learning more about
various shoot/no shoot judgment scenarios, and gunlaws.com provides
a wealth of resources on related subjects like gunfight tactics, carry
options and gear, self defense, crime avoidance, firearm safety, gun
politics, laws in other states and more.

*Applicants for a permit are required to certify they have a copy of the
statutes in Chapters 4 (justifiable use of deadly force) and 31
(misconduct with weapons), and that they are knowledgeable about
those provisions.* The Arizona Gun Owner's Guide *includes the full
required sections of law.*

To apply for a CCW permit you complete a *DPS Concealed Weapon
Permit Application*, available from your trainer or DPS. The form
requires your name, address, social security number (optional),
telephone, origin/race, sex, height, weight, eye and hair color, and
date and place of birth. A photo requirement (there isn't one) has been
talked about since inception. Certificate of completion is on the back.

There are check boxes to indicate if you are applying for a permit, a
set of boxes confirming that you are an eligible applicant (no prior
felonies, etc., as listed above), and a place for your signature and the
date. Two boxes concern naturalized citizens and people here on
green-card immigration status. You are not required to identify the
firearm you will carry, which means you can use your permit with any

arms you prefer. Filling out the form untruthfully is perjury, a class 4 felony. The complete application includes:

1–A Concealed Weapon Permit Application form.

2–A valid document showing successful completion of an acceptable training program or a qualified previously issued carry permit;

3–Two sets of fingerprints—which are scanned and stored digitally by the FBI in the national AFIS system;

4–A fee set by the DPS Director, currently $60, that must be paid by cashier's check, certified check or money order, payable to Arizona Department of Public Safety. Personal checks and cash are not accepted. The fee is non-refundable, and subject to change.

You should also note that:

• If the form is incomplete or all the elements are not properly submitted, the application will be returned within 10 business days with an explanation.

• Only original DPS forms are accepted—do not send photocopies, but you should keep a photocopy for your own records.

• Fingerprint cards come with the application form, which you must take care of on your own—DPS won't take your prints. Local police departments, private firms (found online or in a phone book) or most often, your trainer can take care of this for you.

Application Background Checks

When DPS receives your completed application, they conduct a background check and digitally send your fingerprints to the FBI for a national check. DPS must by law complete all checks in 60 days, and if you pass, issue your permit within 15 working days of your qualifying. Although the forms indicate you should allow 75 days for processing, department policy is to approve applicants as quickly as practical, it has generally been a speedy process and "customer satisfaction" is generally high. Now that permits are no longer required, applications have dropped off dramatically and backlogs are a thing of the past. DPS does not accept calls inquiring about the status of an individual permit application. You'll be checked out through the: Arizona Criminal Justice Information System (ACJIS); National Crime Information Center (NCIC); Arizona Crime Information Center (ACIC); National Instant Background Check System (NICS); Interstate Identification Index (III); Automatic Fingerprint Information System (AFIS); and Federal Bureau of Investigations (FBI). All this to certify the innocent, using scarce resources that could instead go into tracking and catching crooks. But it sure does make some cool lists of people.

Application Denials

If DPS denies your permit after the qualification check, they must notify you in writing within 15 working days and state why your application was denied. When you receive the denial, you have 20 days to submit additional documentation to DPS. When DPS receives this material they must reconsider their decision and, within 20 days, inform you of their reconsideration. If you are denied again, you can schedule an administrative hearing, and then if necessary you have the right to appeal in Superior Court.

Duration and Renewals

A permit is valid for five years and renewable every five years. To renew you complete the DPS-required paperwork (available online) and pay the tax again. Trainers offer optional refresher courses, which is a good idea, since required two-hour refreshers were repealed in 2006. Fingerprint cards are only due with your original application. The first renewals came due in Sept. 1998, and about 27,000 people became eligible in that year. (Until 2005, CCW classes were 16 hours, renewals 4 hours, and the permit and renewal period was four years. Now, training and refresher courses are optional, the same as for open carry since statehood. Training is important and highly recommended. Visit **TrainMeAZ.com** for a wide array of training opportunities.)

You can only apply for a renewal within 90 days of your permit's expiration, or up to 60 days afterwards. If you miss the 150-day window you must reapply. A 90-day grace period was added in 2005 for active-duty military personnel deployed overseas, upon their return. The renewal tax is currently $43.

Remember that, although you can apply for renewal up to 60 days after your permit expires, an expired permit is invalid and you lose the sales, reciprocity, school-zone and other advantages of the permit. DPS now notifies people when their permits are up for renewal—but you should watch the calendar carefully yourself. DPS must conduct a background check within 60 days of getting your renewal application, before your permit can be renewed.

Suspension and Revocation

DPS will suspend or revoke your permit if you become ineligible and will notify you in writing, stating the reasons, normally within 15 working days of the suspension or revocation.

Residency

Now that any U.S. citizen may apply for a CCW permit here, residency rules have limited impact (formerly, only Arizonans could apply). DPS relies upon the residency guidelines for car registration, found in §28-2001. A non-U.S.-citizen living in Arizona should check with DPS for eligibility. Also note that Arizona residents can no longer rely on out-of-state permits for use in the state—state residents must use the Arizona CCW permit. Newcomers who want a permit must apply since out-of-state permits are not transferrable (but are valid until you gain residency). If you get and use another state's permit because you can't qualify for an Arizona permit, you're in violation of the law.

When DPS was running standardized training, it established minimum requirements, and though no longer required, the list still retains value. Chapter 8 has some self-tests (DPS had required a 20-question test):

1–Familiarization with loading, unloading and accessories for single action and double action revolvers, and single, double and select action semiautomatic pistols.

2–Firearms choices for handling comfort, stopping power, controllability and holstering options.

3–Safety issues, including the basic safety rules, gun safes, locking devices, ammunition storage, loaded firearms in the home and training household members.

4–Legal information from A.R.S. Title 4 (liquor laws); Title 13 (criminal law) including chapters 4 (justification), 5 (responsibility), 12 (assault), 13 (kidnapping), 15 (trespass and burglary), 29 (public order), 31 (weapons and explosives); and federal, county and other states' laws as relevant.

5–Shooting techniques including isosceles stance, Weaver and modified-Weaver stances, one- and two-hand grip options, dominant eye, sight alignment, sight picture, target identification, trigger contact and trigger control.

6–Judgmental shooting for shoot/don't shoot situations.

7–Behavior for contact with peace officers while carrying a concealed weapon, declaring CCW, approaching law enforcement during volatile situations, responsibilities for reporting shooting incidents.

8–Mental conditioning for use of deadly force, including white, yellow, orange and red modes of awareness, critical-incident stress and post-shooting trauma.

9–Gun cleaning and maintenance, level of disassembly, unloading weapon, field stripping, cleaning procedures, lubrication and safety checks for re-assembly.

10–A ten-round marksmanship test, at an NRA TQ15 target or equivalent (where the secondary scoring ring is not greater than 14" x 16"), without time limit, 5 rounds fired at 5 yards and 5 rounds fired at ten yards, with shots outside the secondary scoring ring not counting as hits, that students complete with at least 70% accuracy.

Some training programs conduct classes far exceeding these minimum requirements, and some a good bit less. You may want to consider taking an introduction-to-firearms class if you're new to this, since CCW classes are often advanced programs geared more toward those who already know how to handle and shoot firearms.

RECIPROCITY IN GENERAL

Historical Note: A national movement is afoot to ease the stranglehold state laws have placed on law-abiding travelers. Introduced at state and federal levels, *reciprocity laws* seek to guarantee that people who may legally carry in their home states can carry when in another state. It seems the Second Amendment is providing no protection for travelers, and a legislative solution is being sought.

Your home state's rules would not apply when you go "abroad." You would be subject to laws, regulations and customs of the state you are in at the time.

Most proposals seek to obtain this relief for individuals with government-issued permits only. Supporters typically cite the portion of Article IV of the Constitution, known as the *Full Faith and Credit clause*, which says in pertinent part, "Full Faith and Credit shall be given in each State to the public Acts, Records, and judicial Proceedings of every other state;". This sets a model similar to marriage and driver licenses.

Other efforts seek to free people not acting criminally from harassment or arrest for simple possession of a legally owned firearm, independent of the state involved or the method of carry. A distinction would then exist between so-called *"right to carry"* (which requires government taxes and papers) and *"freedom to carry"* (which simply leaves government out of your personal affairs). This is sometimes referred to as Vermont- or Alaska-style carry, where such systems exist. The law that established this level of freedom for simple possession of private property here in Arizona is *Constitutional Carry*, enacted in 2010.

This emulates the way free people are basically free to speak their minds regardless of their location (and no license to exercise the First Amendment is required at this time, except perhaps that broadcasts are forbidden without government permission). It fully respects constitutional guarantees.

Some states take the approach that, if your permit is similar to ours, and your state formally honors ours, then we will honor yours. A method is then set up to determine if the two state's requirements are a rough match. Such comparisons are problematic because they once again subject your rights to bureaucratic review, as in the days before "shall issue" permits, and indeed, states have experienced great difficulty in agreeing if their "standards" match. When the officials decide there is no match, they remove the right to carry between those states. To link all 50 states to each other and thus restore rights (for properly government-licensed individuals only) would require 1,225 pacts (49+48+47... etc.).

Each state's requirements are of course quite different. Studying the laws of your home state (a common requirement) hardly prepares you and is certainly not a match for the laws in any other state. Florida used to have no shooting test for its permit, Virginia asks for proof of demonstrated competence with a gun but does not define it further, Texas requires 50 shots at three distances with all shots timed, Arizona had required seven hits out of ten, and so it goes, state to state.

Some states are considering honoring anyone who has a state-issued permit, and Arizona adopted a form of this in 2006. Some will issue a permit to anyone qualified, resident or not, getting around the problem in yet another way (we have that provision here too). A few states have no permit system, leaving them out of the picture when their residents are on the road, or for you when you visit. A few have introduced laws that would allow you to drive through their states on a "continuous journey," or to enter the state but only for competition or special events. You *should* have rights. You have a mess.

Federal bills have so far unsuccessfully sought to require all states to honor the permits of all other states. Residents in Vermont are excluded because they need no permit to carry in the first place (and you need none while there; possession of personal property, absent some overt criminal act, has simply not been outlawed). The 98% of Americans who bear arms but who have refused to sign up for a government carry-rights permit are left out completely.

Rumors are swirling about which state has adopted what policy, and relying on a rumor where no rule exists can get you arrested. Viewing the printed statute yourself is a good way to help avoid rumors. Laws may offer less protection when new, before on-the-street police policy is established and well known throughout the law enforcement rank and file. As noted earlier, a state can revoke a deal without notice.

Do not assume from the information below or any other listings you may be able to find that reciprocity or recognition exists, only that the states are looking into the possibilities, and you might want to too.

It would be nice if there was a rock-solid reliable place to call to find out exactly where reciprocity exists, but there is none at the present time, and none is expected. Besides, a complete answer with precisely all the do's and don'ts is more than you can possibly get over the phone. The job of telling you is not the role of the police, the sheriff, the DA, the AG, the library or anyone else. Why, you'd need a book the size of this one for every state you visited.

One solution that addresses the core problems is the proposed American Historical Rights Protection Act, or something like it. This basically says that if a person has a gun, the person isn't a criminal, and the gun isn't illegal, then that is not a crime, based on the 14th Amendment. For a copy of this draft statute contact Bloomfield Press or visit gunlaws.com.

ARIZONA RECIPROCITY

Starting in 1998 DPS was required under §13-3112 to enter into written *reciprocity agreements* if a state had a CCW law "substantially similar" to ours. After seven years, only six states made the list, (and one, Utah, went on then off and then back on and off again, confusing everyone). In 2003, to help improve results, conditions were spelled out more clearly, but that didn't work very well either. The state has now adopted a policy called *recognition*, where properly state-issued permits are honored, and the reciprocity concept of signing deals with other states to honor each other's carry permits was repealed in 2006.

Permit-and-License-List Caution

These lists change rapidly and are available through private, commercial and government websites. Most rights organizations have a version posted, and they are linked from our National Directory at gunlaws.com. The accuracy, timeliness, and what it actually means to be on such a list can be hard to tell, and is usually undercut by disclaimers accompanying the lists. Info below is from sources believed to be reliable in 2011.

Arizona Recognizes Them. Prior to 2006, DPS relied on a changing list of states it believed should be recognized here by law. Now, Arizona recognizes any firearm permit issued by any other state or subdivision of a state if: the permit is valid where issued, the permit holder is at least 21 years old, here legally, not an Arizona resident, and not a prohibited possessor. DPS is still required to sign written agreements with other states if the other state requires it for mutual recognition. DPS has warned that states on a list are "for information purposes," this "does not constitute an endorsement," and "it is each individual's responsibility to ensure that they are in compliance" with law.

Eight states that have **signed reciprocity agreements with Arizona:** Alaska, Arkansas, Idaho, Ohio, Pennsylvania, South Dakota, Texas and West Virginia. Michigan and possibly other states only recognize permits from people who live in the issuing state. Utah, popular for its easy, thrifty, widely recognized permit was eliminated from the Arizona reciprocity list in Oct. 2005, because they issued permits to Arizonans who couldn't qualify under our laws.

They Recognize Arizona. Subject to change, DPS believes another 26 states do (and 15 states do NOT) currently recognize Arizona's permit, and has posted its beliefs on its website. **In addition to the states above,** DPS believes these also recognize the Arizona permit: Alabama, Colorado, Delaware, Florida, Georgia, Indiana, Iowa, Kansas, Kentucky, Louisiana, Michigan, Mississippi, Missouri,

Montana, Nebraska, Nevada, New Hampshire, New Mexico, North Carolina, North Dakota, Oklahoma, South Carolina, Tennessee, Utah, Virginia, Wisconsin (as of 11/1/11), Wyoming.

DPS has issued multiple warnings for people who plan to rely on an Arizona permit when out of state, since laws differ, recognition changes, and you should contact the state you are visiting prior to going there. One of the main reasons reciprocity works at all is because people do carry discreetly. By not having contact with authorities, you avoid those who can get quite jumpy when they learn you are from out of state and have a gun, regardless of confusing recognition and reciprocity laws. DPS says **these states do NOT recognize** an Arizona permit: CA, CT, HI, IL, ME, MD, MA, MN, NE, NV, NJ, NY, OR, RI, VT, WA.

Freedom to Carry (no permit needed to discreetly bear arms): Alaska, Montana (outside city limits), Texas (in vehicles), Vermont, Wyoming (for residents only at this time), and of course, Arizona. Check with these states for special conditions that may apply.

Get Another State's License. These 21 states may issue licenses to qualified non-residents: Arizona, Connecticut, Florida, Idaho, Indiana, Iowa, Maine, Maryland, Massachusetts, Minnesota, Nevada, New Hampshire, New Jersey, North Dakota, Oregon, Pennsylvania, Rhode island, Tennessee, Texas, Utah, Washington.

These states passed laws that allowed some bureau in the state (indicated in parenthesis) to cut deals with a bureau in another state, or have other conditions that might lead them to recognize others' permits—check with them for details:

Alaska (no authority named), Arizona (Dept. of Public Safety), Arkansas (State Police), Connecticut (Commissioner of State Police), Georgia (County Probate Judge), Kentucky (Sheriff), Louisiana (Deputy Secretary of Public Safety Services), Massachusetts (Chief of Police), Mississippi (Dept. of Public Safety), Missouri (County Sheriff), Montana (Governor), New Hampshire (Chief of Police), North Dakota (Chief of the Bureau of Criminal Investigation), Oklahoma (State Bureau of Investigation), Pennsylvania (Attorney General), Rhode Island (Attorney General), South Carolina (Law Enforcement Div.), Tennessee (Commissioner of Safety), Texas (Dept. of Public Safety), Utah (Dept. of Public Safety), Virginia (Circuit Ct.), West Virginia (Governor).

The different authorities named in that list are a measure of the consistency of the laws from state to state. If you read these lists and get the sense that reciprocity schemes don't solve the problem and truly unshackle innocent citizens, well, you're not alone. Instead of a vigorously protected civil right to arms, your rights have been eagerly reduced to a short list of government-approved states, a bewildering array of conditions, and expiration dates, for licensees only, under the complex infringement of reciprocity schemes.

HOW CAN YOU CARRY A GUN?

With Constitutional Carry in place, all law-abiding adults in Arizona are free to carry pretty much any way they choose. The top two images used to be legal only with a government-issued permission slip. Now they are perfectly lawful—it's just the simple possession of private property, no crime committed, no victims, no one harmed. Discreet possession has become the civilized norm in modern Arizona.

The woman having a beverage would be in violation only if she's in a bar and there's alcohol in the glass—did you rush to any judgments on that one? You are free to possess arms loaded or unloaded, state law makes no distinction (but arms legally transported by minors must be unloaded). Open carry hasn't changed since statehood in 1912.

The law no longer contains any general ban on peacefully carrying discreetly, and although the law frees you to carry firearms in a typical holster or other standard way, it doesn't *require* that they be carried that way. A gun tucked in a belt or sticking out of a pocket violates no statute, but is unsafe, not recommended and may attract attention you won't want. Carrying a gun in your hand will attract more attention than you want, could lead to serious charges, and is not advisable when out in public. If you walked down the street with an armful of guns or multiple holsters you'd be asking for unwanted attention, and you'll surely get it. Culturally, it's routine to carry long guns in cases and sidearms holstered or in some suitable container of your choice (as you would any valuable property you might carry). Hunters learn how to safely bear arms before going afield.

Police can always cite a person for threatening and intimidating, or disorderly conduct or worse, which are gray areas subject to police and court discretion. As a general safety rule, a sidearm should always be holstered or possessed discreetly unless ready to use. Be smart, act tastefully and just use common sense when outside. And remember, it's illegal to carry discreetly and not tell a law-enforcement officer you're armed, *but only if and when asked during an official stop.* You only have to show a CCW permit, if you have one, when asked by an LEO in a bar or licensed restaurant that allows permitees as customers. (A $300 fine applies and they can suspend your permit if you don't have it with you, but you can completely fix that later in court.)

The same rules apply in a car or other means of transportation—for a law-abiding adult legally in the state, who's not committing or about to commit a crime, and in a place that isn't restricted—any typical means of possession is legal. General principles of civil behavior apply.

In general, people between 18 and 21 are free to carry, on themselves or within their immediate control in a vehicle, in a wholly or partially visible holster or case, but you need to see the many fine details, in Chapter 1. Minors under 18 must be with an adult and meet other conditions, also in that chapter.

Special federal conditions for minors, guns on or near school grounds, guns in bars and other restricted places, and the effect of various posted signs are detailed in Chapters 1, 2 and 7.

WHERE ARE GUNS FORBIDDEN?

WHERE ARE GUNS FORBIDDEN?

The prohibited places listed may not apply to the proper authorities in the performance of their duties—peace officers, members of the military, licensed bodyguards, prison guards, special exempt agents of the government and many more. The federal list alone includes more than 50 different statutes that exempt special people from gun laws that the rest of us must obey. Today, prohibited places present serious infringement on an unfettered public right to simply bear arms.

Simple Prohibited Places

Additional restrictions may exist, and new ones may be added in what is sometimes referred to as *infringement creep*.

* Going into a polling place with a gun, on the day of an election, is a class 1 misdemeanor. §13-3102

* Bringing or having a gun in a nuclear or hydroelectric generating plant is a class 4 felony. See also *Parking Lots* in Chapter 1. §13-3102

* It's a class 2 felony to bring a gun into a correctional facility or its grounds, or into or around a secure care facility. §13-3102

* Firearm possession is prohibited for the general public on the gate side of airport passenger security checkpoints. §28-8429

* A special set of rules for active, retired and off-duty peace officers, dubbed LEOSA, was enacted in 2007, with both protections for and bans on carry, §38-1102, 18 USC §926 B, C.

* Possession of firearms on a military base is subject to control by the commanding officer.

* The gun ban in the National Parks and Refuges, repealed in 2010, freed the public to bear arms there the same as elsewhere in Ariz. Fearful cries of impending bloody doom never materialized, the same as with every other repeal of gun-rights infringements.

* As long as firearms are out of sight in a locked vehicle they are generally legal parked, as of 2009 (§12-781), but there are risks and narrow exceptions, see *Parking Lots* earlier in this chapter.

Checking Guns at Entrances

You must "check" deadly weapons you carry (relinquish possession) on entering any public establishment or any public event, after people in charge make a reasonable request for you to give them custody of ("check") the weapons, *only if* they provide a proper *secure storage facility* for storing the weapon as required under the law. (§13-3102)

A *public establishment* is a structure, vehicle or craft owned, leased or operated by government in Arizona. A *public event* is a named or sponsored event of limited duration run by government, or by a private entity with a government permit or license. It does not include an unsponsored gathering of people in public. Those phrases do not describe a private enterprise.

A *secure storage facility*, sometimes referred to as *lockers*, must be readily accessible on entry and allows for immediate retrieval on exit. No record of you or the weapon may be recorded if you use the facility. Without facilities, no legal demand for checking can be made. CCW permits have no effect on any of this. They may take the weapons (watch the muzzle!) or let you put them in the lockers.

A sign banning weapons at an entrance is considered a reasonable request, though it doesn't provide actual, dispositive proof that you knew possession of your property was a violation. If you were to enter and it becomes evident you are armed, and someone brings to your attention this is not allowed, you could be asked to leave, check the weapon, or even face a misconduct with weapons charge, under §13-3102, a class 1 misdemeanor. Your attitude could play into the result.

Nothing prevents any *private place* from putting up any type of sign that asks people who exercise the civil right to bear arms to keep out. They do this without realizing that discriminating against any other civil right would bring cries of injustice and serious criminal charges against them, along with boycotts and social opprobrium.

Denial of civil rights under color of law is a federal crime, 18 USC §241 et seq., widely unenforced (it's complicated). Places that hang signs banning guns typically do nothing to keep guns out, they just hang the signs, which creates "make-believe" gun-free zones. Walking past them creates the potential for charges to be brought.

In a private place, if it becomes evident you're armed and someone brings it to your attention, you could be asked to leave (which is most typical), check the weapon, or face a class 1 misdemeanor trespass, charge under §13-1502 or -1503. Nothing requires a private place to provide lockers or anything else, although they are free to take this very dangerous option, and make people handle loaded firearms in public the way government facilities presently require to keep you out.

Many places are understandably reluctant to check guns because the staff is unqualified to handle a variety of firearms that creates liabilities, are dangerous, expensive, subject to theft, leave you defenseless, deny your civil rights under color of law (a federal offense, 18 USC §241 et seq.) etc. The most prudent course it would seem, recommended by many experts, is to let honest people simply "come and go in peace," and many places do. Many government facilities however have taken to installing lockers of various types to make individuals check their arms while they are at the site and retrieve them when they leave.

Some otherwise innocent people in Arizona, carrying fully discreetly, and failing to notice signs of varying design, have entered all types of places, with and without signs, taken care of their affairs, and left without incident. It has been known to occur.

Places Licensed to Serve Alcohol

You can't bring a gun, openly or discreetly, into a place licensed to serve alcohol except:

– The licensee can, and may also authorize employees
– Hotel or motel accommodations are permissible
– Gun shows, meetings, classes and similar events may be allowed
– For aid in an emergency you may enter, if you get no alcohol
– CCW permitees are a special case, described below

Along with bars this includes restaurants that serve alcohol, even if you steer clear of the bar area. Places that only sell packaged alcohol, like stores, are not part of this ban. A violation in a place that serves alcohol is a class 3 misdemeanor under §4-244.

It's illegal for a liquor licensee to allow a person with a firearm (except for specified officials) to remain on the premises. It's illegal for the licensee to supply you with alcohol knowing you're armed. These are both class 3 misdemeanors. A licensee must call the police to remove an armed person, if necessary. The State Liquor Board can suspend, revoke, or refuse to renew a liquor license for failure to comply.

CCW Permits and Liquor Service

As of 2009, CCW permitees can enter bars and other liquor-serving places, but only if they don't imbibe, maintain concealment, and the place doesn't have properly posted official no-guns-allowed signs.

See *No-Guns-Allowed Signs* in Chapter 1 to understand the rules for CCW signage. For the rest of the public, bars and most restaurants are off limits if you are armed. An effort is being made to free the rest of the public to eat at licensed restaurants without having to disarm before entering. In an ironic paradox, police are advising people not to leave firearms in cars, due to frequent thefts. The no-guns signs not only defeat the self-defense purpose, it helps arm the criminal element.

School Grounds

Under Arizona state law it is a class 1 misdemeanor to knowingly have a firearm on school grounds , unless it is:

- directly related to hunter or firearm safety courses; or
- for use on school grounds in a program approved by a school; or
- unloaded within a means of transportation under the control of an adult. If the adult leaves, the vehicle must be locked and the gun must not be visible from outside. See Chapter 7 for federal rules.

A school is a public or nonpublic kindergarten program, common school, or high school. A violation of this law is a class 6 felony if it occurs in connection with other specified crimes. A CCW permit does not convey any special state privileges with respect to schools the public does not have. See §13-3102. A valid CCW permit does exempt you from the controversial and unenforced federal gun-free-school-zone rule, see Chapter 7.

School boards are exempt from preemption (§13-3108) to make and enforce policies banning weapons on school grounds, except for peace officers and anyone with a specific authorization from the school administrator, and to report any dangerous incidents, under §15-341. School personnel must immediately report violations to the school administrator, who must immediately report violations to a peace officer, per §15-515.

Public colleges and other public educational institutions must develop their own rules, as required by §13-2911. A pupil may be expelled for more than a year, under §15-841, for use, display or possession of a gun, or for bringing one to school, at the school authority's discretion. Federal rules also apply, described in this chapter and Chapter 7. A CCW permit does exempt a person from a so-called 1,000-foot federal gun-free zone around school property, but this controversial concept, enacted in 1995, covers virtually all populated area of the country and is unenforceable, a feel-good paradox that serves no practical purpose and perplexes officials and the public alike.

Federal Facilities

Guns are generally prohibited in federal facilities (18 USC §930). Knowingly having a gun or other dangerous weapon (except a pocket knife with a blade under 2-1/2 inches) in a federal facility carries a fine and jail time. Exceptions include authorities performing their duties, and according to statute, lawful carrying "incident to hunting or other lawful purposes."

However, test cases on whether CCW (or other routine legal carry) will qualify are less than perfect, and federal authorities routinely post the rights-restriction law without posting the exception, a deplorable practice. The feds have used the courts, regulations (39 CFR §232.1) and 39 USC §410 (which indicates Title 18 does not apply to the Post

Office altogether) in an effort to skirt the inconvenient (for them) "lawful purposes" protection of the statute, and effectively forecloses possession. It hardly matters that the law says you can't be convicted unless notice is conspicuous at each public entrance, or if you had actual notice (which, it could be argued, you now do). A federal facility is a building (or part), federally leased or owned, where federal employees regularly work. It appears to be unsafe (legally) to be armed in federal facilities, including parking lots.

A WORD TO THE WISE

Changes may be made to any of these laws, without notice. Sometimes these changes are administrative, sometimes they affect how you carry, and they can make what once was legal illegal, and vice versa. You need to be aware of these changes and ensure that you comply with all the current rules and regulations to avoid even innocent violations.

Officials don't agree on everything, and how law enforcement officers interpret the law may be different from how an attorney interprets it or how you understand it from your own study and training. Courts have been known to "interpret" a law in direct contradiction to what it says. Unfortunately, the law is not always black and white. The statutes may appear to clearly say one thing but an officer on the scene or a court may interpret it very differently when it addresses the facts of any particular case or when it applies past court precedents.

The elements of this book will undoubtedly change. Remember that you may face serious repercussions for what may be seemingly minor infractions. _The Arizona Gun Owner's Guide_ is just one tool for helping you on a long road to knowledge, and neither the road nor this book is perfect. That road has many turns and pitfalls—you should not rely on a single vehicle for such a complicated route, and be extremely cautious as you travel its course. Take steps to stay current.

Bloomfield Press prepares **updates** periodically. To receive free news about updates send us a stamped, self-addressed envelope, or visit our website and sign up for the free updates. Addresses are on page two.

For the complete list of states currently probably recognizing CCW:
http://www.dps.state.az.us/ccw • 602-256-6280

CCW Records

DPS maintains records comparing the number of permits requested, issued and denied, and reports the information annually to the governor and the legislature. As of the summer of 1997, Arizona had 53,121 permit holders (about 1.3% of the population), 692 qualified instructors and 292 approved training organizations. In 2004 there were 67,689 permits (1.2%), 1,208 instructors, and 384 organizations. By 2005 that grew to 72,820, 1,439 and 470, and in 2007 it was 86,939, 1,414 and 528. In 2009 it stood at 131,830 (roughly 2% of the population), 1,472 and 624. By August of 2011 there were 162,408 permit holders (2.5% of the population), and no DPS-approved schools or instructors, since DPS was removed from certifying the training. By Nov. 2014, it reached 225,587 folks, about 3.4% of Arizonans. The book *Concealed Handgun Manual* is available at gunlaws.com and has similar statistics for all 50 states, as well as a 50-state license guide and other very valuable information. Breakouts by age, race, gender and county for Arizona are posted on the DPS website.

A special DPS hotline phone is available for any questions you may have about the discreet-weapons program. In the Phoenix area call 602-256-6280. Outside Phoenix call toll-free, 1-800-256-6280. The website is www.azdps.gov/ccw/default.asp

Note that a CCW permit generally doesn't allow you to go anywhere you couldn't otherwise go with a firearm, except *conditional* access to liquor-licensed establishments and school zones, described earlier.

TYPES OF WEAPONS 3

There are weapons and there are weapons. Arizona is an enviably free state, and people here are free from government interference in legal ownership, possession and use of a vast variety of firearms, knives and methods of carry. However, if a gun is modified in certain ways, it becomes a *prohibited weapon* and it may be a crime to possess it at all. In the years from 1994 to 2004, certain firearms and accessories, under the so-called "assault-weapon" ban, could only be owned if they were made before Sep. 13, 1994 (that law has ended). *Assault*, by the way, is a type of behavior, not a type of hardware, despite political and "news" media ranting otherwise. The definitions of legal firearms are a moving target, just like the gun laws themselves, see Chapter 1.

Weapons include *dangerous instruments*—things that can be deadly depending on their use, like fireplace tools, kitchen knives or baseball bats. *Deadly weapons* specifically refers to things designed for lethal use. Guns are only one kind of deadly weapon. Concealed-weapon-permit holders, and now all law-abiding adults under the 2010 Constitutional Carry law, may discreetly carry guns and other arms.

It makes sense for American citizens to be educated and have an understanding of the different types of firearms, their methods of operation, selections for personal defense, holstering options, ammunition types, loading and unloading, cleaning and maintenance, accessories and more, even if you currently own no guns. Many fine books cover these areas, and all gun owners ought to be familiar with such information. This chapter of *The Arizona Gun Owner's Guide* only covers weapons from the standpoint of those that are illegal, restricted or otherwise specially regulated.

PROHIBITED WEAPONS

In 1934, responding to mob violence spawned by Prohibition, Congress passed the National Firearms Act (NFA), the second major federal law concerning guns since the Constitution (the first was the Militia Act of 1792, which actually required keeping arms). The NFA was an attempt to control so-called "gangster-type weapons" and reduce crime. Items such as machine guns, silencers, short rifles and sawed-off shotguns were put under strict government control and registration. These became known as "NFA weapons."

This gave authorities an edge in the fight against crime. Criminals never registered their weapons, and now simple possession of an unregistered "gangster gun" was a federal offense. Failure to have paid the required transfer tax on the weapon—the enormous sum (at the time) of $200—compounded the charge. Regular types of personal firearms were completely unaffected.

Political assassinations in the 1960s led to a public outcry for greater gun controls. In 1968 the federal Gun Control Act was passed, which absorbed the provisions of earlier statutes, and added bombs and other destructive devices to the list of strictly controlled weapons. Arizona calls these *prohibited weapons,* though a more accurate title might be *controlled weapons,* as you'll see under Machine Guns. It is generally illegal to make, have, transport, sell or transfer any prohibited weapon without prior approval and registration. Violation of this is a class 4 felony under state law, and carries federal penalties of up to 10 years in jail and up to a $10,000 fine.

Defaced Deadly Weapons
Removing, altering or destroying the manufacturer's serial number on a gun is a class 6 felony. Knowingly having a defaced gun is a class 6 felony. See §13-3102 for the letter of the law.

Federal Weapon Bans
Congress has been considering a variety of selective and categorical firearms bans. You would be well advised to follow developments and remain keenly aware of any firearms or accessories that were formerly legal and then declared illegal. The Striker-12 shotgun is an example, described later in this chapter.

"ILLEGAL" GUNS

(Sometimes also referred to as NFA weapons, prohibited weapons or destructive devices)

Frequently but inaccurately termed illegal, these devices are among those that are legal only if they are pre-registered with the Bureau of Alcohol, Tobacco, Firearms and Explosives (BATFE):

1–A rifle with a barrel less than 16 inches long;
2–A shotgun with a barrel less than 18 inches long;
3–A modified rifle or shotgun less than 26 inches overall;
4–Machine guns;
5–Silencers of any kind;
6–Firearms over .50 caliber;
7–Street Sweeper, Striker-12 and USAS-12 shotguns.

Guns with a bore of greater than one-half inch (except regular shotguns) are technically known as destructive devices. Some antique and black powder firearms have such large bores but are not prohibited, as determined on a case-by-case basis by BATFE.

STUN "GUNS"

A new body of law in 2005 introduced rules for stun guns, see §13-3117. A *remote stun gun* is an electronic device that emits an electrical charge, designed to incapacitate a person or animal, by touching them with electrodes on the device, or remotely through probes wired to the device, or by a spark, plasma, ionization or other conductive means from the device.

An *authorized remote stun gun* (ARSG) is a remote stun gun that also: puts out less than 100,000 volts and under nine joules of energy per jolt, has an ID on all projectiles discharged from it, blows out labeled "confetti" identifying material when fired that is traceable to the original buyer through records kept by the manufacturer, and includes an offered training program. The statute in effect addressed the products and practices of Scottsdale-based TASER International, Inc., the inventor of the ARSG. Their newest models actually record the date and time of every trigger squeeze.

ARSGs present new use-of-force issues, because one could be deployed in a situation where a firearm might not be justified, and yet if a firearm is needed, reaching for an ARSG could be a life-endangering choice. Rules and liability issues for ARSGs are in an early state of flux and may not shake out for a while.

Now available to the general public, a TASER device is a legitimate new self-defense tool and the company has sold more than 230,000 to the public by 2011. It stands between defenselessness and deadly force, a one-shot reloadable weapon with its own special appeal and utility. It stakes out a place in the continuum of force, from bare hands to handguns. *TASER* is a brand name, like Colt, and not the name of a product, even though TASER Int'l. was the only firm that made such devices for many years. The firm obtained opinions from the BATF in 1993, 1994 and 1998 that their design, using compressed gas to expel tethered projectiles, does not meet the federal definition of a firearm.

Using or threatening to use an ARSG against a police officer on official business is a class 4 felony, and other charges may apply. No penalty has been specified for using an ARSG against an individual, and an appropriate level of response against a criminal ARSG attack is unclear. Because an ARSG attack is incapacitating, and an officer's duty weapon could be seized, some police departments have considered using deadly force against an ARSG assault. Using an ARSG in the commission of a crime is an aggravating factor for sentencing purposes (§13-701).

"AFFECTED" WEAPONS

Historical Note: The federal Public Safety and Recreational Firearms Use Protection Act (also called the Crime Bill, also called the assault-weapons ban, expired Sep. 13, 2004), allowed citizens to have certain firearms and accessories only if they were made before Sep. 13, 1994. New products required a date stamp and were off-limits for the public. Having an affected weapon or accessory that had no date stamp was presumption that the item was not affected (that is, it was a pre-crime-bill version) and was OK. This law has now expired, none of these conditions apply any longer, and we can see the value of laws with expiration dates. Even the *New York Times* admitted, after the law expired, that it had absolutely no effect on crime. For the record, the affected weapons (there were about 200) included all firearms, copies or duplicates, in any caliber, known as:

Norinco, Mitchell, and Poly Technologies (Avtomat Kalashnikovs (all models); Action Arms Israeli Military Industries Uzi and Galil; Beretta AR-70 (SC-70); Colt AR-15; Fabrique National FN/FAL, FN/LAR, and FNC; SWD M-10, -11, -11/9, and -12; Steyr AUG; Intratec TEC-9, -DC9 and -22; and revolving cylinder shotguns, such as (or similar to) the Street Sweeper and Striker 12, and, any **rifle** that can accept a detachable magazine and has at least two of these features: a folding or telescoping stock; a pistol grip that protrudes conspicuously beneath the action; a bayonet mount; a flash suppressor or threaded barrel for one; and a grenade launcher, and, any **semiautomatic pistol** that can accept a detachable magazine and has at least two of these features: a magazine that attaches outside of the pistol grip; a threaded barrel that can accept a barrel extender, flash suppressor, forward handgrip, or silencer; a shroud that is attached to, or partially or completely encircles, the barrel and permits the shooter to hold the firearm with the nontrigger hand without being burned; a manufactured weight of 50 ounces (3-1/8 lbs.) or more when unloaded; and a semiautomatic version of an automatic firearm, and, any **semiautomatic shotgun** that has at least two of these features: a folding or telescoping stock; a pistol grip that protrudes conspicuously beneath the action; a fixed magazine capacity in excess of 5 rounds; and an ability to accept a detachable magazine, and, any **magazines**, belts, drums, feed strips and similar devices if they can accept more than 10 rounds of ammunition (fixed tubular devices for .22 caliber rimfire ammo are not included).

OTHER ILLEGAL DEADLY WEAPONS

A number of dangerous devices, some of which are not guns, are prohibited under federal or state law. Possession of these is a class 4 or 5 felony (§13-3102, defined in §13-3101) under Arizona law:

- Explosive, incendiary or poison gas: bombs, grenades, mines or rockets with more than four ounces of propellant (with an exception for fireworks that comply with state law)*

- Molotov cocktails*

- Nunchaku—a martial-arts weapon made of two sticks, clubs, bars or rods, connected by a rope, cord, wire or chain. Nunchaku are not prohibited in lawful martial-arts pursuits.

- Gas-pressure bombs—chemical substances placed in a container so that emitted gases will build up pressure and cause the container to rupture, or cause an explosion or detonation of the substances (added in 2002, expanded in 2008)

- "NFA weapons" without proper BATFE approval (e.g., short rifles or shotguns, devices to muffle a firearm, full-auto firearms)

- Improvised explosive devices—a device using explosives, or destructive, lethal, noxious, pyrotechnic or incendiary chemicals designed to destroy, disfigure, terrify or harass (added in 2008)*

- Dry ice with intent to cause injury, death or property damage

- Federal law adds mortars to the list, and

- Missiles with an explosive or incendiary charge over 1/4 ounce

- Armor-piercing ammunition (handgun bullets with at least a core of one or a combination of tungsten alloys, steel, iron, brass, bronze, beryllium copper, depleted uranium, or a fully jacketed handgun bullet larger than .22 caliber if the jacket exceeds 25% of the total weight. Excluded are nontoxic shotgun shot, frangible projectiles designed for target shooting, projectiles intended for industrial purposes, oil- and gas-well perforating devices, specified fireworks and flares, and ammo intended for sporting purposes.)

NOTE: Effective 3/1/94, Street Sweeper, Striker-12 and USAS-12 shotguns are classified as destructive devices, subject to NFA regulations (similar to machine guns), and *must now be registered*. The tax is waived for all such weapons owned before 3/1/94. If you own and do not wish to register such a weapon, or wish to transfer ownership without filing federal transfer papers, you may transfer the weapon to a properly qualified dealer, manufacturer or importer (with their permission), or to a law enforcement agency.

* The ban includes possession of parts or materials designed and intended for making these items.

MACHINE GUNS

Under strictly regulated conditions, most private citizens who can own regular firearms can own certain other weapons that would otherwise be prohibited. An example is the machine gun.

Unlike normal firearm possession, the cloak of privacy afforded gun ownership is removed in the case of so-called "NFA weapons" (technically, Title II devices), including full autos, suppressors, "sawed off" long guns, and more—those originally restricted by the National Firearms Act of 1934. The list has grown since that time, through subsequent legislation. For a law-abiding private citizen to obtain an NFA weapon, five conditions must be met. These requirements are designed to keep the weapons out of criminal hands, or to prosecute criminals for possession.

1–The weapon itself must be "available,"—registered in the National Firearms Registry and Transfer Records of the Treasury Dept. This list of arms includes about 193,000 machine guns.

> The registry was closed to full autos on 5/19/86. New registrations since then can only include the other Title II devices. Any full autos made after that date may now only be transferred to proper government agents, who acquire them regularly.

2–Permission to transfer the weapon must be obtained in advance, by filing "ATF Form 4 (5320.4)" available from the BATFE.

3–An FBI background check is performed to locate any criminal record that would disqualify you from possessing the weapon. This is done with a recent 2" x 2" photo of yourself, fingerprints (FBI FD-258 Fingerprint Card) submitted with the application, and signature approval of your local chief-law-enforcement officer, typically the sheriff or police chief. Corporations are exempt from the photo, fingerprint and CLEO-signature requirements. In 2014, CLEOs were required to provide legal certifications to the public within 60 days, with options if they can't comply for good reason (§13-3121).

4–You must pay a $200 transfer tax to the Internal Revenue Service. For some NFA weapons, the transfer tax is $5.00.

5–The previous owner's name in the National Registry is changed to the new owner's name, and a new tax stamp, showing the weapon's serial number, is issued. The original or a copy of this stamp must always accompany the weapon, and permission to take the weapon across state lines must be obtained in advance.

The three ways to legally obtain a machine gun include:

1–A properly licensed dealer (a Class III FFL) can sell a registered machine gun to a qualified private buyer; 2–A legal owner can obtain permission from BATFE to transfer the firearm to a qualified recipient in the same state, and 3-You can inherit one. Any inherited NFA weapon can be transferred interstate directly to the heir, after the registration papers are approved. Special rules for executors of estates that contain NFA weapons are available from BATFE.

With prior approval you can make NFA weapons (except machine guns), such as short rifles, sawed-off shotguns, suppressors, "gadget guns" (technically, "any other weapons" such as pen, cane or wallet guns), etc. The application process is similar to the process for buying such weapons. Unregistered NFA weapons are contraband, and are subject to seizure. Having the unassembled parts needed to make an NFA weapon counts as having one.

The authorities are generally exempt from these provisions. Open trade in automatic weapons in Arizona is allowed between manufacturers and dealers, and includes state and city police, prisons, the state and federal military, museums, educational institutions, and people with special licenses and permits.

The official trade in machine guns is specifically prohibited from becoming a source of commercial supply. Only those machine guns that were in the National Firearms Registry and Transfer Records as of May 19, 1986 may be privately held. This includes about 6,600 machine guns in Arizona. The number available nationally will likely drop, since no new full-autos are being added to the registry, and the existing supply will decrease through attrition. Arizona has about 18,000 NFA weapons in total.

CURIOS, RELICS AND ANTIQUES

Curios and *relics* are guns with special value as antiquities, for historical purposes, or other reasons that make it unlikely they will be used currently as weapons. The *Curio and Relic List* is a 60-page document available from BATFE. They can also tell you how to apply to obtain curio or relic status for a particular weapon.

Antique firearms, defined as firearms with matchlock, flintlock, percussion cap or similar ignition systems, manufactured in or before 1898, and modern replicas meeting specific guidelines, are exempt from certain federal laws. For complete details contact BATFE. Remember, though, that if it can fire or readily be made to fire it is a firearm under Arizona law.

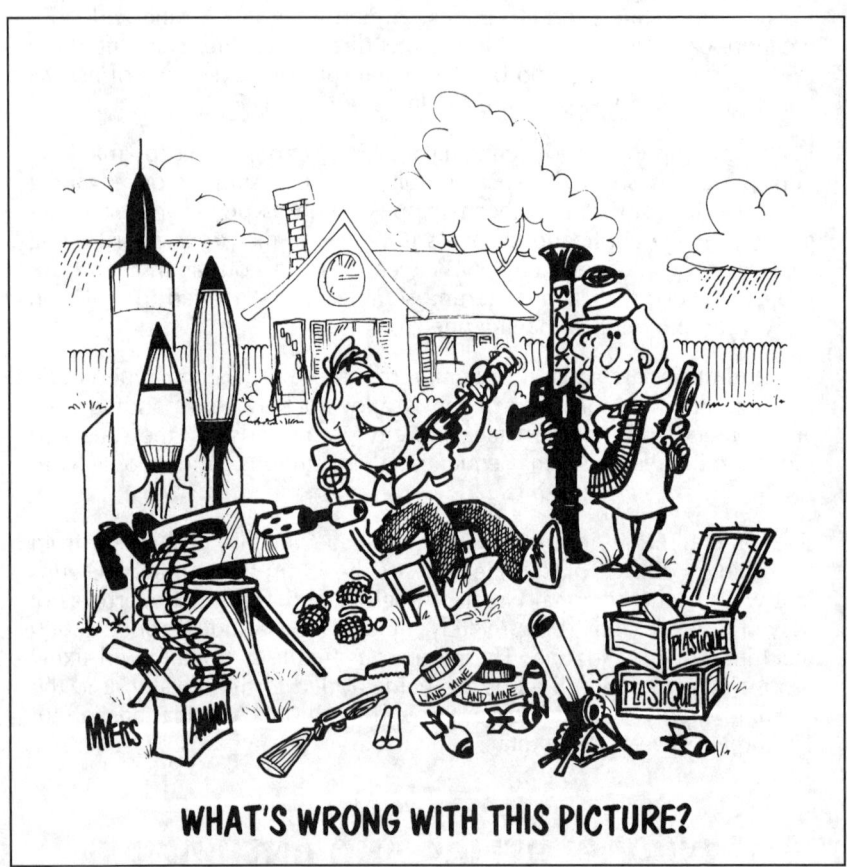

WHAT'S WRONG WITH THIS PICTURE?

These weapons and destructive devices are illegal unless they are pre-registered with the federal Bureau of Alcohol, Tobacco, Firearms and Explosives.

- A rifle with a barrel less than 16 inches long
- A shotgun with a barrel less than 18 inches long
- A modified rifle or shotgun less than 26 inches overall
- Street Sweeper, Striker-12 and USAS-12 shotguns
- Machine guns or machine pistols
- Silencers of any kind
- Firearms using fixed ammunition over .50 caliber
- Armor-piercing ammunition
- Explosive, incendiary or poison gas bombs
- Explosive, incendiary or poison gas grenades
- Explosive, incendiary or poison gas mines
- Explosive, incendiary or poison gas rockets with more than 4 ounces of propellant (includes bazooka)
- Missiles with an explosive or incendiary charge greater than 1/4 ounce
- Mortars

Keep in mind that additional weapons may be added to this list in the future.

WHERE CAN YOU SHOOT? 4

Once you own a gun, it's natural to want to go out and fire it. If you've decided to keep a gun, you should learn how it works and be able to handle it with confidence. Public and private ranges provide an excellent and safe opportunity. Many people also enjoy shooting outdoors on open terrain.

The 72.5 million acres of Arizona are regulated by many authorities. The Bureau of Land Management (BLM) published a state map in 1979 called the *Surface Management Responsibility* map, which gives an excellent overview of what's what, despite its age, though it is now out-of-print and hard to find. Precise up-to-date records are kept by BLM, and the department offers maps-on-demand, printed directly by computer from the latest data available. World Wide Maps and More in Phoenix stocks topographical maps of the entire state, hunter's guides, the *Arizona Where-To-Shoot Gun Map* and more.

In order to understand where you can practice marksmanship outdoors in this state, you must first know where you cannot shoot. The restrictions come first when determining if shooting in an area is permissible. Bans on possession in Arizona's parks and preserves were repealed in 2010 and replaced with an essentially uninfringed right to keep and bear arms, but shooting there still has many limitations.

Certain legal justifications may allow shooting, even when it would otherwise be illegal. An example would be self defense. The list of those justifications is found in Chapter 5.

GENERAL RESTRICTIONS

Illegal Trajectory
It is illegal to shoot if the bullet will travel anywhere where it may create a hazard to life or property. In National Forests, you may not shoot from or across a body of water adjacent to a road.

91

Aside from being a violation of several laws, there is a general rule of gun safety here: Be sure of your backstop. Take this a step further: Be sure of your line of fire. Never fire if you are unaware of (or not in full control of) the complete possible trajectory of the bullet. Be sure that the shot poses no threat to life or property. Charges could include endangerment, disorderly conduct with a firearm and more.

The Quarter-Mile Rule

Shooting while hunting is prohibited within one-quarter mile of any residence or building that could serve as a residence whether occupied or not (without the owner's permission), or any other developed facility of any kind. Another vehicle (other than your own) counts as an object that you must be at least a quarter of a mile away from when you discharge your firearm.

Although this rule comes from and applies specifically to hunting regulations, authorities use the quarter-mile rule as a rule-of-thumb for determining if gun use is safe. Don't take chances. Be *at least* a quarter of a mile from *anything* when you are shooting. Localities may also restrict shooting within one-quarter mile of occupied structures.

From Vehicles

It's illegal to fire a gun (without a handicap permit) from a vehicle while hunting. This includes an automobile, pickup, off-road vehicle, motorcycle, aircraft, train, powerboat, sailboat, floating object towed by a sailboat or powerboat or any device designed to carry a person. (Requirements for hunting waterfowl are different.) It's also illegal to knowingly shoot upon, from, across or into a road or railway while hunting, or while in the National Forests.

Once again, hunting regulations provide restrictions that aren't specifically regulated in most other state statutes. However, authorities frown on "road shooting," and it is extremely unsafe. Shooting from vehicles or on or around roads is not a good idea.

Shooting at Structures

Shooting at a residential structure is a class 2 felony. Shooting at a non-residential structure is a class 3 felony. See §13-1210.

Posted Areas

Properly authorized signs can be posted to restrict firearm use, possession, or access to land or premises (details later in this chapter):

• Private Land may be posted by authority of the landowner or lessee to prohibit shooting or trespassing;

• State Land may be posted by the lessee, but only with permission from the Commissioner of the Arizona State Land Dept.;

• National Forests may have areas posted for a number of reasons by the authorities;

• The Arizona Game and Fish Dept. can post areas to restrict hunting.

Protection of the Right to Practice

Enacted in 2014 to overcome abuses that had become severe, state law now requires that no one can be banned ("enjoined") from the lawful discharge of a firearm, air gun or the use of archery equipment except in two ways. First, by action taken by the state attorney general to stop a public nuisance under §13-2917. Second, a private nuisance lawsuit or a negligence suit can be filed by a person, in a permanent residence within 1/4 mile of the shot, with a strict burden of proof, and with the prevailing party collecting attorney's fees and costs. Any claimed damages are subject to clear and convincing evidence, and more, to deter nuisance and frivolous actions, see §12-558.

Preemption of Political Subdivisions

To prevent infringements at the local level, §13-3108 was tightened in 2014 to prevent political subdivisions of the state from using zoning to prohibit or regulate the discharge of firearms, or to regulate land maintenance or improvements (for example, making berms) directly related to shooting, on private land that isn't open to the public on a commercial or membership basis. Localities are also banned from exercising similar controls over land used for agricultural or other non-commercial purposes.

THE LAND OF ARIZONA

Bureau of Land Management Land (BLM)

Nearly 20% of the state's land—more than 14 million acres—is managed by BLM under a doctrine of multiple use and sustained yield. What this means is that recreationists share the lands with ranchers, miners and other users. BLM land is as close as there is to truly "public land."

The Arizona state BLM office in Phoenix maintains the maps (called Master Title Plats) and current records on land status for the entire state. It is an invaluable resource for determining what land is what.

Two maps published by BLM are excellent general references for shooters. The *Surface Management Map* provides an overview of the whole state at a glance. The *Wilderness Status Map* shows all BLM areas under special restrictions as wilderness preserves. Both are out-of-print but provide a good overview if you can find one. BLM now produces maps digitally on demand to your specifications.

Shooting on BLM land is legal as long as you comply with the normal state regulations. A few special considerations apply:

- Observe posted closures. BLM land generally isn't posted, although main entry points may have signs. Special Management Areas and other sections may have posted restrictions;
- Avoid conflicts with lessees;
- Discharging firearms in developed areas is prohibited;
- The Long Term Visitor Area (LTVA) of La Posa in the Yuma district, and the land within one-half mile of the LTVA is closed to shooting and hunting;
- It's illegal to willfully deface, disturb or destroy any personal or public property, natural object or area, structures, or scientific, cultural, archaeological or historical resource;
- It's illegal to willfully deface or destroy plants or their parts, soil, rocks or minerals.

Hunting on BLM land is allowed, subject to the regulations of the Arizona Game and Fish Dept. However, BLM authorities can close sections to shooting, or restrict or close access to public lands, when and where safety or other valid reasons may require.

Knowingly and willfully violating BLM regulations carries a maximum $100,000 fine and up to one year in jail. Violators may be subject to civil damages as well. BLM field offices are listed in Appendix C.

Cities

It is usually illegal to shoot, with criminal negligence, recklessness, knowledge or intent, into or within the boundaries of any city in the state. Under §13-3107, amended in 2000 and nicknamed Shannon's law, discharge within city limits is a class 1 misdemeanor or a class 6 felony, at the prosecutor's discretion, even for a negligent (accidental or unintentional) discharge. The exceptions include:

• *Legally Justified Instances*—Shooting within city limits under certain narrow circumstances called *justification.* An example is self defense. For details see Chapter 5;

• *Animal Attacks*—Shooting within cities in self defense or defense of another person against an animal attack, if a reasonable person would believe that it is immediately necessary and reasonable to protect yourself or the other person from the animal;

• *Firing Ranges*—Shooting within city limits on a properly supervised range. See "Shooting Ranges" in this chapter for a description of such ranges;

• *BB-type Guns*—With adult supervision for shooting air or carbon-dioxide gas-operated guns (be certain that property and people are not endangered or threatened in any way);

• *Designated Hunting Ranges*—An area within a city may be designated for hunting, as established by the Arizona Game and Fish Commission. Discharge may be restricted within 1/4 mile of an occupied structure, unless it's OK with the owner or person in the structure. "Occupied structure" is now limited to a building where a reasonable person, at the time and place the shot was fired, would expect a person to be present (§13-3107); Wherever hunting is legal, government subdivisions are under similar restrictions (§13-3108);

• *Control of Nuisance Wildlife*—A required permit is available for this purpose from the Arizona Game and Fish Dept. or from the United States Fish and Wildlife Service. Problems with nuisance wildlife can often be handled best by contacting an exterminator who has the proper permits;

• *Special Permits*—The chief of police of a city may issue a special permit for firing guns within city limits.

• *Blanks*—The prohibition against firing in cities under §13-3107 does not apply if the firearm is using blanks (though disturbing the peace or other charges could still apply);

• *Remote areas*—Shooting is not prohibited in city areas that are more than one mile from any occupied structure as defined in §13-3101. Some cities have annexed large tracts of land that would qualify under this exception, but it's important to note that this definition of an "occupied" structure would include your own empty vehicle, or pretty much any other object where a person could be, whether occupied or not.

County Land

Arizona is divided into 15 counties: Apache, Cochise, Coconino, Gila, Graham, Greenlee, Lapaz, Maricopa, Mohave, Navajo, Pima, Pinal, Santa Cruz, Yavapai and Yuma. In nine of these, the only lands generally owned by the county are small parcels that contain the sheriff's office, the county courthouse, the jail, vehicle depots or similar facilities. Six counties have a park system, listed in Appendix C.

County parks used to be open to firearm use, but because of increasing population and the relatively small sizes of these parks, firearm use is now extremely limited. In general, rifled firearms and target practice are unavailable in county parks. Shotgun (smooth bore) hunting on these lands is regulated by the Arizona Game and Fish Dept. If and when prudent wildlife management requires, strictly controlled rifled firearm hunting may be allowed by AGFD in cooperation with the park authorities.

County land may contain authorized shooting ranges, and in fact one of the state's best equipped ranges was under county control for many years, through its parks department. The land under the Ben Avery Range (west of I-17 on Carefree Highway), is now owned by the Arizona Game and Fish Dept. Named for a former state legislator and newspaper reporter, Ben Avery wrote many of Arizona's gun laws, along with Sandra Day O'Conner, who served as the first female Justice on the U.S. Supreme Court, from 1981 to 2005.

Large tracts of county land are open to private ownership for homes, ranching, agriculture, mining, business and other uses. In 2014, to protect firearms and related uses, §11-812 was amended so that nothing contained in the statutes could prevent, restrict or otherwise regulate the lawful discharge of firearms, air guns or use of archery equipment on a private lot or parcel of land—as long as it is not open to the public on a commercial or membership basis. If it becomes open to the public that way it would be subject to business regulation.

State Parks, Local Parks and Preserves

Arizona has 25 state parks on about 45,000 acres of land. These are managed by Arizona State Parks. Hunting in the state parks is regulated by the Arizona Game and Fish Dept. Civil-rights bans for gun possession in local parks and preserves were repealed in 2010, so firearms may be carried openly or discreetly in the parks. Because of the relatively small size of these parks and the large number of people using them, use of firearms is very limited. Standard rules for checking weapons apply.

Parks (and other local authorities) have leeway under preemption (§13-3108) to ban shooting within 1/4 mile of an occupied structure, but preemption prevents local authorities from prohibiting shooting:

• In cases of legal justification, such as self defense;

• In defense against an animal attack if a reasonable person would believe that deadly physical force against the animal is immediately necessary and reasonable under the circumstances to protect yourself or another person;

• On a properly supervised range;

• On properly approved and posted hunting areas;

• To control nuisance wildlife with a proper permit;

• With a permit from the chief law enforcement officer of the locality;

• By an animal-control officer performing official duties.

Indian Country

Twenty-two federally recognized Indian tribes—better than 360,000 people as of 2014—live in Arizona on reservations. More than 19 million acres are included in this land, some 27.2% of the state.

Carrying firearms while traveling on a public road that passes through Indian land is subject to standard state regulations.

Each reservation maintains its own government, and operates as an independent nation when convenient, or a dependent of the federal government at other times. A Tribal Council, headed by a Chairman, Chairperson, President or Governor, makes laws regarding guns on Indian land. You must contact a specific reservation to get current information and valid permits for their land. No state license, permit or tags are required by the state for hunting in Indian Country. The address and telephone number for contacting each reservation is listed in Appendix C, or easily found on the Internet.

Many reservations encourage hunting (and other use) of their land, with proper tribal permits and within regulations. Hunting does not necessarily mean firearms are allowed. For example, hunting is permitted by the Navajos on the largest reservation in the state, but a tribal code prohibits the use of firearms. Some tribes offer no guidelines on the subject, or create rules on an ad hoc basis.

Overlapping federal, state, tribal and local authority creates confusion when laws are violated in Indian Country. Enforcement of laws on

Indian reservations can cause a fundamental conflict over jurisdiction. Actual penalties for violations may be the subject of dispute. The Arizona Commission on Indian Affairs calls for the federal government to take ultimate responsibility for prosecution of crimes committed on Indian lands by non-Indians, but this can be a messy Catch-22.

National Forests

15.3% of Arizona—about 11 million acres—is made up of National Forests operated by the Forest Service of the U.S. Dept. of Agriculture. You are free to carry arms at anytime and anywhere in the National Forests, as long as you are in compliance with the law (not a prohibited possessor, legal weapons, etc.).

Hunting is allowed in the National Forests, but requires proper licenses. Contact the Arizona Game and Fish Dept. for details. Also see the separate section on "Hunting Regulations" in Chapter 6.

Target shooters are required to use removable targets. Clay pigeons, bottles, trash and other targets that leave debris are prohibited. Black powder shooters should use extra caution to prevent fires. Your choice of a target site should be against an embankment that will prevent bullets from causing a hazard. Your location should be remote from populated sites—it's safer, and noise complaints will cause you grief.

The laws controlling the National Forests are in a book called *Code of Federal Regulations, Title 36,* available at larger libraries and online. These federal rules prohibit shooting:

- Within 150 yards of a residence, building, campsite, developed recreation site or occupied area;
- Across or on a Forest Development road;
- Across or on a body of water adjacent to a Forest Development road;
- In any way that puts people at risk of injury or puts property at risk of damage;
- That kills or injures any timber, tree or forest product;
- That makes unreasonable noise;
- That damages any natural feature or property of the U.S.

Violation of these restrictions carries a maximum $5,000 fine and a prison sentence of up to six months under federal law.

The Forest Supervisor may issue special restrictions on firearm possession or use, or close a section to access if it seems necessary to protect public safety, or for other good reason. Anything you can do to minimize your impact on the forest and other forest users will help preserve access to the forest for marksmanship and recreational shooting. Restricted areas often prohibit many uses, such as camping, grazing, vehicles, time-of-day or time-of-year limits, shortcutting switchbacks, use by large groups, equipment storage, possessing glass containers, etc. The following list describes areas where shooting is specifically restricted in Tonto National Forest. Other restrictions apply to these sites, and the other National Forests in Arizona may have their own restricted sites. Approximate locations appear in parenthesis, contact the Forest Service for precise maps:

Order 12-100, 7/1/92. Cholla Recreation Site. Discharging a firearm, air rifle or gas gun. (Named recreation area, W. shore of Roosevelt Lake)

Order 12-101, 7/21/92. Burnt Corral Recreation Site and adjacent areas. Discharging a firearm, air rifle or gas gun. (Named recreation site, NE. tip of Apache Lake)

Order 12-110, 4/27/93. Grapevine Recreation Site. Discharging a firearm, air rifle or gas gun. (Named recreation site, S. shore of Roosevelt Lake)

Order 12-16-5R, 11/1/93. Roosevelt Lake Wildlife Area. No access without specific authorization. (S. shore area nr. E. tip of Roosevelt Lake, and large area of N. shore)

Order 12-17, 9/16/94. Diversion Dam Recreation Area. Discharging a firearm, air rifle or gas gun, except authorized hunting. (Salt River nr. E. entry to Roosevelt Lake)

Order 12-99-R, 6/19/95. Windy Hill Recreation Site and Entrance Road #82. Discharging a firearm, air rifle or gas gun. (Isthmus area on S. shore of Roosevelt Lake)

Order 12-137-2R, 3/19/97. Needle Rock Area. Discharging a firearm, air rifle or gas gun, except authorized hunting. (E. and W. of Verde River from Ft. McDowell reservation to N. of Needle Rock)

Order 12-161, 8/20/97. Sears Kay Ruin Recreation Area. Discharging a firearm, air rifle or gas gun, except authorized hunting. (Just N. of Cave Creek Rd. entry to forest)

Order 12-165, 11/22/97. Exchange Pasture - ATV Area. Discharging a firearm, air rifle or gas gun. (S. of Globe)

Order 12-5-6R, 11/10/99. Lower Salt River Recreation Area. Discharging a firearm, air rifle or gas gun, except authorized hunting. (N. and S. of Salt River from Saguaro Lake to Granite Reef Dam)

Order 12-59-2R, 7/14/00. Superstition Wilderness Area. Discharging a firearm except for authorized hunting. (6-mile stretch E. of Apache Junction)

Orders 12-146-R and 12-182, 8/7/01. Discharging a firearm or gas gun, except authorized hunting. (Note: These two orders removed all 80,000 acres of commonly used decades-old metro-Phoenix target-practice areas, E. of Carefree, N. of Scottsdale, W. of Bush Highway, and N. of Mesa and Apache Junction, raising a firestorm of protest that failed to prevent the closures, and now requires metro-Phoenix residents to push far further into the forest for recreational shooting and outdoor marksmanship practice.)

Order 12-08-234R 6/18/09. Discharging a firearm, air rifle or gas gun (36 CFR 261.58(m) on designated lands in the Cave Creek, Mesa and Globe Ranger Districts (detailed maps were issued, q.v.), except for lawful hunting, self defense and defense of a third person. Areas are high use recreation and forest-urban interface where "indiscriminate discharge of a firearm is likely to pose a substantial risk to public safety."

When special closures are made they should be posted, but sometimes they are not. It's always wise to check with a representative of the Forest Service about any piece of National Forest land you're planning on using. See National Forest Service field offices in Appendix C.

National Park Service Land

The National Park Service of the U.S. Dept. of the Interior manages 22 national sites in Arizona, more than any other state, totaling more than 3 million acres. This represents 4.2% of the state and includes National Parks, National Monuments, National Historic Sites and National Recreation Areas.

Limited hunting privileges exist in National Recreation Areas by special agreement of the Dept. of the Interior and the Arizona Game and Fish Dept. The unconstitutional federal ban on mere possession in our National Parks and National Wildlife Refuges, implemented by bureaucrats without an act of Congress, was lifted on Feb. 22, 2010, and now, state rules for carry apply on these lands.

Private Land

About 9.5 million acres, or 13% of Arizona, is owned privately or by corporations. You can shoot on your own land as long as you and your guns are in compliance with the law. That means you need enough land to shoot safely, at least a quarter-mile from any roads, outside of municipal boundaries, with legally possessed arms, without disturbing the peace, in an area not subject to other restrictions and so forth. Recently enacted or amended laws to protect such activity include at least §11-812, §12-558, §13-3107, §13-3108 and §17-601, which you should read and understand. As a land owner, you need to know precisely where you are located and all the regs that apply to the land you own before opening fire in your backyard.

Land owners may grant permission for others to shoot on their land and may allow access to the public, though if you charge or run a commercial venture other regulations apply. You can withdraw your permission at will. To prohibit shooting on or access to private land, the landowner or lessee must put up plainly legible signs (§17-304), at least eight by eleven inches in size, no more than a quarter-mile apart, around the entire protected area.

State and Federal Military Land

The 2.8 million acres of land reserved for military use (3.7% of the state), whether under the jurisdiction of the National Guard or a branch of the federal armed forces such as the Army or the Air Force, is controlled by a military commander. What a commander says, goes. As a practical matter, possession or use of firearms on a military base is subject to control by the commanding officer, although no statute specifically prohibits private arms.

You pretty much can't do anything on military land without prior approval. Where limited hunting privileges are available, they are subject to the regulations of the Arizona Game and Fish Dept. *and* the base commander. Anyone on military land is subject to a search. For details concerning a specific military installation, contact the base provost marshal or the base commander's office.

Military ranges are frequently available to the public or to organized groups on a controlled basis. Federal law actually says that a rifle range built with any federal funds may be used by the military, "and by persons capable of bearing arms" (10 USC §4309). The rules for use are set by whoever controls the range, and the military has first call on use of the range.

Under the federal Civilian Marksmanship Program laws (36 USC §40701) the Army cooperates with civilians to provide practice and firearm instruction for citizens and for youths in the Boy Scouts, 4-H and similar clubs. For details see the entry in Chapter 7. This program is part of the long historical record of cooperation between the government and the citizens in keeping the population trained in marksmanship and the use of small arms.

Carrying firearms while traveling on a public road that passes through military land is subject to standard state regulations.

State Land

12.9% of Arizona is managed by the Arizona State Land Dept., and leased out under guidelines that require productive use of the land. You must have a permit to be on the 9.4 million acres of state land. Trespassing is a class 2 misdemeanor.

State land, even though it may be under lease for grazing, agriculture, or any other purpose, is usually open to licensed hunting and fishing. Wildlife on state land belongs to the state, and so it is regulated by the Arizona Game and Fish Dept.

A person with valid licenses and tags, engaging in a lawful hunt, is allowed on state land. In effect, a hunting license validly used is a written exemption from the "No Trespassing – State Land" signs. Other people using the land, or hunters engaging in any other activities besides those normally involved in a lawful hunt, would be trespassing unless they had received special authorization.

Recreation permits are available for camping and other non-consumptive use of state land, but use of firearms is not included in these specially issued permits.

While you are on state land, it's illegal to intentionally or wantonly destroy, deface, injure, remove or disturb anything made and put there by people, or to harm or take away any natural feature, object of natural beauty, antiquity or other public or private property. Violation is a class 2 misdemeanor.

Shooting Ranges

Officially approved shooting ranges may be the best place to learn and practice the shooting sports. A properly supervised range may be legally set up in Arizona as long as it is operated by:

• A club affiliated with the National Rifle Association, The Amateur Trapshooting Association, The National Skeet Association, or any other nationally recognized shooting organization;

• Any agency of the federal government;

• An agency of this state, or a county or city government that will have the range within its boundaries;

• Any public or private school; or

• With adult supervision for shooting in underground ranges on private or public property;

• With adult supervision for shooting air- or carbon-dioxide-gas-operated guns.

The definition of a shooting range was expanded in 2014 to include, "Any area that is used for shooting on a private lot or parcel of land that is not open to the public on a commercial or membership basis." This is designed to stop various authorities that have been harassing the public for using air guns and other implements in their backyards, without harming anyone, as a matter of pure anti-rights bias (§17-601). Use of BB guns and similar training tools and toys in Arizona has always been understood to be protected under §13-3107, simply with adult supervision as plainly stated in statute. This also protects ranges people can simply set up on sufficient tracts of private land.

Outdoor shooting ranges have been built around Arizona by state government for public use. Managed loosely in good faith for decades, in 2011, the Arizona Game and Fish Commission was formally charged under §17-231 with responsibility to set: hours of operation, use fees, regulation of groups and events, operation of related range facilities, types of firearm and ammunition that may be used, safe handling of firearms at the range, required safety equipment for anyone using the range, sale of firearms, ammo and shooting supplies at the range, and authority of range officers to enforce the rules, including removal of violators from the premises and denying access for repeat offenders. World-class facilities like the Ben Avery range at the northern edge of Phoenix, and the Joe Foss range in Buckeye, are available for low daily fees and offer a tremendous array of shooting sports. See the entire list of state ranges at azgfd.gov. You can also use the *Arizona Where-To-Shoot Gun Map* from Wide World Maps and More, or TrainMeAZ.com, to find a range near you.

Shooting Range Protection

A special fund is set up under §17-273 to be used by the Arizona Game and Fish Dept. on shooting ranges open to the public and run by government or non-profit groups for:

1–shooting range engineering and studies;

2–noise abatement;

3–safety enhancement;

4–shooting range design;

5–new range sites and construction;

6–range relocations; and

7–other projects needed to operate and maintain ranges under good practices and management.

The Dept. may also accept private grants, gifts and contributions to carry out these goals. The Game and Fish Director and State Land Commissioner are directed to work together to identify state trust land suitable for new or relocated ranges.

Beginning in 2014, §17-273 requires money from goods sold at shooting ranges to go into the firearms safety and ranges fund and not into the AGFD general fund (with an exception for federal grant program income). Range fund money can now be used for two new purposes: shooting sports programs, and inventory for goods sold at ranges (targets, books, eye and ear wear, etc.).

Under §17-601 thru §17-605 extensive measures were put in place in 2002 to protect ranges from encroachment, nuisance lawsuits and arbitrary closings. A range is "a permanently located and improved area that is designed and operated for the use of rifles, shotguns, pistols, silhouettes, skeet, trap, black powder or any other similar sport shooting in an outdoor environment." Loosely defined archery, air gun and indoor ranges are excluded.

The state claims sole responsibility (preemption) for noise regulation, sets the standards ranges must meet, requires sound measurements (with interesting specs in that section), and empowers anyone to take the measurements. Zoning authorities are required to provide noise attenuation for certain communities near ranges properly constructed before July 1, 2002, and may negotiate with developers and land owners to do so. Ranges on land zoned for a school, hotel, motel, hospital, church, or for residential use, must close from 10 p.m. to 7 a.m. The proper authorities have the option to keep it open all night just for themselves, with adequate public notice, implying they need training more than the public does, and pointing out that "authorities" increasingly have powers and privileges denied to the public.

An affirmative defense against any civil liability is provided for ranges in compliance with the law. In such a lawsuit, the loser pays the costs. This is the real incentive to limit nuisance suits.

The general plan of a city with more than a million people must have, under §9-461.05, "protections from encroaching development" on certain outdoor ranges owned by the state before July 1, 2004. A one-half-mile buffer zone is created around such ranges to ban uses that might be incompatible with the range, such as residential, or a school, hotel, motel, hospital or church. Any such zoning already in place is grandfathered, and may remain. Such cities must file public records identifying the range and its area, and warnings about noise. A variety of threats to our nationally famous, official "Point-of-Pride" Ben Avery Shooting Facility, prompted this range protection bill, and Ben Avery is the only one fitting the description. This state law prevents the city of Phoenix and others from actions that might adversely affect the range. There were some pretty outrageous stories afoot. If the anti-rights folks can ban ranges, the Second Amendment would be gutted.

The protective zoning under this law does not apply to the National Guard, ranges owned by the state before 2002, and loosely defined archery, air gun and indoor ranges.

To prevent capricious action, under §17-621, the Game and Fish Commission, responsible in large measure for running Ben Avery, cannot close the range without meeting eight conditions, including a unanimous vote and an executive order from the Governor.

WHAT'S WRONG WITH THIS PICTURE?

1–Shooting within city limits is normally prohibited.

2–It's illegal to shoot or harm a cactus.

3–It's illegal to deface signs.

4–Trespassing is illegal.

5–You can't use targets that leave debris.

6–Shooting at wildlife requires a permit or license.

7–The target has no backstop. The shooter is not controlling the entire trajectory of the bullet.

8–The shooter isn't wearing eye or ear protection.

THERE'S NOTHING WRONG WITH THIS PICTURE!

Practicing the shooting sports outdoors is a perfectly natural and wholesome pursuit as long as you comply with the laws.

- The shooters are at a remote location, on land that isn't restricted.
- The target leaves no debris.
- The target has a backstop preventing bullets from causing a potential hazard.
- No wildlife or protected plants are in the line of fire.
- The shooters are using eye and ear protection.
- The sun is shining, they're improving their skills, and they're thoroughly enjoying themselves and their time spent outdoors.

DEADLY FORCE and SELF-DEFENSE LAWS 5

"I got my questionnaire baby,

You know I'm headed off for war,

Well now I'm gonna kill somebody

Don't have to break no kind of law."

– from a traditional blues song

There are times when you may shoot and kill another person and be guilty of no crime under Arizona law. The law calls this *justification,* and says justification is a complete defense to any criminal or civil charges (§13-103 to §13-421), but that's not perfectly airtight. See for example the entry about double jeopardy in this chapter. The specific circumstances of a shooting determine whether the shooting is justified, and if not, which crime has been committed. Whenever a shooting occurs, a crime has been committed. Either the shooting is legal as a defense against a crime or attempted crime, or else the shooting is not justified, in which case the shooting itself is the crime.

Your civil liability in a shooting (a lawsuit) can be a greater risk than criminal charges, you can be hit with both, and your legal protections are less vigorous in civil than in criminal cases. Overcoming criminal charges does not necessarily protect you from a civil suit—you can be tried twice. Justification in killing someone does not provide criminal or civil protection for recklessly killing an innocent third person in the process. A stray shot you make can be as dangerous to you legally as committing a homicide. Using lethal force is so risky legally it is yet another reason to avoid it if at all possible—for *your own* safety.

USE OF DEADLY PHYSICAL FORCE

A reasonable person hopes it will never be necessary to raise a weapon in self defense. It's smart to always avoid such confrontations. In the unlikely event that you must resort to force to defend yourself, **you are generally required to use as little force as necessary to control a situation. Deadly force can only be used in the most narrowly defined circumstances, and it is highly unlikely that you will ever encounter such circumstances in your life.** You have probably never been near such an event in your life so far. Your own life is permanently changed if you ever kill another human being, intentionally or otherwise.

The cover of this books asks, **"When can you shoot?"** The other part of the question is, **"...and expect to be justified in the eyes of the law."** You are only justified when the authorities or a jury determine—after the fact—that your actions were justified. *You never know beforehand.*

An argument can be made against the whole notion of *shoot to kill* on moral and legal grounds. In a true self-defense case, your goal—your intention and mental state—is not to kill, but to protect. *Shoot to stop,* or *shoot to neutralize the threat,* are other ways of saying it. In true self defense, you shoot to live.

No matter how well you understand the law, or how justified you may feel you are in a shooting incident, your fate will probably be determined much later, in a court of law. Establishing all the facts precisely is basically an impossible task and adds to your legal risks.

What were the exact circumstances during the moments of greatest stress, as best you remember them? Were there witnesses, who are they, what will they remember and what will they say to the authorities—each time they're asked—and in a courtroom? What was your relationship to the deceased person? How did you feel at the moment you fired? Did you have any options besides dropping the hammer? Can you look at it differently after the fact? Has there been even one case recently affecting how the law is now interpreted? Was a new law put into place yesterday? How good is your lawyer? How tough is the prosecutor? How convincing are you? Are the police on your side? Does the judge like your face? What will the jury think?

Be smart and never shoot at anyone if there is any way at all to avoid it. Avoiding the use of deadly force is usually a much safer course of action, at least from a legal point of view. You could be on much safer ground if you use a gun to protect yourself *without* actually firing a shot. Even though it's highly unlikely you'll ever need to draw a gun in self defense, the number of crimes that are prevented by the presence of a citizen's gun—*that isn't fired*—are estimated to be in the millions. And yet, *just drawing a gun can subject you to serious penalties*. Think of it in reverse—if someone pulled a gun on you, would you want to press charges because they put your life in danger? You must be careful about opening yourself up to such charges.

Still, the law recognizes your right to protect yourself, your loved ones and other people from severe criminal acts. In the most extreme incident you may decide it is immediately necessary to use lethal force to survive and deal with the repercussions later. *Shooting at another human being is a last resort, reserved for only if and when innocent life truly depends on it. If it doesn't, don't shoot. If it does, don't miss.*

You are urged to read the actual language of the law about this critical subject, and even then, to avoid using deadly force if at all possible. Get the annotated criminal statutes in a library and read some case law to get a deeper understanding of the ramifications of using deadly force—and dealing with the legal system after the fact.

The Arizona Gun Owner's Guide **is intended to help you on a long journey to competence. Do not rely solely on the information in this book or on any other single source, and recognize that by deciding to prepare to use deadly physical force if it ever becomes necessary you are accepting substantial degrees of risk.**

Even with a good understanding of the rules, there may be more to it than meets the eye. As an example, shooting a criminal who is fleeing a crime is very different than shooting a criminal who's committing a crime. You may be justified in shooting in a dire circumstance, and you might miss and only wound, but if you ever shoot to intentionally wound you'll have a very tough defense. The law is strict, complex and not something to take chances with in the heat of the moment if you don't have to.

It's natural to want to know beforehand just when it's OK to shoot and be able to claim self defense later. Unfortunately, you will never know for sure until *after* a situation arises. You make your moves whatever they are, and the authorities or a jury decides. The law doesn't physically control what you can or can't do—it gives the authorities guidelines on how to evaluate what you did after it occurs. **There are extreme legal risks when you choose to use force of any kind.**

A person who gets shot, or is merely threatened with a gun, is often thought of as a victim and in need of protection. There is a distinct tendency to think of the person holding the smoking gun as the perpetrator, later as the suspect, and finally as the defendant. If you ever come close to pulling the trigger, remember that there is a likelihood you will face charges when it's all over. The effects of the shot last long after the ringing in your ears stops.

> The "§" (section) symbol refers to the related section of the Arizona Revised Statutes, which can be found in Appendix D.

"The quotations that follow are plain, conversational expressions of the gist of the law." This is followed by a more precise description of the law. Finally, each subject is cross-referenced to the actual section ("§") of the law. Court cases that may set precedents are *not* included.

Common Law and Affirmative Defenses
"Self defense and similar justifications are controlled by statute."

All common-law offenses and affirmative defenses are now abolished. Justification defenses are explicitly not affirmative defenses. In other words, self defense and similar legal protections are not subject to the former abusive standard where you had to prove your innocence. See §13-103 for the letter of the law.

Burden of Proof
"The state must prove your guilt beyond a reasonable doubt."

Justification defenses are explicitly not affirmative defenses. Justified conduct describes behavior that, if not justified would be an offense, but if justified is not criminal or wrongful. If evidence of justification is presented by a defendant, the state must prove beyond a reasonable doubt that the defendant did not act with justification. See §13-205 for the letter of the law, and the Precautionary Note in this chapter.

Maintaining Order
"The person in charge can keep the peace."

If you are responsible for keeping order in a place where people are gathered you are justified in using deadly physical force if it is reasonably necessary to prevent death or serious physical injury. A person responsible for keeping order on a common motor carrier of passengers is similarly justified. See §13-403 for the letter of the law.

Self Defense
"Only when someone is about to kill or maim you can you shoot at them."

You are justified in threatening or using deadly physical force against another person to protect your self, only if a reasonable person would believe that your life or limb is immediately and illegally threatened by the other person. If your life or limb is being threatened by someone because of criminal activities you are doing, self defense is probably not a valid claim. You have no duty to retreat before threatening or using deadly physical force under this law if you are in a place where you can legally be and aren't engaged in an unlawful act. See §13-404 and §13-405 for the letter of the law.

The law says that if you provoke another person to attempt to use deadly force on you, you may lose your justification. However, it also says that if you provoke someone, then back down and they don't back down, you may be justified. You are never justified in response to verbal provocation alone. See §13-404 for the letter of the law.

Defense of a Third Person

"You can protect someone else the same as you can protect yourself."

You are justified in threatening or using deadly physical force to protect a third person under the same circumstances as you would to protect yourself: if a reasonable person would believe that your actions are immediately necessary to protect the third person against the use of unlawful deadly physical force. See §13-406 for the letter of the law.

Defense of Premises

"You can threaten deadly force but not shoot to protect your property."

You or someone acting for you is justified in threatening to use deadly physical force in order to stop someone from criminally trespassing on your land or premises. Using deadly physical force is *not* justified unless you are actually defending your life, the life of a third person, or if one of the crimes listed under "Crime Prevention" (see below) is being committed. See §13-407 for the letter of the law.

Law Enforcement

"You can shoot to control certain criminal activities related to arrest and escape."

NOTE: On September 15, 1989, this section of the law was changed to prohibit a private citizen from shooting at a fleeing suspect. The language used to make the change unexpectedly altered other parts of this law, which basically describes your rights and limits for firearms use in law enforcement situations. For example, the new law now conflicts with the self-defense laws. Under certain circumstances it says if you are being shot at, you can only threaten to shoot back. Although some experts agree that this is an unintentional error needing correction, other experts feel it is acceptable as is. It is the law until changed by the state legislature, and its effects on an actual case are uncertain. See §13-410 for the letter of the law.

Crime Prevention

"You can shoot to prevent certain crimes."

You are justified in using physical force or deadly physical force if you reasonably believe it is immediately necessary to prevent someone from the imminent or actual commission of:

1–Arson of an occupied structure (§13-1704)
2–First or second degree burglary (§13-1507, 8)
3–Kidnapping (§13-1304)
4–Manslaughter (§13-1103)
5–First or second degree murder (§13-1104, 5)
6–Sexual conduct with a minor (§13-1405)
7–Sexual assault (§13-1406)
8–Child molestation (§13-1410)
9–Armed robbery (§13-1904)
10–Aggravated assault (§13-1204, A, 1 & 2)

The justified threat or use of physical force or deadly physical force to prevent crimes listed in this statute include your home, residence, place of business, land you own or lease, any type of conveyance or any other place in the state where you have a right to be. (An activist judge, legislating from the bench, had decided this law only applied in your home, which was found nowhere in the law; new language was added in 2006 to eliminate his arbitrary precedent.) There is no duty to retreat before acting under this law. See §13-411.

Some experts feel that the second-degree burglary justification would be very difficult to defend in court. Anytime you have an opportunity to avoid conflict and do not, your defense in court can be more difficult.

The Castle Doctrine
"You can stand your ground against certain serious criminal attacks."

You are justified in threatening or in using physical force or deadly physical force against a person if you reasonably believe you or another person are in imminent peril of death or serious physical injury, and the person you act or threaten to act against had unlawfully or forcefully entered or was unlawfully or forcefully attempting to enter a residential structure or occupied vehicle, or had removed or was attempting to remove another person from the residential structure or occupied vehicle against their will. You have no duty to retreat before threatening or using physical force or deadly physical force in such situations. Residential structure is described in §13-1501. Vehicle means a conveyance of any kind, motorized or not, designed to transport people or property. See §13-418 for the letter of the law.

Presumption of Reasonableness
"Your actions are considered reasonable if you act as defined here."

Acting reasonably is a key element in any legal defense for the threat or use of any force. You are presumed to reasonably believe the threat or use of physical or deadly physical force is immediately necessary, under §13-419, for the purposes of the defense-against-crime statutes

§13-404 through §13-408, §13-418 and §13-421, if you know or have reason to believe that the person against whom you threaten or use such force is unlawfully or forcefully entering or has unlawfully or forcefully entered and is present in your residential structure or occupied vehicle.

For the purpose of those statutes, a person who is or has unlawfully or forcefully entered and is present in a residential structure or occupied vehicle is presumed to pose an imminent threat of unlawful deadly harm to any person in the residence or vehicle. This law, strengthened in 2011, forces courts to presume you are acting reasonably, and a criminal intruder poses a sufficient threat, to justify taking action, if the various conditions are met. These legal presumptions do not apply if:

1–The person you act against has the right to be in or is a lawful resident of the residential structure or occupied vehicle, which includes an owner, lessee, invitee or titleholder, and an order of protection or injunction against harassment has not been filed against that person;

2–The person you act against is the parent, grandparent, or has legal custody or guardianship of a child or grandchild sought to be removed from the residential structure or occupied vehicle;

3–If you are engaged in an unlawful activity or are using the residential structure or occupied vehicle to further an unlawful activity when you threaten or use the physical or deadly physical force; and

4– You act against a law enforcement officer who enters or attempts to enter a residential structure or occupied vehicle in the performance of official duties.

It's unclear whether the vagueness of item 3 might remove protection for tangential things like sexually active youngsters, visiting certain web sites on the Internet, incorrectly filed taxes, unknowing possession of certain contraband, unpaid traffic tickets and more. With so much activity criminalized by government, any generalized requirement to be crime-free is a dangerous Catch-22.

Public Duty
"Deadly force is justified if it is required or authorized by law."
This includes circumstances such as combat during war, executions, and certain actions of peace officers. It could be applied to a person who is commanded to assist a peace officer or who comes to the aid of a peace officer, if a reasonable person would believe such conduct is required or authorized. It also applies if a reasonable person would believe such conduct was required or authorized by a court or tribunal, or for legal process such as serving a warrant. See §13-402, §13-2403 and §13-3801 thru §13-3804 for the letter of the law.

Domestic Violence
"A domestic violence victim's state-of-mind is a legal issue."

If a person has been a victim of domestic violence, their state of mind may be taken into account in certain justifiable homicides. See §13-415 for the letter of the law. A person who uses or displays a firearm threateningly during domestic violence (§13-3601) is subject to arrest and many other conditions, covered in Chapter 1. The federal government has enacted a controversial *ex post facto* measure concerning domestic violence, described in Chapter 7.

Use of Reasonable and Necessary Means
"Private prison security officers can control their prisoners."

A special justification was added in 1997 for security officers at private prisons, to help them keep the prisoners under control and in custody. See §13-416 for the letter of the law.

Necessity Defense
"The common-law doctrine of *competing harms* is codified."

A special justification was added in 1997 to allow conduct, which would otherwise be prohibited, by a reasonable person who has "no reasonable alternative to avoid imminent public or private injury greater than the injury that might reasonably result from the person's own conduct." The necessity defense is unavailable for an offense involving homicide or serious physical injury. It recognizes that a person might justifiably break a law to avoid a greater imminent harm, such as trespass to prevent a wildfire, or intoxicated driving to escape an assault, which must be the only option and provable. The effect of the law on gun use is unclear (§13-417)

Self Defense During An Animal Attack
"You can defend against a dangerous animal attack."

Added by Shannon's law in 2000, §13-3107 allows shooting within cities in self defense or defense of another person against an animal attack, if a reasonable person would believe that it is immediately necessary and reasonable to protect yourself or the other person from the animal. This right to defend against an animal attack is also protected under the preemption law. (§13-3108)

Defensive Display
"Defensively 'going for your gun' is a justified act."

In many situations, reaching for, handling or mentioning a firearm can be charged as an assault. This was addressed in 2009 with a law to protect the legitimate defensive display of a firearm. Defensive display is justified when and to the extent a reasonable person would believe that physical force is immediately necessary to protect yourself against the use or attempted use of unlawful physical force or deadly physical force. You're not covered if you provoke the other person, or if the gun is used in a serious offense (§13-706) or violent crime (§13-901.03).

Defensive display includes verbally telling the other person that you have or can get a firearm; showing the firearm in a way a reasonable person would understand is meant for legitimate protection against someone using or attempting to use unlawful physical or deadly force; and placing your hand on a firearm while it's in your pocket, purse or other means of containment or transport. Defensive display is not a requirement before the use of physical force or the threat of physical force if you are otherwise justified in the use or threatened use of physical force. See §13-421 for the letter of the law.

PRECAUTIONARY NOTE
"Sometimes guilty people go free, sometimes innocent people do not."

Many factors make reliance on justification laws quite risky. Yes, the laws support the use of physical force or deadly physical force in life-threatening emergencies, and yes, your right to self defense is an invaluable and fundamental right. People are indeed often acquitted under justification, but remember that justice is not always served, and if you're acquitted, people often wonder afterwards if you were actually guilty and walked, a stigma that can hang over you for a lifetime.

Remember that you are only justified if the authorities or a jury agree, *after the fact*, that you were justified. You get to sweat it out the whole time the case is pursued, which can take years. Changes to the law can complicate your defense, such as when the burden of proof law, §13-205, was quietly changed to favor prosecutors in 1997, again in 2006 to favor defendants, and perhaps again—after this book goes to print.

In early years, if you claimed justification, the prosecution had the burden to prove beyond a reasonable doubt that your acts were not justified. In a stunning late-night legislative reversal quietly slipped in by prosecutors, you had to prove, by a preponderance of the evidence, you were justified, a huge blow to the protections Arizonans once enjoyed. Then in 2006, after a difficult legislative battle, the innocent-unless-proven-guilty standard was reinstated. The lobbying and legal wrangling can be an ugly business. The "laundry list" justifications in §13-411 have been a legal and judicial football at times.

Remember that a prosecutor's role is to work hard to get convictions, regardless of your guilt or innocence, and conviction rates approach 100%. You might hope that's because they only pursue bad apples. Many convictions though come from plea bargains, where regardless of guilt or innocence, you plead to a lesser charge to avoid the huge cost, humiliation, inconveniences—and risk—of a lengthy trial. Plea bargains help manage the huge case loads and have been called everything from wise to pragmatic, and from expedient to extortion.

The pursuit of high conviction rates may lead to what some would consider dirty lawyer tricks—with your future on the line. An added charge can be dangled before you, known as *charge stacking*, to get you to cop to a lesser plea. There's an old saying that has some merit here, "Better a criminal goes free than a lien on your home." Other folk wisdom advises, "It's better to be tried by twelve than carried by six." It is admittedly a very tough and risky choice.

RELATED LAWS

Use of firearms can lead to charges being brought against you if your actions are not justified by law. The basic penalties listed below may be significantly increased depending upon the circumstances.

Aggravated Assault
"You can't shoot or threaten to shoot someone without a legal reason."
Intentionally, knowingly or recklessly shooting a person (or causing serious bodily injury in any other way, for that matter) without legal justification, is aggravated assault, generally a class 3 felony, but it may range from class 2 to 6, depending on circumstances. Threatening to shoot someone is also aggravated assault. Taking or attempting to exercise control over a peace officer's firearm, other weapon, or any other implement (as defined, except handcuffs) is aggravated assault. See §13-1204 for the letter of the law.

Endangerment
"You can't just point a gun at someone."
It's against the law to recklessly put another person at substantial risk of imminent death or physical injury. When a risk of death is involved, endangerment is a class 6 felony. In all other cases, endangerment is a class 1 misdemeanor. See §13-1201 for the letter of the law.

Threatening or Intimidating

"You can't threaten a person with a gun."

Attempting to terrify anyone by threatening or intimidating them with physical injury or serious damage to their property ranges from a class 1 misdemeanor to a class 4 felony. Causing an evacuation is a class 1 misdemeanor. See §13-1202 for the letter of the law.

Disorderly Conduct

"You must act seriously with guns."

It's illegal to recklessly handle, display or fire a gun with the intention of or knowingly disturbing the peace or quiet of a neighborhood, family or person. This is a class 6 felony. Making unreasonable noise with the intention of or knowingly disturbing the peace and quiet of a neighborhood, family or person is a class 1 misdemeanor. See §13-2904 for the letter of the law.

Hindering Prosecution

"It's illegal to help someone evade the law."

Providing a person with a gun to help them avoid a felony, is a class 5 felony. Providing a gun to someone to help them avoid a misdemeanor or petty offense, is a class 1 misdemeanor. See §13-2510 thru 2512 for the letter of the law.

Criminal Nuisance

"It's illegal to endanger other people."

Recklessly creating or maintaining a condition that endangers the safety or health of others is a class 3 misdemeanor. See §13-2908 for the letter of the law.

Reporting Gunshot Wounds

"It's a crime to treat a gunshot wound and not report it."

A physician, surgeon, nurse or hospital attendant who is called on to treat a gunshot wound that may have resulted from illegal activity must immediately notify the authorities, and report the circumstances. Failure to make a report is a class 3 misdemeanor. See §13-3806 for the letter of the law. Hunters must report hunting accidents. (§17-311)

Aiding a Peace Officer

"You must aid a peace officer who commands you to do so."

It is a class 1 misdemeanor to refuse or fail to assist a peace officer in making an arrest or preventing a crime, if the officer commands you to help. A person who complies with such a request is granted a degree of protection against liability for any damages that might result. You may also be required to assist authorities in keeping the peace, and in maintaining law and order. See §13-2403 and §13-3801 to §13-3804.

Firing a Warning Shot
<u>"There is no justification for firing a warning shot."</u>

There is no statute that allows for warning shots. Any such shot in a city would be at least a class 1 misdemeanor, as a discharge within city limits (§13-3107), and other charges could be brought. Because warning shots are dangerous to bystanders (even a mile away when the round comes down) they are ill advised, and causing an injury in the process could be a felony.

The justification to shoot in self defense or in resisting certain crimes does not in any way allow using a firearm as an audible warning device, and it can attract more police attention to you (since the bad guys will have long since split) than you ever wanted. The firearm used may be subject to confiscation, and you really don't want to have to explain your innocence to uniformed officers at your door.

If the situation isn't immediately life or death, don't fire. If you really are locked in mortal combat, don't waste a potentially life-saving shot making scary noises. Firing a warning may serve as evidence that you didn't believe the situation presented an immediately deadly threat, and that you really did fire without justification. A warning shot is an irresponsible tool of Hollywood ignoramii (who constantly promote this dangerous crime), that has little place in the real world.

Bullet-Proof Vests and Body Armor
<u>"A crime committed while wearing a bullet-proof vest carries greater penalties."</u>

There is no law against owning or wearing "bullet-proof vests" (or as the trade refers to them, bullet-resistant vests or ballistic vests), and in fact, they are basically expensive defensive tools owned by many citizens. As of 1999, committing a felony while wearing body armor (defined in §13-3116) is itself a class 4 felony, and is considered an aggravating circumstance (§13-701) that can increase the penalty for a conviction. Wearing a vest for self defense but then finding yourself charged after an incident will complicate your defense in court.

Keeping Control of Your Firearms
<u>"You could be liable for damage others cause with your guns."</u>

You could face civil lawsuits for negligently letting a minor or other incompetent person get possession of a firearm you own, if it is used to cause injury or damage. This is a volatile area of law controlled more by lawyerly zeal, activist judges and unpredictable court precedents, than by statute. Some legal arguments attempt to spread blame to people other than those who commit criminal acts. It points to the wisdom in controlling access to your firearms at all times.

Responsibility
"Not everyone is equally criminally responsible for their acts."

A person who is guilty except insane at the time of commission of a criminal act is subject to special sentencing (§13-502). Temporary voluntary intoxication is not insanity and provides no defense for criminal acts (§13-503). The long-standing law (§13-501) that said a person under the age of fourteen could not be charged criminally for a shooting, unless there was clear proof that the person knew the conduct was wrong when it took place, was quietly repealed in 1997, at the same time that minors aged 15 to 18 were deemed adults for serious gun-related charges (a response to increased gang activity).

Aiming a Laser at a Peace Officer
"It's illegal to shine lasers or bright lights at the police."

Introduced in 2000, intentionally or knowingly shining a laser at another person if you know or reasonably should know that the person is a peace officer is a class 1 misdemeanor (§13-1213). *Laser* is broadly described to include any visible light beam used for aiming, targeting or pointing out features.

Hoax Bombs
"You can't go around scaring people with phony bombs."

It is a class 5 felony to intentionally terrify, intimidate, threaten or harass anyone with a simulated explosive device (§13-3110). Placing or sending such a device is considered prima facie evidence of illegal intent if the device does not have conspicuous written notice attached that it is inert and only serves as a curio, relic, display or similar.

Forensics Firearms Identification System
"DPS is officially running a database on firearm information."

The Dept. of Public Safety was authorized in 2000, under §13-3115, to establish and run an identification system to provide investigative information on criminal street gangs and the unlawful use of firearms.

Possession of Military Equipment
"You can't take your military gear with you."

It's a class 5 felony to keep state or federal military property you're not supposed to have, including arms. If the value is under $50, it's a class 2 misdemeanor. All such property is subject to seizure. (§26-178)

Diversion Programs
"Certain plea bargains are not allowed for firearm offenses."

A criminal complaint may be dropped if you successfully finish a diversion program, but you may not take one if the crime involves shooting, using or threatening display of a gun. (§9-500.22)

DNA Testing
"DNA samples are taken and filed for certain gun offenses."

DNA samples are now required from people convicted of offenses involving shooting, using or threatening display of a gun, along with many other offenses. (§13-610)

Terrorism
"Terrorism is broadly defined."

Terrorism includes, among many other things, intentionally using a firearm to "influence the policy or affect the conduct of" any part government in the state, or to cause substantial damage to or interruption of public infrastructure (§13-2308). For the purpose of the new terrorism law, the term "explosive agent" does not include firearms. Terrorism is a class 2 felony. (§13-2308.01)

Dangerous Offense and Serious Offense
"Certain crimes can be categorized to provide greater punishment."

In 2008 Arizona's entire sentencing structure was revamped, with certain extreme crimes designated *serious offense* (listed in §13-706), and "an offense involving the discharge, use or threatening exhibition of a deadly weapon or dangerous instrument..." called a *dangerous offense*. These aggravate sentencing, meaning more jail time. A felony designated as "dangerous" (§13-701 et seq.), which prosecutors have a degree of discretion in charging, permanently removes the right to keep and bear arms. The "serious" category encompasses the grim felonies that automatically remove your rights. The threat of adding these charges can be used to encourage a plea agreement, a manipulative ploy denounced by some observers. Some elements of the overhaul appear contradictory and may be updated in the future.

Citizen's Arrest and False Arrest

"A person can make an arrest, but a false arrest is a crime."

Under proper circumstances, one person can arrest another person who appears to have committed a crime (§13-3884 et seq.), but this is quite risky, since you can't tell if it's a crime for sure until a court decides, and the person arrested can sue you. Holding a person at gunpoint, which is a more difficult task than movies might lead you to believe, can lead to many charges including false arrest.

No Duty To Protect

"The state and the police have no obligation to protect you."

Government promotes the idyllic notion that police are there to "serve and protect," but courts have repeatedly and correctly decided that the fact that governments are established doesn't confer on all people an individual right to protection from harm. A police force has a general duty to society, but no duty of any kind to protect you personally. You aren't required to defend yourself, and "the proper authorities" aren't either. Courts are full of cases where you would imagine police must be required to act, but they just let people die and are blameless in the eyes of the law (e.g. *DeShaney v. Winnebago* 489 U.S. 189 (1989)). Defense of yourself and family is ultimately up to you. Remember, when seconds count, the police are just minutes away, with luck.

Double Jeopardy and Criminal vs. Civil Law

"You can be tried more than once for the same act."

The idea that "you can only be tried once" under *double jeopardy* protection in the Fifth Amendment is false. In a self-defense shooting, you face a possible criminal trial for your actions, and a second civil trial for harm you may have caused. That's two trials, and you can actually face more if separate civil-rights violations are filed, for the same single self-defense act. This bears repeating—it's always better to avoid a gunfight than to win one.

Your rights in a civil trial are much weaker and may be a greater threat to you than possible criminal charges described in this book. You have no right to an attorney, and usually no jury. Instead of 4th Amendment protection against search and seizure, you are *required* to turn over any evidence you have or the other party requests, if it's reasonably connected (called *discovery*), *especially* if it hurts you. You have no 5th Amendment protection against self-incrimination, which means no right to silence—refusing to answer questions is used to infer that your answer would harm you. Simply brandishing a gun can enable someone to sue for fear of death or injury, assault, mental distress, etc.

The standard for guilt in a criminal trial is *beyond a reasonable doubt*, a very high bar. Civilly it's *a preponderance of the evidence*, which means whoever has the slightest edge prevails, a very low threshold for protecting the innocent, and by the way, there is no presumption of innocence in civil trials. In a criminal trial, government comes after you with a prosecutor and team. Typically, in a civil action, someone hires a lawyer (and maybe a team) and you have to hire an attorney to defend yourself. There is no public defender if you have no money. Sometimes the government can sue you civilly too.

You can actually face many trials—criminal charges from the state and the federal government is two, and civil suits from anyone you harmed plus the federal government, that's four altogether. It gets even bigger if you realize everyone claiming harm can file a separate suit against you, and every criminal charge—they can get stacked pretty high—is an entire procedure of its own, with evidence, testimony and a separate finding of guilt or innocence.

One brief act on your part, lots of jobs for the judicial industry. You didn't get much of this in school now, did you. It's not the pure justice your social-studies teacher believed and inculcated you with, is it. Some observers claim students are poorly educated on such things on purpose, and believe a better educated public would be bad for the power structure, but a good thing for the public. For a rapid education, read *After You Shoot: Your gun's hot. The perp's not. Now what?*

Check for updates at
GunLaws.com

WHEN CAN YOU CONCEAL A FIREARM?

Remember this image? It was a basic element of Arizona gun law until 2010, when the infringement on discreet carry was lifted by our legislature. Now, the question of "When can you legally conceal" is just a footnote in history, a fading memory, replaced with the robust liberty of Constitutional Carry. The new approach to uninfringed carry is now years into the history books, other states are joining the trend, and it is working out just fine. The incessant, mythical, fear-mongering, and crude hoplophobic gloom-and-doom predictions from anti-rights advocates who have never been right and have belligerently projected their own internal personal fears on every decent advance in the public's civil rights and Second Amendment freedoms turned out to be false, although they received massive positive media coverage. We are still awaiting corrections and retractions, believing facts matter.

IF YOU SHOOT A CROOK OUTSIDE YOUR HOUSE DO YOU HAVE TO DRAG HIM INSIDE?

IF YOU SHOOT A CROOK OUTSIDE YOUR HOUSE DO YOU HAVE TO DRAG HIM INSIDE?

No! Acting on this wide-spread myth is a completely terrible idea. You're talking about tampering with evidence, obstructing justice, interfering with official procedures and more. If you're involved in a shooting, leave everything at the scene just as it is and tell your attorney to call the police and an ambulance right away. You do have an attorney, right?

Don't think for a minute that modern forensics won't detect an altered scene of a crime. At any shooting a crime has been committed. Either the shooting is justified, which means you were within your rights and the person shot was acting illegally (you're the crime victim), or you exceeded your rights in the shooting, regardless of the victim's circumstance (you're the offender, then the defendant). The situation will be investigated to determine the facts, and believe it, the facts will come out. Police tell time-worn jokes about "black heel marks on the linoleum." And once you're caught in a lie, your credibility is shot.

If you tamper with the evidence, you have to lie to all the authorities to back it up. Then you have to commit felony perjury to follow through. Can you pull it off? And say, where's your lawyer?

If the guy with the mask was shot from the front, armed as he is, the homeowner has a good case for self defense. If the masked man was shot from behind, the homeowner has a case (much weaker) for acting to prevent 1st degree burglary. Either way, he's better off leaving the body where it falls.

Suppose you shoot an armed intruder coming through your window, and the body falls outside the house. You'll have a better time convincing a jury that you were scared to death, than trying to explain how the dead crook in your living room got blood stains on your lawn.

The reason this fable gets so much play is because there is a big difference between a homeowner shooting a crook in the kitchen, and one person shooting another outdoors. Shooting at a stranger outside your house (or even inside!) can be murder, depending on the exact circumstances, and you won't know until authorities sort it all out, often many years later. It's always better to avoid a gun fight than to survive one.

CAN YOU POINT A GUN AT SOMEONE?

CAN YOU POINT A GUN AT SOMEONE?

No matter how many aces a person is holding, you can't settle the matter with a gun. This also shows how the law can be interpreted in more than one way.

If the gun you draw is loaded, you create a substantial risk of imminent death, a class 6 felony called *endangerment*. (Without the risk of death endangerment is a class 1 misdemeanor.) Using a gun to put a person in reasonable fear of imminent physical injury is *aggravated assault*—a class 3 felony. A more lenient view would be to say that this is "reckless display of a gun," which is *disorderly conduct,* a class 6 felony. Merely flashing a gun can be *threatening or intimidating,* a class 1 misdemeanor. At the very least this is *criminal nuisance*, a class 3 misdemeanor.

When you go to court, it could be argued that this is actually *attempted murder,* a class 2 felony. And if the guy with the gun is angry enough to take back his money, it becomes *armed robbery,* also a class 2 felony—even though he's being cheated.

By drawing your gun, the other guy may be able to shoot you dead and legally claim self defense. You may never pull a gun to leverage an argument.

If someone pointed a gun at you, would you get angry and want to see them arrested? Consider how someone would feel if your roles were reversed, and it was you who pulled the gun when it wasn't absolutely necessary to prevent a life-threatening situation.

Despite all this, the law recognizes your right to defend yourself, your loved ones, and other people, and this was strengthened with a "defensive display" law. The law also recognizes a person's right to act to prevent certain crimes. These cases, when you *can* point a gun at another person, are described in Chapter 5.

HUNTING REQUIREMENTS 6

Hunting regulations are complex, highly detailed and mandatory requirements issued annually by the Arizona Game and Fish Department (AZGFD). The regulations are based on *Arizona Revised Statutes, Title 17.* You *must* get in touch with AZGFD before even considering hunting or shooting at any wildlife. *The Arizona Gun Owner's Guide* only covers those parts of hunting rules that apply to firearms use.

AZGFD offers a 20-hour course of instruction online that teaches safe handling of firearms, ethics and responsibilities, wildlife management and identification, survival, first aid and more, including class and field work (hunter-ed.com). AZGFD sets rules for its voluntary training programs, and in-person classes, contact them for details.

Land open to hunt is not always open to all shooting. Many sections of Tonto National Forest, for example, are closed to all shooting except licensed hunting (see chapter 4). Some land that may be hunted, like the 14-million-plus acres of the Navajo Indian Reservation for example, has a ban against firearms altogether.

Here are the key rules about using guns while hunting. Remember that hunting regulations are not limited to guns, and include bow and arrow and other devices.

- The Arizona Game and Fish Department specifies the types of guns and ammunition that are allowed when hunting each different type of game. The specifications are designed to help insure a quick clean kill. Different types of game may only be hunted in specified areas during specified seasons. It is illegal to otherwise hunt. Main hunting areas are on land regulated by the U.S. Forest Service, the Bureau of Land Management, the State Land Department, Indian Country and private land.

- No one under ten years of age may hunt big game.

- No one between ten and fourteen years of age may hunt big game without first passing the Ariz. Hunter Education Course from AZGFD.

- A person between the ages of ten and fourteen may hunt wildlife other than big game without a license, if accompanied by a properly licensed hunter who is 18 years or older. There is a limit of two children per license holder.
- Anyone over 14 years of age needs a license to hunt wildlife.
- When hunting, you must have in your possession either a Class G General Hunting License, a Class F Combination Hunting and Fishing license, or a Class H Three-Day Hunting License (not valid for big game), plus any required tags, permit tags, or stamps.
- It's illegal to shoot while taking wildlife within a quarter mile of an occupied or possibly occupied farmhouse, cabin, lodge, trailer home or other building, without the permission of the owner or resident.
- It's illegal to shoot from a vehicle while hunting, without a special "challenged access" permit. Special rules apply to hunting waterfowl.
- Shooting from, across or into a road or railroad while hunting is illegal.
- It's illegal to be intoxicated while hunting.
- It's illegal to handle or fire a gun in a careless or reckless manner while hunting, or with wanton disregard for the safety of human life or property.
- A person involved in a shooting accident while hunting must:

    1–Render every possible assistance to the injured person;
    2–Immediately report the accident to and cooperate with the nearest law enforcement officer;
    3–File a written report of the incident within 10 days to the Arizona Game and Fish Department.

- Poaching (hunting outside of the established regulations) is strictly illegal. To anonymously report a suspected violation, call Operation Game Thief, 1-800-352-0700, 24 hours a day.

    Rewards are anonymously paid for tips leading to arrests through the Operation Game Thief program, by AZGFD and these organizations: Arizona Bowhunters Association, Tucson Rod and Gun Club, Arizona Desert Bighorn Sheep Society, Arizona Bowhunters and Field Archers Association, *Western Bowhunter* Magazine, Arizona Muzzleloading Association, Western Bowhunters Association, Central Arizona Bowhunters, Sportsman's Voice, Phoenix Varmint Callers and the Arizona Trapper's Association. Rewards can be as high as $1,000.

- Legal shooting time while hunting is during daylight hours. Weather conditions can alter actual times—you must be able to see well enough to shoot safely, to be legal. A few special exceptions apply.
- It's illegal to destroy, injure or molest livestock, growing crops, personal property, notices or signboards, or other improvements while hunting.
- It's illegal to shoot game and let any edible meat go to waste. Abandoning a carcass is illegal. In 2014, the law became more clear by describing the edible parts and by exempting meat damaged by the method of taking.
- As of 2014, there is no longer a ban on the possession of legal arms, ammunition or devices while hunting, as long as such items are not actually used for hunting. Only weapons and ammo authorized for specific

hunting are allowed for hunting. Use of unauthorized weapons and ammo for hunting is a class 1 misdemeanor. For example, an old prohibition, such as the ban on possession of a sidearm during rifle- or shotgun-only seasons no longer applies, but the sidearm cannot be used for taking game. The exact effects of all of this new law, §17-305 are not perfectly clear.

- The former prohibition on hunting with silencers (also known as suppressors or modulators), was lifted in 2014. Some observers have noted that if OSHA were active in this field, silencers would have never been banned, as they protect hearing, improve the environment and would be an economic stimulus because they would be popular.

- The use or possession of lead shot is prohibited in areas designated as nontoxic shot zones.

- Hunting with rifled firearms is prohibited within the Maricopa County Parks System. Limited deer hunting with rifled firearms, by special permit, may be allowed for a limited time by the Maricopa County Park Commission in cooperation with the Arizona Game and Fish Commission.

- Rifled firearms are prohibited in the Base and Meridian Wildlife Areas, and centerfire rifled firearms are prohibited in the Robbins Butte Wildlife Area. Many other Wildlife Area restrictions apply.

- A special permit is available from the Phoenix office of AZGFD that allows a physically disabled person to shoot from a motor vehicle, if a) the vehicle has a current handicapped license plate or disabled shooter's permit, b) is standing still, c) is not on a maintained public roadway, d) has its engine off, and e) is not used at any time to hunt or pursue wildlife (Challenged Hunter Access Mobility Permit, CHAMP).

- Since 2006, interfering with the rights of hunters legally hunting is a class 2 misdemeanor. This includes placing yourself in the line of fire, disturbing wildlife or hunters, blocking access points and more.

Hunting Penalties

- Hunting license privileges may be revoked for up to five years for careless use of firearms resulting in human injury or death; destroying, molesting or injuring livestock; destroying or damaging crops, personal property, signs or other improvements; littering; letting someone else use your big game tag; or unlawful taking or possession of wildlife.

- Unless a penalty is otherwise specifically described by law, violation of hunting regulations is a class 2 misdemeanor.

- Taking wildlife, or attempting to obtain a hunting license while your hunting privilege is suspended is a class 1 misdemeanor.

- Knowingly taking, having or transporting big game unlawfully is a class 1 misdemeanor.

- Knowingly selling, bartering or offering for sale any big game that was taken unlawfully is a class 6 felony.

- Any peace officer who knowingly fails to enforce a hunting regulation is guilty of a class 2 misdemeanor.

- Anyone who unlawfully wounds, kills or has possession of certain wildlife is subject to civil suit by the Arizona Game and Fish Dept. in addition to other penalties. The list includes any endangered species, elk, bighorn sheep, buffalo, all eagles, deer, antelope, mountain lion, bear, turkey, javelina, beaver, goose, raptors, duck, small game animals, small game birds, game fish and non-game birds.

- A firearm seized by the authorities acting under the hunting laws must be returned to the person it was taken from after the case is resolved. If that person can't be found the firearm may be sold. It may not be destroyed unless it is a prohibited or defaced weapon. A report of seized weapons is kept, and proceeds go to the game and fish fund.

A Hunter's Pledge

Responsible hunting provides unique challenges and rewards. However, the future of the sport depends on each hunter's behavior and ethics. Therefore, as a hunter, I pledge to:

- Respect the environment and wildlife
- Respect property and landowners
- Show consideration for non hunters
- Hunt safely
- Know and obey the law
- Support wildlife and habitat conservation
- Pass on an ethical hunting tradition
- Strive to improve my outdoor skills & understanding of wildlife
- Hunt only with ethical hunters

By following these principles of conduct each time I go afield, I will give my best to the sport, the public, the environment and myself. The responsibility to hunt ethically is mine; the future of hunting depends on me.

The Hunter's Pledge was created cooperatively by:

International Association of Fish and Wildlife Agencies; Izaak Walton League of America; National Rifle Association; Rocky Mountain Elk Foundation; Tread Lightly! Inc.; Sport Fishing Institute; Times Mirror Magazines Conservation Council; U.S. Dept. of Agriculture Extension Service; Wildlife Management Institute.

NOTES ON FEDERAL LAW 7

Although federal laws regulate firearms to a great degree, the same laws prohibit the federal and local governments from encroaching on the right to keep and bear arms. This is seen in the 2nd, 4th, 9th, 10th and 14th Amendments to the U.S. Constitution, and in more than 270 federal statutory gun laws, as of 2011.

Dealers of firearms must be licensed by the federal Bureau of Alcohol, Tobacco, Firearms and Explosives (BATFE). Federal law requires licensed dealers to keep records of each sale (18 USC §923(g)), but prohibits using this information in any sort of national registration plan (18 USC §926(a)). The information is permanently saved by the dealer but is not centrally recorded by the federal authorities. If a dealer goes out of business the records are sent to a central federal depository for storage (or a state site if approved by the Justice Dept.). Although a federal law prohibits using these records to establish a national firearms registration system, several federal attempts to do so have apparently been made. Reportedly, fingerprints submitted to the FBI for background checks are stored by that agency until the individual reaches 99 years of age.

Paperwork required by the Brady law is collected by local authorities, but must be destroyed shortly after it is used to conduct background checks, and by law, no records of the checks may be kept. Local authorities are required to certify their compliance with record destruction, to the U.S. Attorney General, every six months. The Justice Department reports that compliance with this requirement has been quite low.

In theory there's no central place for anyone to go and see if a given individual owns a firearm (except perhaps in the case of those people who have registered for a concealed-weapon permit, if you assume they all own guns). Firearm ownership in America is traditionally a private matter. For someone to find out if you have a gun they would have to check all the records of all the dealers in the country, a daunting task, and only BATFE is authorized to check the records of manufacture, importation and sale of firearms. As a practical matter, however, the authorities are increasingly able to easily determine which people have chosen to own firearms. Local authorities occasionally ask to see a dealer's records, and dealers may feel it's in their best interests to cooperate, even if it isn't required by law.

The dealer's records allow guns to be *traced,* a very different and important matter. When a gun is involved in a crime, BATFE can find out, from the manufacturer's serial number, which licensed dealer originally received the gun. The dealer can then look through the records and see who purchased the weapon. It's a one-way street—a gun can be linked to a purchaser but owners can't be traced to their guns. One study of successful traces showed that four out of five were of some value to law enforcement authorities.

When President Reagan was shot by John Hinckley Jr., the weapon was traced and in fourteen minutes time, a retail sale to Hinckley was confirmed.

Buying, selling, having, making, transferring and transporting guns is in many cases regulated by federal laws. These regulations are generally covered in *The Arizona Gun Owner's Guide,* but for the most part, only state penalties are noted. There may be federal penalties as well.

Under the Assimilative Crimes Act, 18 USC §13, state law controls if an offense occurs on a federal site and there is no federal law on the subject—the feds use state language to make the federal charge. Recognize that there can be a question of jurisdiction in some cases.

A long history of federal regulation exists with regard to firearms and other weapons. For a detailed examination of the historical record, read Stephen Halbrook's book, *That Every Man Be Armed.* For an unabridged copy of the federal laws, get *Gun Laws of America*, both available at gunlaws.com.

The main federal gun laws in effect today include:

- 2nd, 4th, 9th and 10th Amendments to the Constitution (1791)
- Fourteenth Amendment to the Constitution (1868)
- National Firearms Act (1934)
- Federal Firearms Act (1938)
- Omnibus Crime Control and Safe Streets Act (1968)
- Gun Control Act (1968)
- Organized Crime Control Act (1970)
- Omnibus Crime Control Act (1986)
- Firearms Owners' Protection Act (1986)
- Brady Handgun Violence Prevention Act (1993)
- Public Safety and Recreational Firearms Use Protection Act (The Crime Bill, aka Assault Weapons Ban) (1994, repealed 2004)
- Promotion of Rifle Practice and Firearms Safety Act (1996)
- Antiterrorism and Effective Death Penalty Act (1996)
- Omnibus Consolidated Appropriations Act for FY 1997 (Domestic Violence Gun Ban, Gun Free School Zones)
- Omnibus Consolidated & Emergency Supplemental Appro-priations Act, 1999 (numerous requirements detailed later in this chapter)
- Smith & Wesson-preference ban (P.L. 106-398, 10/30/00, DOD FY 2001); The Patriot Act: Anti-terrorism measures (P.L. 107-56, 10/26/01); Aviation Security Act: Arm the pilots (P.L. 107-71, 11/19/01); Homeland Security Act: Arm the government measures (P.L. 107-296, 11/25/02)
- Vision 100—Century of Aviation Reauthorization Act (2003) (Deputize Cargo Pilots so they may be armed)
- Reauthorization of the ban on undetectable firearms. (2003)
- Consolidated Appropriations Resolution (2003)
- Law Enforcement Officers Safety Act, LEOSA (2004)
- Protection of Lawful Commerce In Arms Act (2005)
- Disaster Recovery Personal Protection Act (2006)
- NICS Improvement Amendments Act (2007)
- Numerous other laws described in this chapter

Additional federal requirements may be found in the Code of Federal Regulations (CFR) and the United States Code (USC). Changes and additions to statutes are posted at gunlaws.com.

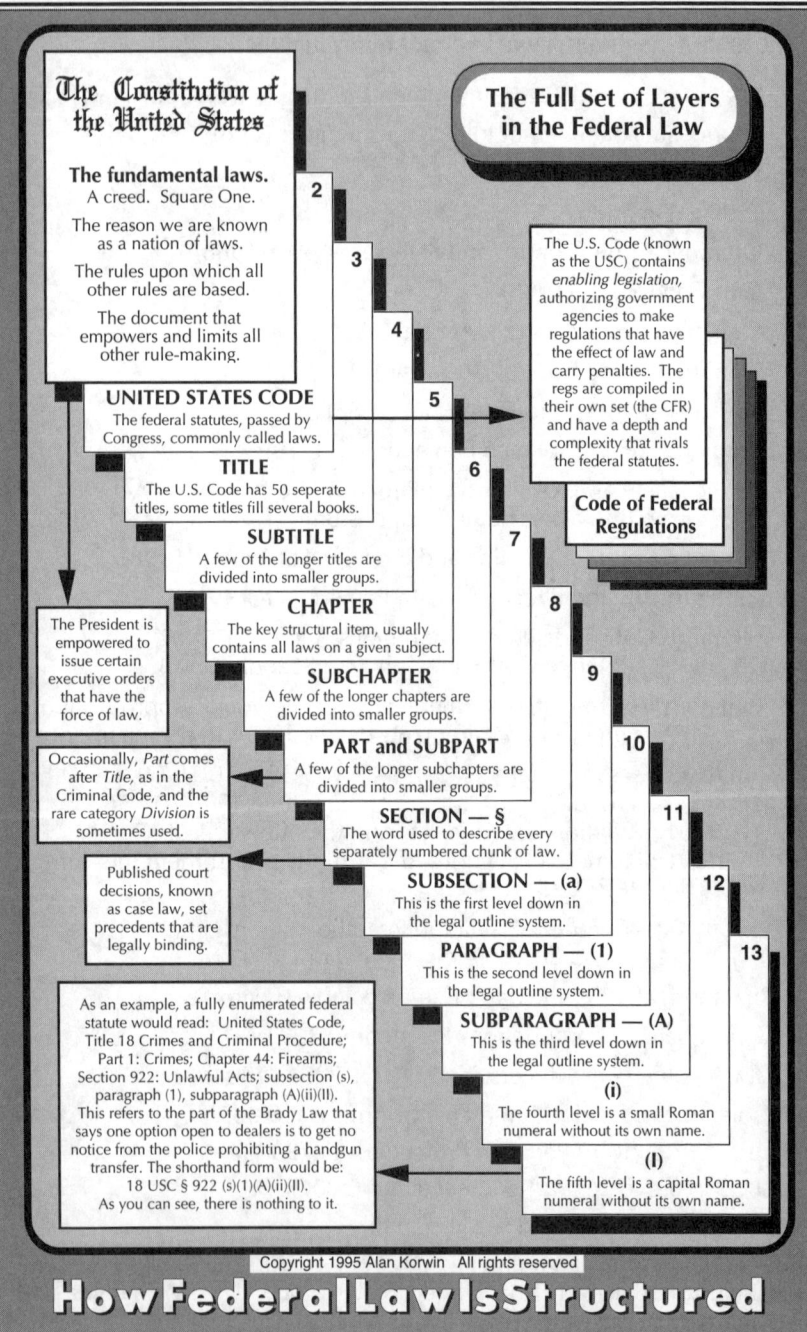

HowFederalLawIsStructured

FEDERAL FIREARMS TRANSPORTATION GUARANTEE

Passed on July 8, 1986 as part of the Firearms Owners' Protection Act, federal law guarantees that a person may legally transport a firearm from one place where its possession is legal to another place where its possession is legal, provided it is unloaded and the firearm and ammunition are not readily accessible from the passenger compartment of the vehicle. The law doesn't say it in so many words, but the only non-accessible spot in the average passenger car is the trunk. If a vehicle has no separate compartment for storage, the firearm and ammunition may be in a locked container other than the glove compartment or console.

There have been cases, especially in Eastern states, where local authorities have not complied with this law, creating a degree of risk for people otherwise legally transporting firearms. To avoid any confusion, the text of the federal guarantee is printed here word for word:

Federal Law Number 18 USC § 926A
Interstate transportation of firearms

Notwithstanding any other provision of any law or any rule or regulation of a State or any political subdivision thereof, any person who is not otherwise prohibited by this chapter from transporting, shipping, or receiving a firearm shall be entitled to transport a firearm for any lawful purpose from any place where he may lawfully possess and carry such firearm to any other place where he may lawfully possess and carry such firearm if, during such transportation the firearm is unloaded, and neither the firearm nor any ammunition being transported is readily accessible or is directly accessible from the passenger compartment of such transporting vehicle: Provided, That in the case of a vehicle without a compartment separate from the driver's compartment the firearm or ammunition shall be contained in a locked container other than the glove compartment or console.

Anyone interested in a complete copy of the federal gun laws, with plain English summaries of every law, can get a copy of *Gun Laws of America*, published by Bloomfield Press. See the back section of this book for details.

The Brady Law

Enacted in 1993 as the Brady Handgun Violence Prevention Act, the Brady law in reality turned out to be five things:

1–Centralized federal control over all handgun and long gun retail sales;

2–A $200 million funding mechanism for a national computer system capable of checking out any individual from a single FBI location;

3–The establishment of a national ID card infrastructure (based on drivers' licenses and social security numbers) for all original firearm purchases;

4–The most thorough commerce tracking system on earth, initially only for retail sales of firearms in America; and

5–A mechanism for preventing known criminals from personally purchasing firearms at retail and paying sales tax.

The widely publicized five-day waiting period was largely a myth, and never existed in most states (Arizona never had one). The effect of the Brady law on crime reduction is essentially unknown, since the hundreds of thousands of criminals reportedly identified by the system (the number is hotly disputed) are on the loose—very little effort to track or apprehend them has been made. It is a five-year federal felony for criminals and other disqualified persons to attempt to purchase a firearm.

Part 1 of the law, the handgun part, was promoted to get the law passed, set to expire 60 months after enactment, and is described below in small type (it expired Nov. 30, 1998). Brady Part 2, the National Instant Background Check (dubbed NICS by the FBI, who displaced BATFE to operate the system), automatically replaced the handgun law, and controls rifles, shotguns and handguns, and is described as it appears in the federal statute. Complex regulations to implement the new law, which are basically transparent in this state, are not covered (available in their entirety on the FBI and BATFE Internet sites).

The FBI's use of the Brady computer system to record the name and address of every retail gun buyer in America, in violation of long-standing law (strictly forbidden in both the McClure Volkmer Act, 1986, and the Brady law itself), prompted outcries from the public and Congress, but continued unabated throughout and then after the Clinton administration. In addition, the Justice Dept. under Clinton attempted but failed to levy a tax on the sale of firearms, to benefit the FBI, with no apparent authority to do so (taxes are supposed to originate in Congress). The Bush administration appeared intent on correcting such abuses, but it is distressing to see how politicized administration of the laws has become. States that agree to cooperate with the FBI, as Arizona has done, would avoid the proposed tax on its licensed dealers. The taxing proposals have been dropped at present.

For updates and detailed analysis of the complex Brady machinations, check our website, gunlaws.com.

The Brady Law, Part 1 (First Five Years, expired 11/30/98)

The Brady Handgun Violence Prevention Act was signed into law on Nov. 30, 1993. Its provisions for common carriers, reporting multiple handgun sales and license fee increases are among the rules affecting private individuals that took effect immediately. The waiting-period provisions took effect on Feb. 28, 1994, and were set to expire on Nov. 30, 1998.

In addition to the regulation of private citizens described below, the Brady Law: places special requirements on dealers, sets timetables and budgets for the U.S. Attorney General to implement the law, provides funding, sets basic computer system requirements, mandates criminal-history record sharing among authorities, enhances penalties for gun thieves and more. Your federal legislators can send you the full 12-page Brady Law.

The Brady Law refers to a "chief law enforcement officer," defined as the chief of police, the sheriff, an equivalent officer or their designee. The description below refers to such persons as "the authorities." Where the law refers to an individual who is unlicensed under §923 of USC Title 18, this description says "private citizen" or "you." Federally licensed dealers, manufacturers and importers are referred to as "dealers." The act of selling, delivering or transferring is called "transferring." The law defines *handgun* as, "a firearm which has a short stock and is designed to be held and fired by the use of a single hand." A combination of parts which can be assembled into a handgun counts as a handgun.

Under the Brady Law, to legally obtain a handgun from a dealer you must provide:

• A valid picture ID for the dealer to examine;

• A written statement with only the date the statement was made, notice of your intent to obtain a handgun from the dealer, your name, address, date of birth, the type of ID you used and a statement that you are not: 1–under indictment and haven't been convicted of a crime which carries a prison term of more than one year, 2–a fugitive from justice, 3–an unlawful user of or addicted to any controlled substance, 4–an adjudicated mental defective, 5–a person who has been committed to a mental institution, 6–an illegal alien, 7–dishonorably discharged from the armed forces, or 8–a person who has renounced U.S. citizenship.

Then, before transferring the handgun to you, the dealer must:

• Within 1 day, provide notice of the content and send a copy of the statement to the authorities where you live;

• Keep a copy of your statement and evidence that it was sent to the authorities;

• Wait five days during which state offices are open, from the day the dealer gave the authorities notice, and during that time,

• Receive no information from the authorities that your possession of the handgun would violate federal, state or local laws.

The waiting period ends early if the authorities notify the dealer early that you're eligible. The authorities "shall make a reasonable effort" to check your background in local, state and federal records. Long guns are unaffected by the Brady Law until the National Instant Check described below comes on line, and Brady does not apply to getting your own handgun (or a replacement) back from a dealer you gave it to (e.g., a repair shop, pawnbroker, etc.).

The Brady Law excludes you from the waiting period:

1–If you have a written statement from the authorities, valid for 10 days, that you need a handgun because of a threat to your life or a member of your household's life

2–With a handgun permit, in the state that issued it, if the permit is less than five years old and required a background check (Arizona's concealed-weapon permit meets this requirement)

3–In states that have a handgun background check (Arizona's Handgun Clearance Center qualifies. Established on Oct. 1, 1994 by state law and operated by DPS, it conducts instant background checks by phone or fax, for handgun purchasers, eliminating the need for residents to wait for handgun purchases)

4–If the transfer is already regulated by the National Firearms Act of 1934, as with Class III weapons

5–If the dealer has been certified as being in an extremely remote location of a sparsely populated state and there are no telecommunications near the dealer's business premises.

If a dealer is notified after a transfer that your possession of the handgun is illegal, the dealer must, within one business day, provide any information they have about you to the authorities at the dealer's place of business and at your residence. The information a dealer receives may only be communicated to you, the authorities or by court order. If you are denied a handgun, you may ask the authorities why, and they are required to provide the reason in writing within 20 business days of your request.

Unless the authorities determine that the handgun transfer to you would be illegal, they must, within 20 days of the date of your statement, destroy all records of the process. The authorities are expressly forbidden to convey or use the information in your statement for anything other than what's needed to carry out the Brady process.

The authorities may not be held liable for damages for either allowing an illegal handgun transfer or preventing a legal one. If you are denied a firearm unjustly, you may sue the political entity responsible and get the information corrected or have the transfer approved, and you may collect reasonable attorney's fees.

The Brady Law Part 2—National Instant Check: The Brady law required the U.S. Attorney General (AG) to establish a National Instant Criminal Background Check system (NICS) before Nov. 30, 1998. Once it began (30 days after the AG notified all FFLs that the system was running and how to use it), the previous process (above, in small type) was eliminated. In order to transfer *any firearm, not just handguns,* with the NICS system in place, a dealer must verify your identity from a government-issued photo-ID card, contact the FBI's system (based in Clarksburg, W. Va.), identify you and either:

• get a unique transfer number back from the system, or

• wait three days during which state offices are open and during which the system provides no notice that the transfer would violate relevant laws.

Originally, Arizona was one of 31 "Point of Contact" states designated by the FBI. This meant that dealers here contacted the DPS Firearms Clearance Center (previously named the Handgun Clearance Center) for all gun sales, as they had done for the first five years under the Brady law. Then the DPS statewide instant check automatically included a check of the NICS system, and the process was transparent to Arizona buyers (except when the NICS system was down, freezing most guns sales nationwide). Arizona abandoned this approach in 2002, and dealers now contact the NICS center directly by phone, fax or on the web.

The NICS system is required to issue the transfer number if the transfer would violate no relevant laws, and it must instantly destroy all records of approved inquiries except for the identifying number and the date it was issued. The FBI, however, has in various ways recorded the name and address of every person buying a gun at retail, and in that light, official assurances about how much is recorded, and for how long, are skeptically received. If the transfer is approved, the dealer includes the transfer number in the record of the transaction (a redesigned 4473 form). The NICS system is bypassed under conditions similar to 2, 4 and 5 listed above (in small type) as exceptions to the Brady process (with number 2 broadened to include "firearms" permit). *Proceed, delay* or *denied* are the words the dealer hears.

A licensed dealer who violates these requirements is subject to a civil fine of up to $5,000 and suspension or revocation of their license, but only if the system would have shown that the customer would have been ineligible to make a purchase.

It's important to note that the NICS law plainly says you only have to use NICS if it exists and it's running (18 USC §922 (t)(5)), a clause specifically put there by lobbyists who were afraid the system might never be implemented, ending gun sales altogether. But BATFE and the FBI have re-interpreted that clause to mean you can't sell a gun when NICS is down—rewriting the statute from their bureau desks—and dealers are too terrified to follow the law and oppose the government agents. The state police insta-check departments nationwide haven't been willing to stand up for states' rights and force the issue either. So when NICS is off, retail gun sales grind to a halt nationally, and this has occurred scores of times, and even on a regional basis.

If you are denied a firearm due to a NICS check, the law says you may request the reason directly from NICS and it must present you with a written answer within five business days. You may also request the reason from the AG, who must respond "immediately," according to the law. You may provide information to fix errors in the system, and the AG must immediately consider the information, investigate further, correct any erroneous federal records and notify any federal or state agency that was the source of the errors.

Multiple sales of handguns, (two or more from the same dealer in a five day period) are already reported to the Bureau of Alcohol, Tobacco, Firearms and Explosives, and must now be reported to local authorities as well. Congress specifically omitted similar authority for long-gun reporting. Local authorities may not disclose the information, must destroy the records within 20 days from receipt if the transfer is not illegal and must certify every six months to the AG that they are complying with these provisions.

Common or contract carriers (airlines, buses, trains, etc.) may not label your luggage or packages to indicate that they contain firearms. Federal law requires you to notify the carrier in writing (verbal notice is often accepted) if you are transporting firearms or ammunition. The long-time labeling practice had been responsible for the frequent theft of luggage containing firearms. Contact carriers early to avoid issues.

Licensing fees for a new dealers' license went up to $200 for three years. The fee for renewing a current license is $90 for three years.

With the passage of Arizona's concealed weapon law in April, 1994, effective July 17, 1994, CCW permit holders are exempt from the paperwork, additional background checks and potential delays of the Brady law, since you're already recorded in the criminal database. This cash-and-carry aspect of the permit is one of its greatest appeals, despite the fact that it reflects a perpetually monitored class of people.

New laws may be passed at any time, and it is your responsibility to be up to date when handling firearms under all circumstances.

Failure to comply with new laws and regulations can have serious personal consequences, even if you believe your fundamental rights have been compromised.

Public Safety and Recreational Firearms Use Protection Act

This law, popularized as the 1994 Crime Bill and sometimes referred to as the assault-weapons ban, affected three areas of existing firearms law: 1–Possession and use of firearms by juveniles; 2–Possession of firearms by people under domestic violence restraining orders; and 3–It created a new class of regulated firearms and accessories. The information on juveniles is found in Chapter 1 since it relates to who can bear arms. The new class of prohibited purchasers (for domestic violence cases) is also in Chapter 1, as part of the list of prohibitees for federal form 4473—the form dealers use with all sales.

Historical Note: The portion of the law that created the illegal *assault-weapons* category expired on Sep. 13, 2004. Nothing was actually banned—Americans could still buy, own, sell, trade, have and use any of the millions of affected firearms and accessories.

What the law actually did was to prohibit *manufacturers and importers* from selling newly made goods of that type to the public (and it was a crime for the public to get them). Maybe that is a ban, but not in the sense that was reported. Ten years later, after the end of the ban, there was widespread recognition that it had no effect on crime, and its expiration didn't spawn anything adverse. The list of affected weapons is preserved for history in Chapter 3. More laws should be enacted with expiration dates.

The net effect of the law was to motivate manufacturers to create stockpiles before the law took affect, then to introduce new products that were not affected, and to step up marketing efforts overseas for affected products. Demand and prices skyrocketed for the fixed supply of goods domestically, and then adjusted downward when it became obvious that supplies were still available. When it was over, a normal 17-round magazine for a sidearm dropped from more than $100 to around twenty bucks.

Rifle Practice and Firearms Safety Act (1996)

The Civilian Marksmanship Program, run by the U.S. Army, has served as the federal government's official firearms training, supply and competitions program for U.S. citizens, since 1956. Its history traces back to the late 1800s, when programs were first established to help ensure that the populace could shoot straight, in the event an army had to be raised to defend the country. The program is privatized by this act, now 36 USC §40701 et seq..

The federal government transfers the responsibility and facilities for training civilians in the use of small arms to a 501(c)(3) non-profit corporation created for this purpose. All law-abiding people are eligible to participate, and priority is given to reaching and training youth in the safe, lawful and accurate use of firearms.

Functions formerly performed for this program by the Army are now the responsibility of this new corporation. The Army is required to provide direct support and to take whatever action is necessary to make the program work in its privatized form.

Official federal policy, as stated in the program goals, is to:

1–Promote safety in the use of firearms;

2–Teach marksmanship to U.S. citizens;

3–Promote practice in the use of firearms;

4–Conduct matches and competitions;

5–Award trophies and prizes;

6–Procure supplies and services needed for the program;

7–Secure and account for all firearms, ammunition and supplies used in the program;

8–Give, lend or sell firearms, ammunition and supplies under the program. Priority must be given to training youths, and reaching as many youths as possible.

Any person who is not a felon, hasn't violated the main federal gun laws, and does not belong to a group that advocates violent overthrow of the U.S. government, may participate in the Civilian Marksmanship Program.

What do you think would happen if Americans everywhere knew of this fine new law, and enrolled their children in programs that teach responsible use of firearms and gun safety? It would build understanding and self-esteem, replacing the gun ignorance fostered by wildly violent senseless TV shows, with knowledge and respect for the power and proper use of firearms. The Civilian Marksmanship Program is listed in Appendix C.

Antiterrorism Act of 1996

A wide variety of gun-law changes were introduced in this 48,728-word act. Eight sections introduce new law, and other sections make

17 amendments to existing federal law. Much of it deals with intentional criminal acts, and so falls outside the scope of *The Arizona Gun Owner's Guide*. Other sections could lead to unexpected results and are described below.

Section 702. Using a firearm in an assault on any person in the U.S. is a federal crime if:

1–the assault involves "conduct transcending national boundaries" (described below) and

2–if any of the following also exist:

A–any perpetrator uses the mail or interstate or foreign commerce in committing the crime;

B–the offense in any way affects interstate or foreign commerce;

C–the victim is anyone in the federal government or the military;

D–any structure or property damaged is owned in any part by the federal government, or

E–the offense occurs in special U.S. territorial jurisdictions.

The maximum penalty in a non-lethal assault with a firearm is 30 years in a federal prison.

Causing a serious risk of injury to anyone, by damaging any structure or property in the U.S., is a federal crime if the conditions described in 1 and 2 above exist. The maximum penalty is 25 years.

Threatening, attempting or conspiring to commit the above acts is a crime, and various penalties are defined.

The phrase "conduct transcending national boundaries" is defined as "conduct occurring outside of the United States in addition to the conduct occurring in the United States." It is not clear what this might include.

The Attorney General is in charge of investigating "federal crimes of terrorism." Such crimes occur when any of a long list of felonies is committed to influence the government by intimidation or coercion, or to retaliate against government actions. An assault involving conduct transcending national boundaries, described in the first part of this law, is one of the felonies.

Section 727. Using or attempting to use deadly force against anyone in the federal government or the military, if the attack is because of the person's government role, is a federal crime (in addition to existing assault and homicide laws). All former personnel are included. Federal penalties for an attack on anyone in this protected class are defined. In the case of such an assault, a gun is considered a gun, even if it jams due to a defective part.

Omnibus Consolidated Appropriation Act for Fiscal Year 1997; Section 657, Gun-Free School Zone.

Congress was stopped in its attempt to exercise police powers at the state level by the U.S. Supreme Court, when the court declared in 1995 (*U.S. v. Lopez,* 514 U.S. 549), that the 1991 Gun-Free School Zone law was unconstitutional. That law was reenacted by Congress, to the surprise of many observers, as an unnoticed add-on to a 2,000-page federal spending bill in 1996, in a form essentially identical to the one the Supreme Court overturned, and given the same number.

The law makes it a federal crime to knowingly have a firearm at a place that you know, or should reasonably believe, is a school zone. A school zone means in or on the grounds of an elementary or secondary public, private or parochial school, and the area within 1,000 feet from the grounds of the school.

An exemption is granted to anyone who registers with the government for a license to carry the firearm (if the license required the state's law-enforcement agency to verify you were qualified by law to receive the license, the AZ CCW qualifies). In addition, the ban doesn't apply to:

1–Firearms while on private property not part of the school grounds;

2–Any firearm that is unloaded and in a locked container;

3–Any firearm unloaded and locked in a firearms rack on a motor vehicle;

4–Possession of a firearm for use in an approved school program;

5–Possession under a contract with the school;

6–Possession by law-enforcement officers in an official capacity; and

7–An unloaded firearm, while crossing school premises to public or private land open to hunting, if crossing the grounds is authorized by the school.

It is also illegal to fire a gun (or attempt to fire a gun), knowingly or with reckless disregard for safety, in a place you know is a school zone, with the following exceptions:

1–On private property that is not part of the school grounds;

2–As part of a program approved by the school;

3–Under contract with the school;

4–By law enforcement acting in an official capacity.

An exemption for self defense is conspicuously absent, creating a shocking suggestion that self defense or defense of a third person within 1,000 feet of a school could be a federal crime (two actually, for possession and for discharge). An offense is designated as a misdemeanor, but carries a five year federal prison term. States are not prohibited from passing their own laws.

America had 121,855 public and private schools as of 1994. In effect, this law criminalizes the actions of nearly anyone who travels in a populated area with a legally possessed firearm, creating millions of federal offenses every day (see maps and details at gunlaws.com). In stark contrast, none of the 6,000 students who brought weapons to school in 1997 were prosecuted under the law. As with its overturned predecessor, its affect on the very real problem of youth violence is unclear, and of course, any firearm used illegally in America, whether it is near a school or not, is already a serious crime with penalties.

Section 658.
Misdemeanor Gun Ban for Domestic Violence Offense.

Anyone convicted of a state or federal misdemeanor involving the use or attempted use of physical force, or the threatened use of a deadly weapon, among family members (spouse, parent, guardian, cohabiter or similar) is prohibited from possessing a firearm under federal law. This marks the first time that a misdemeanor offense serves as grounds for denial of the constitutional right to keep and bear arms. The number of people affected is unknown, and no provision is made for the firearms such men and women might already possess. Firearms possession by a prohibited possessor is a five-year federal felony.

A number of narrow conditions may exempt a person from this law, including whether they were represented by an attorney, the type of trial and plea, an expungement or set aside, or a pardon or other restoration of civil rights. Because such offenses are often handled in courts-not-of-record, such a determination may not be possible.

The current congressional practice of placing unrelated laws in larger acts, in order to get them passed without debate (or even unnoticed), has raised concerns among many observers. This law, sometimes referred to as the Lautenberg amendment, is an extreme example of such a practice, and caught both firearms-rights advocates and adversaries by surprise.

The law is drafted broadly, affecting sworn police officers nationwide, the armed forces, and agencies such as the FBI, CIA, Secret Service, Forest Service and others, most of whom are accustomed to being exempted from such laws. Many of these groups are currently battling to get themselves exempted from the law. They don't believe they should be prevented from defending themselves or others because of prior minor infractions. Some police departments and other agencies have had to lay off officers who are in violation.

So many problems exist with respect to this legislation that it has raised concerns unlike any recent act of Congress. Indeed, some members reportedly were told before voting that this language had been deleted from the final version, and the vote was held before copies of the 2,000-page act were available for review. Experts close to the issues cite numerous constitutional conflicts, including:

1–It is *ex post facto*—a law passed after the fact to outlaw your former actions (prohibited by U.S. Constitution Art. 1, Sec. 9);

2–It infringes upon the right to keep and bear arms (2nd Amendment);

3–Legally owned property becomes subject to automatic seizure (prohibited by the 4th Amendment);

4–It holds people accountable to a felony without a Grand Jury indictment, represents a second punishment for a single offense creating double jeopardy, and it requires dispossession of personal property without compensation or due process (all prohibited by the 5th Amendment);

5–It denies your right to be informed of an accusation, and to counsel and a public jury trial—because an existing misdemeanor now automatically creates a federal felony (prohibited by the 6th Amendment);

6–Using a misdemeanor (a minor infraction) instead of a felony (a serious crime) to deny civil rights may be cruel and unusual punishment (8th Amendment);

7–Family conflicts, historically an issue at the state level, become federalized (prohibited by the 10th Amendment); and

8–It denies due process, abridges the rights of U.S. citizens by state law, and denies equal protection under the law (violates 14th Amendment guarantees).

Domestic violence does not have a single definition at the state level. Some states' laws require the arrest of at least one party if the police respond to an apparent domestic-violence report. This raises all the issues of judicial process and plea-bargaining after an arrest. A parent who pays a small fine rather than endure a long expensive trial can now be charged with a federal felony; domestic violence pleas have been a standard ploy in divorce proceedings for decades; these charges now deny your right to keep and bear arms, to vote, to hold office and more.

An analogy to cars crystallizes this law's affects. It is as if a former speeding ticket were now grounds for felony arrest if you own a car or gasoline. When a law is scrutinized for constitutionality it is typically held up to a single constitutional provision. The eight constitutional issues in this short piece of legislation may set a record.

Omnibus Consolidated & Emergency Supplemental Appropriations Act, 1999: This 4,000-page budget bill was secretly drafted in committee, rushed to the floor of Congress, voted on two days later, and enacted in October 1998 without any of your representatives actually reading it. It increased federal gun law by almost 6%, with provisions for NICS funding, gun-law enforcement funding, gun-safety devices sold at retail, public gun-safety-training funding, restrictions on aliens, NICS record-keeping and taxing prohibitions, shotguns and certain antiques redefined, undetectable gun law reenactment, relief for importers, a pawn shop NICS glitch fix, the Arms Control and Disarmament Agency disbanded with duties moved to the State Dept., and a special ban on using the U.S. global arms control and disarmament agenda against the public. Detailed analysis is available on our website, gunlaws.com

The USA Patriot Act and the "Arm the Pilots" Law, 2001: Hurriedly enacted as a response to the September 11 attacks, a small part of the huge Patriot Act introduces definitions of terrorism and various gun provisions related to terrorism. Also rushed into law, the Aviation & Transportation Security Act allows pilots to be deputized, so those deputies, whose jurisdiction is solely the flight deck, can be armed. Curiously, there is nothing in current law that prevents pilots from being armed without this bill, it's come down to a plain issue of political pressure, and not law. Pilots are even authorized under existing law to take custody of *your* gun while enroute (though they are not required to do so) in 18 USC §922(e).

Undetectable Firearms Ban Extension, 2003: The ban on these guns, none of which are publicly known to exist, was extended for another ten years, to Dec. 10, 2013, and then again to 2023.

Arming Cargo Pilots, 2003: Air-cargo pilots, omitted from efforts to arm passenger-plane pilots, may now also be deputized and, as federal officers, be armed against terrorism. Bureaucratic foot-dragging has plagued this effort, the same as for passenger pilots.

Consolidated Appropriations, 2003: Many items, including: Dept. of Agriculture may selectively arm its employees; Judiciary may not tax or add fees to the Brady NICS check and must destroy certain records related to retail gun sales; Federal officers get funding for firearm competitions and awards; reiteration of ban on centralizing certain firearms records; no changes to *Curios or Relics* list; continued denial of relief for individuals with federal firearms disability except for corporations; no electronic retrieval allowed for out-of-business dealer records; safeguards against using dealer records in police work; $45 million for prosecutions to reduce gun violence; and a renewed ban against advocating or promoting gun control by the Centers for Disease Control.

Congress continues to churn out gun measures, issuing a national concealed-carry law for active and retired police in 2004 (enacted as HR 218, now 18 USC §926B and C, known as LEOSA). The 1994 Crime Bill, with its list of hundreds of restricted weapons, expired in 2004, and frivolous-lawsuit protection for the firearms industry passed in 2005 with many civilian conditions attached. In 2006, responding to abusive firearm confiscations in New Orleans following the Katrina hurricane disaster, they passed the Disaster Recovery Personal Protection Act to help ban further abuses. The Protection of Lawful Commerce in Arms Act protects manufacturers from frivolous lawsuits by people seeking to hold gun makers liable for the acts of criminals. The NICS Improvement Act in 2008 cleaned up record-keeping requirements and enhanced the process for getting old records corrected or removed. Other smaller changes have also been made. Check gunlaws.com update pages for details.

Infringement Creep: Judicial and legislative activity are underway with regard to federal firearms issues on a practically non-stop basis. Despite some pronouncements about a moratorium on new gun laws, federal gun law grew by more than 13% in 1996 alone. That's more new federal law in one year than we've seen in almost any *decade*.

Multiple Long Gun Sales: In 2012 BATFE began creating a registry of anyone who buys two or more long guns, greater than .22 caliber with a detachable magazine, in a five-day period from the same dealer, in the Mexico-border states, AZ, CA, NM, TX. Federal law specifically bans such a registry, but a court challenge failed to stop the practice. The agency decided to "enact" this without congressional approval after getting caught smuggling guns into Mexico, under the guise of stopping gun smugglers, in the Fast and Furious debacle.

Medical Marijuana: Arizonans can now legally obtain marijuana for medical use with a doctor's prescription. Federal law however bans firearms to anyone "who is an unlawful user of or addicted to any controlled substance." The feds consider pot an illegal drug, even though many states now accept it. The effect on the gun rights of the 50,073 Arizonans (as of 3/28/14) who have obtained prescriptions so far is unknown, and poses a serious risk.

Quarterly Excise Tax on Arms: HR 5552, The Firearms Excise Tax Improvement Act, was signed into law on Aug. 16, 2010, P.L. 111-237, and removes the burden on firearms and ammo makers to pay excise tax every two weeks, an enormous and costly burden. They now pay it quarterly like other conservation industries.

Tonto National Forest: Order #12-08-234R bans certain use of firearms, air rifles or gas guns in parts of Tonto National Forest, except for licensed hunting, self defense, defense of a third person, authorities acting in an official capacity and under specially issued permits, to protect visitors and employees in areas of high recreational use and the forest-urban interface. The order is in effect until June 2014, and other orders apply, listed in Chapter 4. Maps and area descriptions are posted by the Forest Service.

HealthCare: Broadly framed and undefined "injury control," "health promotion" and "wellness programs" woven into the federal takeover of the medical industry has caused concern among some industry observers that these could be used to place gun owners in more expensive insurance brackets, or identify "unhealthy" behavior (firearm possession) for treatment. The national health database will allow data mining for past or current use of red-flagged drugs such as anti-depressants, for special attention, as government advances the argument that "the government has the authority to control private behavior" and enforces compliance with "applicable standards."

LEOSA Improvements: A new bill (SB1132, P.L. 111-272) adds federal agents to the carry-anywhere privilege LEOs have, protects carrying hollowpoint ammo for LEOs, reduces the years of service needed to qualify from 15 to 10, and makes getting the needed ID cards easier. The public is still left out of these plans, only former government agents are granted the power to carry nationally.

National Parks and National Wildlife Refuges: The bans in place for mere possession of firearms in National Parks and National Wildlife Refuges were repealed by HR627 (P.L. 111-024) in 2009, effective in 2010. The bill describes in exquisite detail how these bans violated the right to keep and bear arms, entrapped unwary people, and stood out against the laws of the states the places are located. "Congress needs to weigh in on the new regulations to ensure that unelected bureaucrats and judges cannot again override the Second Amendment rights of law-abiding citizens..." Almost more important than the lifting of the rights bans in 83.6 million acres of NP and 90.8 million acres of NWR, the law makes these places subject to the state laws they are in. In other words, federal authority over this land is overridden by the states, an excellent development in the quest for increased federalism, an end to federal usurpation and recognition of the Tenth Amendment.

Gun rights in the military: The 2011 National Defense Authorization Act has an amendment championed by the NRA: "Section 1062 of the Act prohibits the Secretary of Defense from issuing any requirement, or collecting or recording any information, 'relating to the otherwise lawful acquisition, possession, ownership, carrying, or other use of a privately owned firearm, privately owned ammunition, or another privately owned weapon by a member of the Armed Forces or civilian employee of the Department of Defense' on property not owned or operated by the DOD. It also requires the destruction of any information of the type prohibited by the Act, within 90 days." Fort Riley in Kansas started the fiasco with regulations requiring, "troops stationed there to register privately owned firearms kept off-base and firearms owned by their family members residing anywhere in Kansas. It prohibited soldiers who have carry permits from carrying for protection off-base. And, it authorized unit commanders to set arbitrary limits on the caliber of firearms and ammunition their troops may privately own," according to the NRA. There is no end to the attacks the Second Amendment faces, even from our own military.

The bill also includes an improvement on previous attempts to make military surplus available to the public who funds it all. Section 346 requires, "Small arms ammunition and ammunition components in excess of military requirements, including fired cartridge cases, which are not otherwise prohibited from commercial sale or certified by the Secretary of Defense as unserviceable or unsafe, may not be demilitarized or destroyed and shall be made available for commercial sale." It applies to loaded ammo and other components as well as fired brass. The military is also encouraged to continue granting access to its vast lands for hunting and fishing.

It became evident however, beginning in 2009 in an unanticipated jihadi assault on a U.S. military base in Texas that many military members are kept unarmed on base, leaving them exposed to attack and defenseless, a situation that desperately needs attention.

Spring-Assisted Knives: An attempt by U.S. Customs and the Dept. of Homeland Security to ban importation of spring-assisted knives, or knives that can be opened with one hand, which constitute the vast majority of knives sold in America today, was defeated in 2011. This power grab and attack on the right to arms and on free enterprise was beaten back, and Customs dropped the effort after massive public outcry and some inside lobbying that never made the news.

The Switchblade Knife Act of Aug. 12, 1958 (P.L. 85–623, now 15 U.S.C. §§ 1241–1245), says that whoever knowingly introduces, or manufactures for introduction, into interstate commerce, or transports or distributes in interstate commerce, any switchblade knife, shall be fined or imprisoned, or both. Notably, possession or use of the knives is not covered. And of course, use of any knife in the commission of a crime is a serious crime with commensurate penalties.

Switchblades are defined in 19 CFR §12(a) as "any imported knife... including "balisong", "butterfly"... knives, which has one or more of the following characteristics or identities: (1) A blade which opens automatically by hand pressure applied to a button or device in the handle of the knife, or any knife with a blade which opens automatically by operation of inertia, gravity, or both..." including kits or knives that can be easily converted to such operation, and knives with a spring-powered blade that shoots out of the handle.

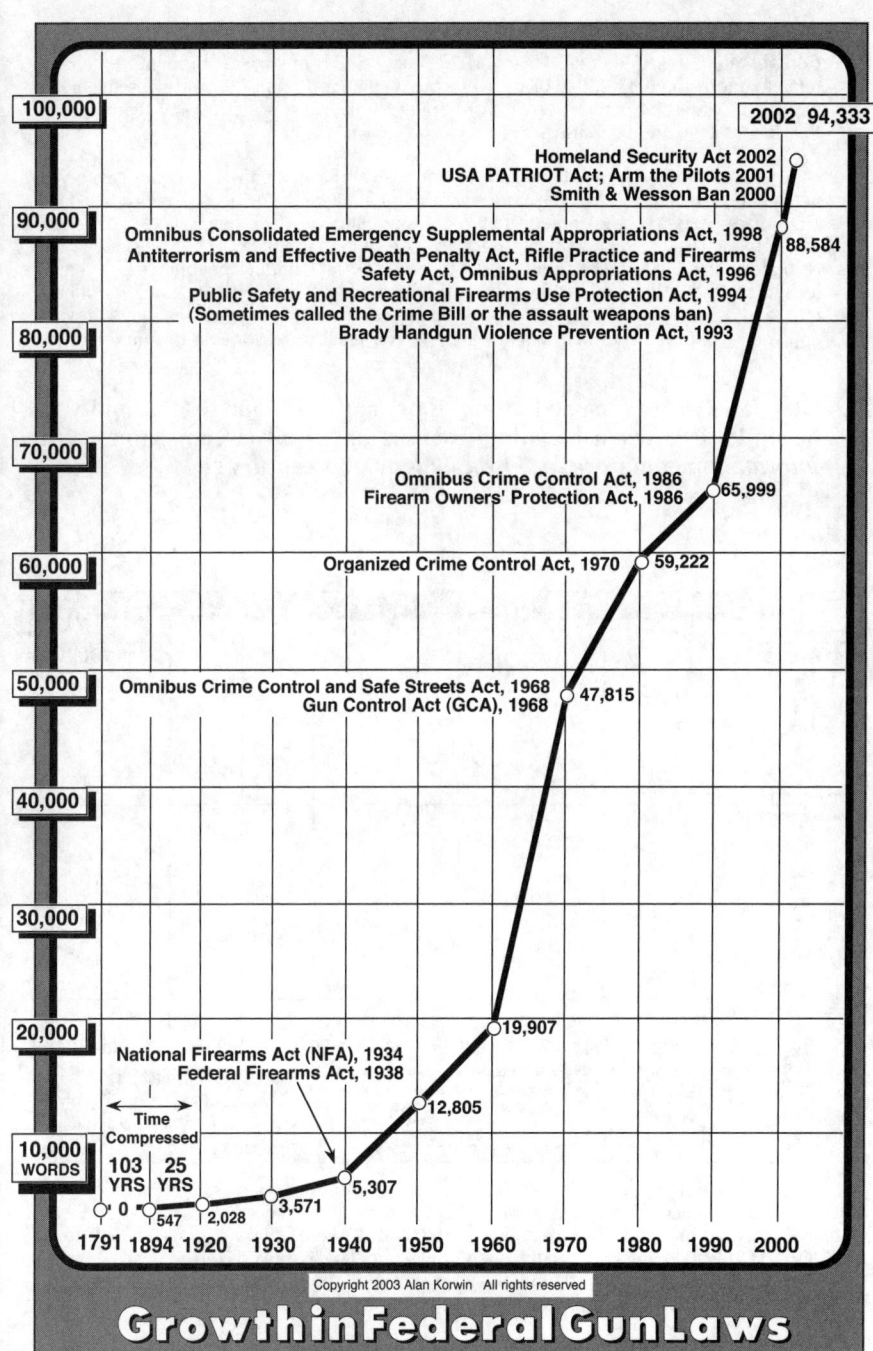

100,000   2002 94,333

Homeland Security Act 2002
USA PATRIOT Act; Arm the Pilots 2001
Smith & Wesson Ban 2000

90,000

Omnibus Consolidated Emergency Supplemental Appropriations Act, 1998
Antiterrorism and Effective Death Penalty Act, Rifle Practice and Firearms
Safety Act, Omnibus Appropriations Act, 1996   88,584
Public Safety and Recreational Firearms Use Protection Act, 1994
(Sometimes called the Crime Bill or the assault weapons ban)
Brady Handgun Violence Prevention Act, 1993

80,000

70,000

Omnibus Crime Control Act, 1986
Firearm Owners' Protection Act, 1986   65,999

60,000

Organized Crime Control Act, 1970   59,222

50,000

Omnibus Crime Control and Safe Streets Act, 1968
Gun Control Act (GCA), 1968   47,815

40,000

30,000

20,000   19,907

National Firearms Act (NFA), 1934
Federal Firearms Act, 1938

Time Compressed

12,805

10,000 WORDS

103 YRS | 25 YRS

5,307

0   547   2,028   3,571

1791 1894 1920 1930 1940 1950 1960 1970 1980 1990 2000

GrowthinFederalGunLaws

Only two decades in U.S. history—the 1960s and 1970s—saw more gun law enacted by Congress than in 1996 alone. Nearly 10,000 new words of gun law brought the federal total to more than 83,000 words. This represented a 13.43% increase for the year, which, measured by percentage or word count, set records for the federal regulation of the right to keep and bear arms.

Failure to comply with new laws and regulations can have serious consequences to you personally, even if you believe your constitutional rights have been compromised. In fact, many experts have noted that increasing latitudes are being taken by some governmental authorities with respect to constitutional guarantees. Legislative and regulatory changes present serious risks to currently law-abiding people, since what is legal today may not be tomorrow. The entire body of U.S. law is growing at a significant rate and it represents some potential threats to freedoms Americans have always enjoyed. It is prudent to take whatever steps you feel are reasonable to minimize any risks.

New laws may be passed at any time, and it is your responsibility to be up-to-date when handling firearms under all circumstances. *The information contained in this book is* guaranteed *to age.*

GrowthinFederalGunLaws

The net reduction in words since 2002 results mainly from losses due to codification of the Public Laws since 1995, plus repeals, expirations and amendments. In several cases amendments expanded a law's scope but reduced its word count (e.g., 610 words less in 18 USC §1114). Expiration of the assault-weapon law removed 1,105 words, and the 3,710-word list of approved guns. The increase in numbered statutes is a net gain, accounting for repeals and new enactments. New statutes since 2002 added 4,339 words.

THE NOBLE USES OF FIREARMS

In the great din of the national firearms debate it's easy to lose sight of the noble and respectable place firearms hold and have always held in American life. While some gun use is criminal and despicable, other applications appeal to the highest ideals our society cherishes, and are enshrined in and ensured by the statutes on the books:

- Protecting your family in emergencies
- Personal safety and self defense
- Preventing and deterring crime
- Detaining criminals for arrest
- Guarding our national borders
- Deterring and resisting terrorism
- Preserving our interests abroad
- Helping defend our allies
- Overcoming tyranny
- International trade
- Emergency preparedness
- Obtaining food by hunting
- Commerce and employment
- Historical preservation and study
- Olympic competition
- Collecting
- Sporting pursuits
- Target practice and recreational shooting

News reports, by focusing almost exclusively on criminal misuse of firearms, create the false impression that firearms and crime are directly linked, when in fact almost all guns never have any link to crime whatsoever. The media judiciously ignore stories about legal self defense, which occur almost daily according to the FBI. We get silence on the effect the gun industry has on jobs in the manufacturing sector, contributions to the tax base, capital and investments, scientific advances, national trade and balance of payments, ballistics, chemistry, metallurgy, and, of course, the enjoyment of millions of decent people who use firearms righteously. **Some people associate guns with crime, fear and danger, or they suffer from an irrational hoplophobic condition, and just want guns to go away. Those who associate guns with liberty, freedom, honor, strength and safety understand the irreplaceable role firearms play in our lives.**

It's interesting to note that the top three participant sports in the nation, measured by equipment sales, are exercise, the shooting sports, and golf. People know all about golf tournaments but many don't even know shooting sports exist, an indicator of the massive suppression of real news the media unethically perpetrates on the American public.

THE NOBLE USES OF FIREARMS

GUN SAFETY
and Concealed-Weapon Training   8

Many fine books, DVDs and classes teach the current wisdom on gun safety and use. In Arizona, some of the best public classes are given by the Arizona Game and Fish Dept. and the Arizona State Rifle and Pistol Association, both listed in Appendix C. Private firearms trainers are spread across the state, and can be found at **TrainMeAZ.com**.

When studying firearm safety (and every gun owner should), you will no doubt come across the Ten Commandments of Gun Safety. These well-intentioned lists have serious drawbacks—no two lists are ever the same and there are many more than ten rules to follow for safe gun use. In addition, hunters must learn many rules that don't apply to other shooters. For instance, a hunter should never openly carry game—it may make you an unwitting target of other hunters.

The Commandments of Safety are actually a way of saying, "Here's how people have accidents with guns." Each rule implies a kind of mishap. It's good exercise to look at each rule and read between the lines to find its counterpart—the potential disaster the rule will help you avoid. For example, rule number 1 translates into, "People have accidents with guns they believe are empty." Always keep in mind the prime directive: Take time to be safe instead of forever being sorry.

As of 2010, carrying a weapon discreetly no longer requires mandated classes from government. This puts the burden on you personally to make sure you're adequately trained in the law and for safety.

The Arizona Game and Fish Dept. is authorized, in §15-713, to provide training in the safe handling and use of firearms, to the public-school system on request. The Dept. may develop courses of study, instruction materials, trainer certifications, conduct training programs and issue certificates of completion. This work may be done in conjunction with other agencies or private firms. It would make sense to encourage your local schools to adopt such training, to help reduce the ignorance most youngsters have developed about guns from TV, movies, video games and other sources of gross misinformation, and help increase their general safety.

Training may be offered (§15-714) to anyone who is at least ten years old, on a purely voluntary basis. The Arizona Gun Safety Program (§15-714.01) provides for an elective full-semester one-credit class in gun safety and marksmanship, with a published curriculum. Gun-safety classes at college are approved under §13-2911.

The federal government has been providing public firearms training opportunities for more than a century, using federal facilities and the military in cooperation with civilian leaders. To get involved with the Civilian Marksmanship Program, call their office, listed in Appendix C.

Federal Marksmanship Programs for the Public

10 USC §4309:   Public access to federally funded rifle ranges.

10 USC §4312:   Public national shooting matches and small arms school, with subsidies for youngsters.

18 USC §922(q):   Guns OK at approved school training programs.

18 USC §922(x):   Handguns and ammunition can be transferred temporarily to juveniles for target practice.

Juveniles can have handguns and ammunition for a course of instruction in the safe and lawful use of a handgun.

36 USC §40701:   Civilian marksmanship programs, with special programs for youngsters.

The Gun Owner's Commandments for Safety that follow deal with the routine of gun handling in daily, non-threatening circumstances like range time, hunting, cleaning, transporting, teaching and similar uses of firearms. The gun safety rules for combat, as in crime prevention and personal safety, are another matter entirely.

If you think there are a lot of safety rules for routine gun handling, wait till you read some books on gun handling in tactical live-or-die situations. In stark contrast to the usual safety rules, the so-called Lovejoy's rules of gun safety include: 1–You must have a gun; 2–Keep your gun loaded and ready to fire at all times; 3–The first hit counts more than the first shot, and 4–The best gun is the one you have. Depending on who you ask it is a long list packed with valuable suggestions, e.g., If your shooting stance and sight picture are good, you're probably not moving fast enough or using cover correctly. And the first rule—it's always better to avoid a gunfight than to win one.

THE GUN OWNER'S COMMANDMENTS OF SAFETY

1–Treat every gun as if it is loaded until you have personally proven otherwise.

2–Always keep a gun pointed in a safe direction.

3–Don't touch the trigger until you're ready to fire.

4–Be certain of your target and what is beyond it before squeezing the trigger.

5–Keep a gun you carry holstered or out of sight unless you're ready to use it.

6–Use but never rely on the safety.

7–Never load a gun until ready to use. Unload a gun immediately after use.

8–Only use ammunition that matches the markings on your gun.

9–Always read and follow manufacturers' instructions carefully.

10–At a shooting range, always keep a gun pointed downrange.

11–Always obey a range officer's commands immediately.

12–Always wear adequate eye and ear protection when shooting.

13–If a gun fails to fire: a) keep it pointed in a safe direction; b) wait in anticipation of a delayed firing; c) unload the gun carefully, avoiding exposure to the breech.

14–Don't climb fences or trees, or jump logs or ditches with a chambered round.

15–Be able to control the direction of the muzzle even if you stumble.

16–Keep the barrel and action clear of obstructions.

17–Use extra caution when carrying ammunition that doesn't match the gun you are carrying.

18–Be aware that customized guns may require ammunition that doesn't match the gun's original markings.

19–Store guns with the action open.

20–Store ammunition and guns separately, and out of reach of children and careless adults.

21–Never pull a gun toward you by the muzzle.

22–Never horseplay with a firearm.

23–Never shoot at a hard flat surface, or at water, to prevent ricochets.

24–Be sure you have an adequate backstop for target shooting.

25–On open terrain with other people present, keep guns pointed upwards, or downwards and away from the people.

26–Use extra caution when handling a gun you are not familiar with.

27–Learn to work a gun empty before attempting to load and shoot it.

28–Always start out newcomers with a .22 before more powerful guns.

29–Never lean a firearm where it may slip and fall.

30–Don't use alcohol or mood-altering drugs when handling firearms.

31–When loading or unloading a firearm, always keep the muzzle pointed in a safe direction.
32–Never use a rifle scope instead of a pair of binoculars.
33–Always remember that removing the magazine (sometimes called the clip) from semi-automatic and automatic weapons may still leave a live round, ready to fire, in the chamber.
34–Never rely on one empty cylinder next to the barrel of a revolver as a guarantee of safety, since different revolvers rotate in opposite directions.
35–Never step into a boat holding a loaded firearm.
36–It's difficult to use a gun safely until you become a marksman.
37–It's difficult to handle a gun safely if you need corrective lenses and are not wearing them.
38–Know the effective range and the maximum range of a firearm and the ammunition you are using.
39–Be sure that anyone with access to a firearm kept in a home understands its safe use.
40–Don't fire a large caliber weapon if you can't control the recoil.
41–Never put your finger in the trigger guard when drawing a gun from a holster.
42–Never put your hand in front of a revolver's cylinder when firing.
43–Never put your hand in back of the slide of a semiautomatic pistol when firing.
44–If anyone asks you what kind of gun they should buy, make sure you have them take a class or two first.
45–Never leave ammunition around when cleaning a gun.
46–Clean firearms after they have been used. A dirty gun is not as safe as a clean one.
47–Never fire a blank round directly at a person. Blanks can blind, maim, and at close range, they can kill.
48–Only use modern firearms in good working condition, and ammunition that is fresh.
49–Accidents don't happen, they are caused, and it's up to you and you alone to prevent them in all cases. Every "accident" that ever happened could have been avoided. Where there are firearms there is a need for caution.
50–Always think first and shoot second.

The Eddie Eagle Safety Rules for Kids—If you find a gun:
STOP! Don't touch. Leave the area. Tell an adult.

It is the responsibility of every American to prevent firearms from being instruments of tragedy.

HOW WELL DO YOU KNOW YOUR GUN?

Safe and effective use of firearms demands that you understand your weapon thoroughly. This knowledge is best gained through a combination of reading, classes and practice with a qualified instructor. The simple test below will help tell you if you are properly trained in the use of firearms. If you're not sure what all the terms mean, can you be absolutely sure that you're qualified to handle firearms safely?

☐ Action; ☐ Ammunition; ☐ Automatic; ☐ Ballistics; ☐ Barrel;

☐ Black powder; ☐ Bolt; ☐ Bore; ☐ Break action; ☐ Breech;

☐ Buckshot; ☐ Bullet; ☐ Butt; ☐ Caliber; ☐ Cartridge; ☐ Case;

☐ Casing; ☐ Centerfire; ☐ Chamber; ☐ Checkering; ☐ Choke;

☐ Clip; ☐ Cock; ☐ Comb; ☐ Cylinder; ☐ Discharge; ☐ Strong eye;

☐ Effective range; ☐ Firearm; ☐ Firing Pin; ☐ Firing Line;

☐ Forearm; ☐ Fouling; ☐ Frame; ☐ Gauge; ☐ Grip; ☐ Grip panels;

☐ Grooves; ☐ Gunpowder; ☐ Half cock; ☐ Hammer; ☐ Handgun;

☐ Hangfire; ☐ Hunter orange; ☐ Ignition; ☐ Kneeling; ☐ Lands;

☐ Lever action; ☐ Magazine; ☐ Mainspring; ☐ Maximum range;

☐ Misfire; ☐ Muzzle; ☐ Muzzleloader; ☐ Pattern; ☐ Pistol;

☐ Powder; ☐ Primer ; ☐ Projectile; ☐ Prone; ☐ Pump action;

☐ Receiver; ☐ Revolver; ☐ Rifle; ☐ Rifling; ☐ Rimfire; ☐ Safety;

☐ Sear; ☐ Semi-automatic; ☐ Shell; ☐ Shooting positions; ☐ Shot;

☐ Shotgun; ☐ Sights; ☐ Sighting-in; ☐ Sitting; ☐ Smokeless powder;

☐ Smoothbore; ☐ Squib load; ☐ Standing; ☐ Stock; ☐ Trigger;

☐ Trigger guard; ☐ Unplugged shotgun

CONCEALED-WEAPON TRAINING

Arizona abandoned the state-mandated training model, established with the CCW-permit program in 1994, when it adopted more robust freedom with Constitutional Carry in 2011. DPS has been removed from the burden of designing classes, approving or drafting curricula, testing and approving applicants and instructors, but still has the administrative load of the program for handling application paperwork and tracking innocent people with permits. A wide variety of training opportunities now satisfy the requirements for a permit, for those people who wish to get one for its specific benefits, see chapter 2.

Now that any law-abiding adult in the state can carry arms, discreetly or openly, it makes perfect sense for the entire public to get some gun-safety training, learn more about the popular shooting sports, and exercise the right to arms we have had as Americans since the nation was founded.

Areas of Study and Self-Test

1–Where are firearms prohibited in Arizona?
   (At least eleven places, study chapter 2)

2–What are the possible penalties for improper display of a weapon?
   (At least seven possible charges could be brought, study chapter 5)

3–What risks exist in drawing a firearm in public?
   (Could justify a self-defense claim by another party, accidental discharge, discharge in prohibited area, more, study chapter 5)

4–When does state law justify the use of deadly force?
   (At least 16 circumstances are described, study chapter 5)

5–What factors mitigate the strict legal definitions for justifiable use of deadly force?
   (This is a complex issue frequently subject to debate and interpretation, fact-intensive and specific to the circumstances, study chapters 5 and 8, and other books, such as In The Gravest Extreme, by Massad Ayoob)

6–What responsibility does a shooter have for shots fired that miss the intended target?
   (Severe liabilities and penalties can result from the effect of stray bullets, study chapter 5)

7–Can you bring a firearm into a bar?
   (Usually prohibited, certain exceptions apply, see chapters 1 & 2)

8–What types of weapons are illegal?
   (For federal- and state-law restrictions, study chapter 3)

9–Who can legally bear arms in Arizona?
   (Age, background, mental condition and more are taken into account, study chapter 1)

10–Under what circumstances can minors bear arms?
   (Study chapters 1 and 7)

11–How can firearms be carried throughout the state?
   (Different rules apply for law-abiding adults, for minors and in special places, study chapters 1 and 2)

12– What are the requirements for getting a CCW permit?
   (Personal background and eligibility are involved, study chapter 2)

13–What do you have to do to ship firearms or carry them with you on a train, plane, or as you travel by car?
   (Federal regulations control interstate transit, study chapter 1)

14–How remote need you be to practice target shooting outdoors?
   (Land office rules are plentiful, study chapter 4)

15–How much judgment is involved in deciding whether you can use deadly force in a situation?
   (No easy answers to this, read everything you can find on the subject, study chapters 5 and 8, and recognize that in using deadly force you accept very definite and substantial legal risks)

16–What are the main rules of firearm safety?
   (More than 50 exist, study chapter 8)

17–What types of weapons are suitable for self defense, and what are the best choices for you?
   (Not covered here, discuss this at length with your instructors)

18–How do the various types of firearms operate?
   (This topic should be covered by your instructors)

19–What are the options for carrying a weapon discreetly?
   (This topic should be covered by your instructors)

20–Have any new laws passed that you should know about?
   (This requires ongoing information and vigilance)

21–Are you mentally prepared to use deadly force?
   (Mental conditioning for use of deadly force is a critical practical component, and one that is not easily addressed. Until a moment arrives you may never truly know the answer to this question.)

As you can see, your preparation for carrying a weapon discreetly can go well beyond a basic class or some short program. Make the smart choice and way exceed minimum training by reading extensively, practicing regularly, keeping up on the important issues, and taking additional training programs periodically. Visit TrainMeAZ.com.

Practice Test Questions

The former DPS required test for a CCW permit had ten questions, selected from a larger set. The questions presented here are designed for study—to challenge your understanding, provoke thought and encourage discussion. Some of these have obvious yes-no or true-false answers, while others require a deeper understanding of the issues and must be answered with "maybe" or "it depends." Some defy clear answers. If you have trouble with any of these, ask your firearms safety instructor for assistance.

1–Is it legal to point an empty gun at a person, or at anything?

2–What do we mean by "is it legal" to do something?

3–Do you need a permit to put a handgun in a handbag?

4–Is home defense with a machine gun legal?

5–Never tell family you keep a loaded gun in the house.

6–Always tell family you keep a loaded gun in the house.

7–Arizona requires you to lock your guns in a safe.

8–Arizona requires you to put a trigger lock on your guns.

9–Does the law say you may kill if your life is in danger?

10–Does the law say you may kill if your friend is in danger?

11–If a peace officer is in danger may you shoot to kill?

12–You may conceal weapons in Arizona without a permit.

13–You can only conceal some weapons in Arizona with a permit.

14–A CCW permit prohibits concealing a bayonet.

15–A CCW permit prohibits bringing a gun onto a plane.

16–A CCW permit prohibits concealing explosives.

17–It's always illegal to bring a gun into a bar.

18–A bar's owner may carry a sidearm in the bar.

19–A bar owner may allow the employees to be armed.

20–A bar owner may allow patrons to be armed.

21–Drawing a gun to settle a severe argument is legal.

22–Drawing a gun wrongly may lead to criminal charges.

23–Drawing a gun wrongly is permissible if you don't shoot.

24–If someone else draws a gun you may too.

25–If your life is immediately at risk you may draw a gun.

26–May you draw a gun to stop a serious crime in progress?

27–May you draw a gun to stop a kidnapping?

28–May you draw a gun to stop a robbery?

29–May you draw a gun to stop an armed robbery?

30–May you draw a gun to stop a sexual assault?

31–May you draw a gun to stop child molestation?

32–May you draw a gun to stop a serious traffic violation?

33–May you draw a gun to stop criminal trespass?

34–May you draw a gun to stop an arsonist?

35–May you draw a gun to stop vandals?

36–May you draw a gun to stop a first-degree escape?

37–May you draw a gun to stop shoplifting?

38–May you shoot in items 25 through 37 above?

39–Do you want to ever have to shoot someone?

40–All states treat self-defense shooting the same way.

41–Federal law guarantees your rights no matter what.

42–Shooting criminals is legal if they are "in the act."

43–You should declare you have a CCW permit to police.

44–Never mention your CCW permit unless asked.

45–It's OK to let a concealed weapon show occasionally.

46–If you shoot a criminal you don't have to report it.

47–You should report any shooting incident to authorities.

48–If you shoot a criminal leave the body where it falls.

49–If you shoot a criminal outside your home drag him inside.

50–You're normally aware of everything around you.

51–When danger lurks, your awareness always goes up.

52–Even if you're cautious, danger can surprise you.

53–When you're surprised you're not always predictable.

54–Acting under stress can lead to surprising responses.

55–Name the four modes of mental awareness.

56–Describe the four modes of mental awareness.

57–The only official way to shoot is the Weaver stance.

58–You must grip a firearm with both hands to be legal.

59–Any shooting position you like is legal for self defense.

60–If you get a CCW permit you're perfectly qualified.

61–A CCW permit increases your personal safety.

62–A CCW permit increases your ability to respond.

63–A CCW permit will allow you to take back the streets.

64–With a CCW permit you may go wherever you want.

65–If a man charges you with a knife may you shoot him?

66–If a man charges you with a bat may you shoot him?

67–If a woman charges you with a bat may you shoot her?

68–If a man hits your spouse with a bat may you shoot him?

69–If a man threatens you with a bat may you shoot him?

70–If a man enrages you for no reason may you shoot him?

71–If a man won't let you get gasoline may you change his mind with a gun?

72–If someone starts shooting someone else, may you shoot the first person to stop the attack?

73–Methods for controlling a violent confrontation are something that cannot be learned.

74–Will you need a gun more after you have a CCW permit than you did before you had a permit?

75–Have you ever witnessed a serious crime, such as a kidnapping, armed robbery or murder, that would justify your use of deadly force?

76–Are you more likely to witness a serious crime once you have a CCW permit?

77–Is it a good idea to practice marksmanship with the same gun you plan on carrying regularly?

78–Unless you need to use it in an emergency, you should never let a discreetly carried weapon show.

79–If you sell a gun to a person who uses it to commit a crime can you be charged with a crime?

80–What happens if you are found in Arizona with an unregistered handgun in your possession?

81–What is the legal maximum distance for a self-defense shooting in Arizona?

82–Arizona has preemption, which means that cities and counties may pass their own gun laws.

83–Many cities in Arizona have different gun laws that you must follow.

84–Many locations in Arizona interpret the laws differently and are allowed to do so by their courts.

85–What is a "citizen's arrest," how do you make one, and is it a good idea to make one if you witness a crime?

86–If you see a drug deal going down, may you draw your gun and use deadly force to stop it?

87–If you see a prostitute operating in your neighborhood, may you threaten deadly force, without using it, to make the person leave?

88–If you use a gun legitimately to defend yourself there is a possibility you will be charged with a serious offense.

89–Many people who are charged with murder claim self defense or unintentional discharge.

90–Many people who use deadly force in self defense are charged with murder.

91–The person who survives a lethal confrontation is often referred to as the defendant by the authorities.

92–If someone starts hitting you that's justification for threatening to use deadly force.

93–If someone starts hitting you that's justification for using deadly force.

94–If someone says they're going to start hitting you that's justification for threatening to use deadly force.

95–If someone hits you repeatedly in the face until you're bleeding, and then stops, you may draw your gun and shoot the attacker.

96–If someone comes into your place of business and commits a robbery, may you respond with deadly force?

97–A man says he's going to shoot you and sticks his hand in his pocket. May you shoot him first?

98–A woman says she's going to shoot you and sticks her hand in her pocketbook. May you shoot her first?

99–If you are armed may you operate as a free-lance police officer?

100–The police may use deadly force in certain situations that you may not.

101–Tactics refers to the steps you take in an emergency.

102–Strategy refers to the plans you make in the event you are ever in an emergency.

103–A good crime-avoidance plan includes tactics and strategy.

104–"Shoot first and ask questions later," is bad advice for self defense.

105–It's always better to not shoot someone if you can safely avoid it.

106–If you get a CCW permit, or even if you carry constitutionally without one, does that change anything with respect to the number and seriousness of the threats you normally face in your daily routine?

107–Why does it make sense for you personally to get a CCW permit?

108–Spending regular practice time on a shooting range after you get a CCW permit or decide to carry constitutionally is a good idea.

109–Spending regular practice time on a shooting range if you never get a CCW permit, or even do not have a gun, is a good idea, and fun, just like learning to swim, even if you have no pool.

110–Taking friends and relatives to a range periodically, especially if they have rarely or never been to a range, is a good idea because it increases awareness of key issues Americans should know, teaches responsibility and valuable skills, dispels myths many people unwittingly believe, helps support the freedoms we enjoy in this country, sharpens your own skills, builds good friendships, is the number two participant sport in the nation, and is a whole lot of exciting wholesome fun.

In addition to questions such as the ones presented here, firearm owners should study material and be able to answer questions on topics not covered in *The Arizona Gun Owner's Guide*, such as:

What are the various types of firearms, what are their component parts, and how do they operate; what are the various types of ammunition; what are the criteria for selecting a self-defense weapon and ammunition; what are the options for holsters and carrying weapons; how can you reduce chances of unintentional firing and what are the primary firearm safety rules; what affects aiming and firing accurately; how should guns and ammunition be stored; how are guns cleaned, lubricated and checked, what are the tactics and strategies for personal self defense and having weapons accessible; what alternatives are there to confrontation; how can threatening situations be managed; how can confrontations be avoided.

JUDGMENTAL SHOOTING

Anyone who decides to bear arms should study what Arizona had labeled *judgmental shooting* under the olden permission-slip carry system. The decision to use deadly force is rarely a clear-cut choice. Regardless of your familiarity with the laws, your degree of training, the quality of your judgmental skills and your physical location and condition at the time of a deadly threat, the demands placed on you at the critical moment are as intense as anything you will normally experience in your life, and your actual performance is an unknown.

Every situation is different. The answers to many questions relating to deadly force are subject to debate. To be prepared for armed response you must recognize that such situations are not black or white, and that your actions, no matter how well intentioned, will be evaluated by others, probably long after you act. The chances that you will come away from a lethal encounter without any scars—legal, physical or psychological—are small, and the legal risks are substantial. That's why it's usually best to practice prevention and avoidance rather than confrontation, whenever possible.

Most people can think about it this way: You've gotten along this far in life without ever having to draw down on someone, much less having to fire. The odds of that changing once you decide to carry or get a CCW permit are about the same—fairly small. A carried weapon may make you feel more secure, but it doesn't change how safe your surroundings actually are, in the places you normally travel, one bit. And it certainly isn't safe to think of a carried weapon as a license (or a talisman) for walking through potentially dangerous areas you would otherwise avoid like the plague. One closely guarded secret in the debate about street crime is that it typically happens on the streets you don't frequent, in the bad part of town. Check out the "Gunshot Demographics" maps at GunLaws.com. The "news" media, by making crime seem rampant, increases public fear and with it, political capital to attack the right to arms and increase government power.

Remember: the person holding a gun after a shooting is often thought of as the bad guy—the perpetrator—even if you're the assault victim who acted in self defense. The person shot has a different, sympathetic but false name—the victim—and the benefit of a prosecutor even if, perhaps you learn later it's a hardened thug with a long record. Maybe your defense will improve if it is indeed a serious repeat offender, but you won't know that until after the fact, and don't count on it. If you ever have to raise a gun to a criminal, you'll find out quickly how good they can be at portraying you as the bad guy and themselves as the helpless innocents, at the mercy of a crazed wacko—you.

Shooting Scenarios

Think about the deadly force encounters described below, and discuss them with your firearms trainers (analysis follows):

1–If you are being seriously attacked by a man with a club, is it legal to aim for his leg so you can stop the attack without killing him?

2–If you enter your home and find a person looting your possessions are you justified in shooting?

3–If you enter your home and find a person looting your possessions, who runs out the back door as he hears you arrive, may you shoot him to keep him from escaping?

4–If you arrive home and find someone looting your possessions, who turns and whirls toward you when you enter, literally scaring you to death, may you shoot and expect to be justified?

5–If you enter your home and find a stranger in it who charges you with a knife, may you shoot?

6–A stranger in your home has just stabbed your spouse and is about to stab your spouse again. May you shoot the stranger from behind to stop the attack?

7–As you walk past a park at night you notice a woman tied to a tree and a man tearing off her clothing. May you use deadly force to stop his actions?

8–A police officer is bleeding badly and chasing a man in prison coveralls who runs right past you. May you shoot the fleeing suspect while he is in close range to you?

9–You're in your home at night when a man with a ski mask on comes through an open window in the hallway. May you shoot?

10–You're in your home at night, sleeping, when a noise at the other end of the house awakens you. Taking your revolver you quietly walk over to investigate and notice a short person going through your silverware drawer, 45 feet from where you're standing. The person doesn't notice you. May you shoot?

11–As you approach your parked car in a dark and remote parking lot, three youthful toughs approach you from three separate directions. You probably can't unlock your vehicle and get in before they reach you, and you're carrying a gun. What should you do?

12–From outside a convenience store you observe what clearly appears to be an armed robbery—four people are held at gunpoint while the store clerk is putting money into a paper bag. You're armed. What should you do?

13–You're waiting to cross the street in downtown and a beggar asks you for money. He's insistent and begins to insult you when you refuse to ante up. Finally he gets loud and belligerent and says he'll kill you if you don't give him ten dollars. May you shoot him?

14–You get in your car, roll down the windows, and before you can drive off a man sticks a knife in the window and orders you to get out. May you shoot him?

15–You get in your car, and before you start it a man points a gun at you and tells you to get out. You have gun in the pocket on the door, another under the seat, one in the glovebox and a gun in a holster in your pants. What should you do?

16–Before you get in your car, a man with a gun comes up from behind, demands your car keys, takes them, and while holding you at gun point, starts your car and drives away. May you shoot at him while he's escaping?

17–You're walking to your car in the mall parking lot with two friends after a movie when two armed hoods jump out of a shadow and demand your money. You've got a gun in your back pocket. What should you do?

18–A masked person with a gun stops you on the street, demands and takes your valuables, then flees down the street on foot. You're carrying a concealed firearm. What should you do?

19–A youngster runs right by you down the street, and an old lady shouts, "Stop him, he killed my husband!" May you shoot to stop his getaway?

20–You're at work when two ornery-looking dudes amble in. You can smell trouble, so you walk to a good vantage point behind a showcase. Sure enough, they pull guns and announce a stick-up. You and your four employees are armed and there are several customers in the store. What's your move?

21–Your friend and you have been drinking, and now you're arguing over a football bet. You say the spread was six points, he says four. There's $500 hanging in the balance of a five point game, and it represents your mortgage payment. He pulls a knife and says, "Pay me or I'll slice you up." You've got a gun in your pocket. What should you do?

22–At a gas station, the lines are long, it's hot, and the guy next in line starts getting surly. You're not done pumping and he hits you in the face and tells you to finish up. He shuts off your pump and says he'll kick your butt if you don't move on. Should you pull your gun to put him in his place?

Analysis of the Shooting Scenarios:

1–It's an unlikely case where the justification to use deadly force would be justification to intentionally wound. Firing and missing is a different story, but it could be argued that if the threat wasn't enough to use deadly force then there was no right to shoot at all. Any shooting has lethal potential regardless of your ability to aim under extreme duress; a person can die from fright, loss of blood, infection. In the desperate seconds where such a shot could be fired, attempting the most difficult shot known—winging a moving limb—is a dubious strategy. It costs critical time and wastes a shot that may be crucial to your survival. Law does not provide for justifiable wounding. Hollywood vigorously promotes the shoot-to-wound concept, but it's about as valid as most other depictions of things gun in the movies.

2–Not enough information is provided to make an informed choice.

3–No. The penalty for burglary is jail, not death, and you almost never have justification to kill to prevent a criminal from escaping (kidnapping may be an exception). Once the danger to you is over—and it is once the criminal is fleeing—your right to use deadly force usually ends.

4–Probably. But do you always enter your home prepared for mortal combat? Does your story have other holes a prosecutor will notice?

5–It's hard to imagine not being justified in this situation, but stranger things have happened. Check the answer to number 4 again.

6–It's hard to imagine not being justified in this situation, but stranger things have happened. Will the bullet exit the attacker and wound your spouse?

7–Not necessarily, since you don't know if the people are consenting adults who like this sort of thing. A seasoned peace officer might cautiously approach the couple, weapon drawn, and with words instead of force determine what's happening, and then make further choices depending on the outcome.

8–Probably not, under existing state law (see §13-410) and under recent court rulings about civilians shooting at fleeing suspects, but if the officer enlists your aid (see §13-2403), possibly yes.

9–Probably, though a well-trained expert might instead confront the intruder from a secure position and succeed in holding the person for arrest, which is no easy task. Armed and from good cover, you might also convince the person to simply leave. Drop the hammer and your life changes.

10–Perhaps, but the distance and lack of immediate threat will make for a difficult explanation when the police arrive, and if the perpetrator has an accomplice that you didn't notice, the danger to you is severe. If the perpetrator turns out to be a thief with a long rap sheet, you might not even be charged. If it turns out the intruder is 11 years old your court defense will be extremely difficult. Remember, you're obligated to not shoot if you don't absolutely have to. Has your training prepared you for this?

11–Good question. You should never have parked there in the first place.

12–Call for assistance, go to a defensible position, continue to observe, and recognize that charging into such a volatile situation is incredibly risky for all parties. Remember, a smart robber has an armed lookout you don't see.

13–You are never justified in using deadly force in response to verbal provocation alone, no matter how severe.

14–The prosecutor might make a case that if you could have stomped the gas and escaped, the threat to you would have ended, and the need to shoot did not exist. If you were boxed into a parking space, the need to defend yourself would be hard for a prosecutor to refute. These things often come down to the exact circumstances and the quality of the attorneys.

15–Get out quietly and don't provoke someone who has the drop on you. All your guns are no match for a drawn weapon, and remember that discreet carry is not a particularly good way to win a quick-draw contest. This is where a real understanding of tactics comes into play.

16–No. You are almost never justified in shooting at an escaping criminal. The penalty for grand theft auto is jail time, not death. Once the threat to you is over, so is the justification for using lethal force.

17–You have a split-second life-or-death decision here and no clear answer.

18–Nothing, though you could chase him, but it's extremely unwise and risky to you. You are almost never justified in shooting at an escaping criminal (kidnapping, under certain circumstances, might be an exception). The penalty for armed robbery is jail time, not death. Once the threat to you is over, so is the justification for using lethal force. Anyone crazy enough to rob you at gunpoint must be considered capable of doing anything, and the smart move is to avoid further confrontation and stay alive.

19–You don't have enough information. When in doubt don't shoot.

20–This is where strategy and tactics are critical. If you allow your employees to carry and are prepared for armed defense of your premises you better get plenty of advanced training in gunfighting and self defense. You'll need it to survive, and you'll need it to meet the legal challenges later. If a customer gets shot by one of your own, even if you get the villains, you're in for big-time trouble and grief. If no one gets hurt but the criminals, you'll be a hero. Either outcome remains burned in memory. Tough choice.

21–Too many killings occur between people who know each other.
Your chance of a successful legal defense in a case like this are remote. Would he have really killed you? Probably not. Did you have any other options besides killing him? Probably so. Have you fought like this before? Maybe. What would the witnesses say? Nothing you could count on, and probably all the wrong things. The fact that you have a firearm and can use it doesn't mean you should, the likelihood of absolutely having to use it are small, and using it to settle a bet with a friend over a point spread may not be the worst thing you can do but it's close.

22–Cap your tank and move on, you don't need the grief. Or go into the station and tell them what's happened, preparing yourself mentally for further hostilities. Go to a defensible position and call the police. Avoid a confrontation at all costs. See what the other guy does before you do anything. Decide to take another course in how to handle volatile situations and difficult people. And realize that the fact that you have a firearm and a lot of training doesn't solve any problems or reduce your risks in life.

RECOMMENDED READING

Knowledge is power, and the more you have the better off you are likely to be. Some trainers will require you to read important books on personal safety, crime avoidance, self defense and the use of deadly force. **Whether your instructors require it or not, decide to read up on this critical subject.**

Some of the most highly regarded books on these topics are at the back of *The Arizona Gun Owner's Guide* and are easily available directly from the publisher. Call or email for our **free full-color catalog** for more excellent reading and DVDs. If your instructors don't include these in your courses, get them yourself. The single best book on the subject is probably *In The Gravest Extreme*, by Massad Ayoob.

If you're concerned about preserving your right to keep and bear arms, read up on being effective politically. Too many activists make the mistake of endlessly studying the Bill of Rights and related documents, so that they can win debates. But if you win all your debates you're actually losing. You don't want to win debates, you want to win friends and influence people. Bloomfield Press now carries a line of books with this focus—*Getting To Yes, How To Win Friends And Influence People, Confrontational Politics* and other titles that supercharge your efforts.

You may also choose to obtain a complete copy of the Arizona criminal code, since the laws reproduced in *The Arizona Gun Owner's Guide* are a selected excerpt of gun laws only. The Lexus Nexus company is the official publisher, listed in Appendix C. Remember that no published edition of the law is complete without the legislation passed during the most recent session of the state congress, and that federal laws may be passed at any time. An annotated edition of the law, available in major libraries, provides critical information in the form of court cases that clarify and expand on the meaning of the actual statutes.

DON'T SHOOT AT CACTUS!

Cactus is a treasure that the state of Arizona is lucky to have. They are legally protected plants—it's a crime to shoot at them or harm them in any way. Removing any cactus from the desert without special authorization is against the law. Only the lowest and sleaziest bottom-feeding dregs of society would even think of shooting at these harmless and majestic natives of the state.

Cactus can't shoot back, but there's at least one case on record of a cactus that got even! The scene depicted above actually occurred on February 4, 1982, just west of Lake Pleasant in Maricopa County, when a man was crushed to death by a 23-foot section of the saguaro cactus he had shot with rifled slugs from a 16-gauge shotgun.

APPENDIX A
GLOSSARY OF TERMS

Words, when used in the law, often have special meanings you wouldn't expect from simply knowing the English language. For the complete legal description of these and other important terms, see each chapter of the criminal code and other legal texts dealing with language. *Black's Law Dictionary* is a widely used reference for understanding legalese, but guides specific to a given body of law are also essential, and statutes frequently include definitions for use within the specific statute itself. The following plain English descriptions are provided for your convenience only.

ACT—A bodily movement.

ADEQUATE PROVOCATION—Conduct or circumstances sufficient to make a reasonable person lose self-control.

ARREST—To deprive a person of physical liberty by legal authority.

AUTHORIZED REMOTE STUN GUN— a *remote stun gun*, q.v., that also: puts out less than 100,000 volts and under nine joules of energy per jolt, has an ID on all projectiles discharged from it, blows out labeled "confetti" identifying material when fired that is traceable to the buyer through records kept by the manufacturer, and includes an offered training program. This definition was adopted to identify the TASER-brand stun gun.

AZPOST—Arizona Police Officer Standards and Training board, created 1968.

BB-type GUN—A "nearly" gun designed to forcibly propel a ball, pellet, dart or other projectile using compressed air, carbon dioxide gas or similar.

BATFE—The federal Bureau of Alcohol, Tobacco, Firearms and Explosives, a division of the Justice Dept.

BENEFIT—Anything of value or advantage, now or in the future.

BIG GAME—Antelope, bear, bison (buffalo), deer, elk, mountain lion, peccary (javelina), bighorn sheep and wild turkey.

CONDUCT—The actions you take or refrain from, and your thoughts about them.

CONSTITUTIONAL CARRY—The freedom for law-abiding adults to bear arms, openly or discreetly, without government permission or red tape.

CRIME—A felony or misdemeanor.

CRIMINAL NEGLIGENCE—Failure to recognize a risk so dangerous that a reasonable person would be expected to recognize it.

CCW—Acronym for a concealed-weapon permit, or anything related to the program. Refers to a permit to carry a concealed weapon. Other states often use other acronyms (CHL in Texas and Ohio, CHP in Virginia, CPL in Michigan, CWP in Utah and Montana, CCHP in North Carolina, etc.)

CULPABLE MENTAL STATE—An accountable state of mind. Specifically: intentionally, knowingly, recklessly or with criminal negligence, in the senses described by law.

DANGEROUS DRUG—For a detailed description, see A.R.S. §13-3401.

DANGEROUS INSTRUMENT—An object, though not designed for lethal use, that can readily be used to cause death or serious physical injury.

DEADLY PHYSICAL FORCE—Force that can cause death or serious physical injury.

DEADLY WEAPON—Anything designed for lethal use. The term includes a firearm.

DEAL—To engage in the business of selling firearms at wholesale or to repair or modify firearms, with the principal objective of making a livelihood or profit.

DEFACE—To remove, alter or destroy the manufacturer's serial number.

DPS—The Arizona Department of Public Safety, based in Phoenix, is the rough equivalent of what some other states refer to as the state police.

e.g.,—"for example," from the Latin, *exempli gratia*

ENTERPRISE—A corporation, association, labor union or other legal entity.

et seq.—Latin shorthand for additional information, literally, "and what follows."

EXPLOSIVE—Dynamite, nitroglycerine, black powder, plastic explosive or other similar materials. Ammunition and hand-loading ammunition supplies are excluded.

FELONY—A serious crime. An offense against the law that carries a sentence of imprisonment under the custody of the state Department of Corrections. Felony prison sentences run from 6 months to life imprisonment with no chance of parole until 25 years have been served. A class 1 felony (1st degree murder) carries a possible sentence of death. Arizona uses lethal injection to inflict the penalty of death. Felony fines may be up to $150,000 for an individual, and up to $1,000,000 for an enterprise.

FFL—Federal Firearms License (or Licensee, depending on context).

FIREARM—Any loaded or unloaded handgun, pistol, revolver, rifle, shotgun or other weapon that can fire a projectile by using an explosive or expanding gasses. A permanently inoperable firearm is excluded.

GOVERNMENT—The recognized political structure.

GOVERNMENT FUNCTION—Any activity that a public servant is authorized to do for the government.

GUN—A firearm.

HOMICIDE—Killing of a human being, ranked for punishment as first or second degree murder, manslaughter or negligent homicide.

ILLEGAL—Unlawful. An offense. A crime.

ILLEGAL GUN, see *prohibited weapon.*

IMPROVISED EXPLOSIVE DEVICE—a device using explosives, or destructive, lethal, noxious, pyrotechnic or incendiary chemicals designed to destroy, disfigure, terrify or harass.

INTENTIONALLY or WITH THE INTENT TO—With the objective of causing a specific result.

INTOXICATION—Mental or physical incapacity caused by drugs, toxic vapors or alcohol.

JUSTIFICATION—Legal right to use physical or deadly physical force.

KNOWINGLY—With awareness of your conduct and situation.

LAW—Formal rules by which society controls itself. In Arizona, the written law means the *Arizona Revised Statutes,* abbreviated A.R.S. Cities and other governments within the state may not enact a law that contradicts state law.

LEO—Law enforcement officer, sometimes called a peace officer. Police.

LEOSA—Law Enforcement Officers Safety Act, the 2004 federal law granting qualified law enforcement officers the power to carry firearms nationwide.

LESSEE—A person who leases something from another person.

MACHINE GUN—A firearm capable of shooting more than one shot automatically, by a single pull of the trigger.

MISDEMEANOR—A crime less serious than a felony. An offense against the law that carries a sentence of imprisonment in a local facility, not to the state Department of Corrections. Misdemeanor jail sentences run up to six months. Misdemeanor fines can run up to $2,500 for an individual, and up to $20,000 for an enterprise.

MOLOTOV COCKTAIL— A breakable container that contains a flammable liquid with a flash point of one hundred fifty degrees Fahrenheit or less and that has a wick or similar device capable of being ignited.

MUNICIPALITY—Any city or town and any property fully enclosed within the city or town.

NARCOTIC DRUG—For a detailed description, see A.R.S. §13-3401.

NFA—National Firearms Act of 1934. The initials are commonly used to describe implements regulated by the act, e.g., NFA weapons.

OCCUPIED STRUCTURE—Any building, object, vehicle, watercraft, aircraft or place with sides and a floor that is separately securable from any other structure attached to it, that is used for lodging, business, transportation, recreation or storage, where one or more people either are or could be present, or are so near they could be in possible danger, at the time a gun is fired. Occupied structure includes any dwelling house, whether occupied, unoccupied or vacant.

OFFENSE—Any conduct described in the law that carries a jail sentence or fine. A crime.

OMISSION—Failure to do something required by law.

PEACE OFFICER—Anyone with legal authority to maintain public order and make arrests. Sometimes called a law enforcement officer, LEO.

PERSON—A human being, or, as applicable, an enterprise or government.

PETTY OFFENSE—A minor criminal violation. An offense against the law that carries only a fine as a penalty. Petty offenses run up to $300 for an individual, and up to $1000 for an enterprise.

PHYSICAL FORCE—Force used on another person. Confining another person is considered physical force.

PHYSICAL INJURY—Harm to the physical condition of a person or property.

POACHING—Hunting illegally, by either hunting without a valid license, outside of regulations, taking wildlife during closed season or possessing unlawfully taken wildlife.

POSSESS—To knowingly have or exercise control over property.

POSSESSION—The voluntary act of exercising control over property.

PREMEDITATION—Acting with the intention or knowledge that you will kill another human being. The intention or knowledge must precede the killing by a length of time sufficient to permit reflection. Killing in the instant effect of a sudden quarrel or heat of passion is not premeditation.

PROHIBITED POSSESSOR—A person who may not ship, transport, possess or receive a firearm. See Chapter 1 for a detailed description.

PROHIBITED WEAPON—Guns and other weapons that are a crime to have, make, sell, transport or transfer without federal registration. A National Firearms Act (NFA) weapon, without the necessary paperwork. See Chapter 3 for a detailed description.

PROPERTY—Anything of tangible or intangible value.

PUBLIC SERVANT—Any officer or employee of any branch of government. Public servants may be elected, appointed, or hired. Consultants working for government and peace officers are included. You become a public servant at the time you are selected, which may be before you actually occupy the specific government position. Jurors and witnesses are excluded.

q.v.—Latin abbreviation for a cross reference, literally, "which see."

REASONABLE—This term is used to describe behavior and circumstances that fit into a generally recognized and accepted norm. It is frequently possible to argue about the precise meaning of the word, depending on the situation.

REASONABLE PERSON—An imaginary person who conforms to generally recognized and accepted norms. Reasonableness is a factor in determining if the use of force or deadly force is legally justifiable. See Chapter 5.

RECKLESSLY—With awareness of and disregard for a risk so dangerous that a reasonable person would not ignore it.

REMOTE STUN GUN— an electronic device that emits an electrical charge, designed to incapacitate a person or animal, by touching them with electrodes on the device, or remotely through probes wired to the device, or by a spark, plasma, ionization or other conductive means from the device. Sometimes called a TASER, which is actually the brand name of a product.

RIFLED BARREL—A gun barrel with helical internal grooves for giving the bullet a spin that helps stabilize it in flight. Rifled weapons are restricted in limited areas, notably the Maricopa County Parks. Most handguns are rifled.

SERIOUS PHYSICAL INJURY—Injury that creates a reasonable risk of death. Also, injury that causes serious and permanent disfigurement, loss of any organ or limb, or serious long-term harm to health, an organ or a limb.

TAKING—Pursuing, shooting, hunting, fishing, trapping, killing, capturing, snaring or netting wildlife, or placing any device to capture or kill wildlife.

TASER—The brand name of the original authorized remote stun gun.

TRANSFER—Sell, assign, pledge, lease, loan, give away or otherwise dispose of.

UNLAWFUL—Against the law. Illegal. A crime.

VEHICLE—Any device used for transportation of people or property, on a road, waterway, airway or off-road. Devices using solely human power, and devices that travel on tracks or rails are excluded.

VOLUNTARY ACT—A deliberate bodily movement.

VOLUNTARY INTOXICATION—Getting drunk or high on alcohol, drugs or toxic vapors that you know, or should know, will cause the effect. Taking alcohol, drugs or toxic vapors under medical advice is excluded. Taking such substances under duress may afford a defense.

APPENDIX B
Crime and Punishment Chart

EXPLANATIONS

Type of Crime: Illegal activities are divided into these ten categories, to match the punishment to the crime. The category may be effected by how the crime is committed. Felonies are serious crimes, misdemeanors less serious. Felonies remove the right to keep and bear arms, hold public office, vote, obtain certain types of employment and more. These are state crimes, federal charges may also apply.

Jail Term: These are the ranges for a first offense involving a gun; many crimes have special sentences. The back cover shows maximum sentences for first offense without a gun. The class 1 felony, in addition to life imprisonment with no chance of parole for at least 25 years, carries a possible death penalty for first degree murder, which is carried out by lethal injection. Sentences may be raised or lowered, based on aggravating or mitigating circumstances, involving a degree of court discretion, and using guidelines set out in chapter 7 of the state criminal code.

Fines: These are the maximums, which may be lowered at court discretion. Fines are payable immediately, but a court may grant permission to pay by a certain date or in installments.

Statute of Limitations: The period of time, from the discovery of an offense (or from the time when an offense should have been discovered with the exercise of reasonable diligence), within which a prosecution may begin. When a class 2, 3 or 4 felony involves homicide there is no time limit. The period of limitation is put on hold if you are out of state, or if you have no known abode within the state. Plea bargaining a class 6 felony to a misdemeanor does not change the time limit.

Offenses: This is a partial list and exceptions often apply. For example, sexual assault with a gun carries life imprisonment with no chance of parole for at least 25 years.

CRIME AND PUNISHMENT IN ARIZONA

All penalties are subject to change depending on circumstances

Type of Crime	Jail Term 1st Offense	Max. Fine for Person	Max. Fine for Business	Statute of Limitation
Class 1 Felony	**For Life**	**$150,000**	**$1 Million**	**None**
First-degree murder, second-degree murder.				
Class 2 Felony	**4–10 Yrs.**	**$150,000**	**$1 Million**	**7 Years**
Attempted murder, manslaughter, armed robbery, bringing a gun into a prison, drive by shooting, kidnapping, sexual conduct with minor under 15, sexual assault, child molestation, first-degree burglary of residence, arson of occupied structure, promoting prison contraband, using weapon in terrorism.				
Class 3 Felony	**2.5–7 Yrs.**	**$150,000**	**$1 Million**	**7 Years**
Aggravated assault, assisting a suicide, first-degree burglary of non-residence, second-degree burglary.				
Class 4 Felony	**1.5–3 Yrs.**	**$150,000**	**$1 Million**	**7 Years**
Negligent homicide, possession or sale of a prohibited weapon, first-degree escape, perjury, gun possession by a prohibited possessor, gun possession in nuclear or hydroelectric plant.				
Class 5 Felony	**.75–2 Yrs.**	**$150,000**	**$1 Million**	**7 Years**
Bringing a gun into or around a juvenile correctional facility, first-degree hindering prosecution, second-degree escape, obstructing criminal investigation, any unclassified felony in state law.				
Class 6 Felony	**.5–1.5 Yrs.**	**$150,000**	**$1 Million**	**7 Years**
Transferring firearms to a minor without written consent from parent or guardian, endangerment with a risk of death, disorderly conduct with a gun, defacing a gun, possessing a defaced gun, providing a gun to a prohibited possessor, resisting arrest, third-degree escape, unlawful sale of big game.				
Class 1 Misdemeanor	**6 mos.**	**$2,500**	**$20,000**	**1 Year**
Refusing to leave or legally check deadly weapons at a public place or event when asked, entering a polling place on day of election armed, having firearm on school grounds, endangerment without a risk of death, threatening or intimidating, disorderly conduct, first-degree criminal trespass, refusing to aid peace officer if asked, poaching big game, shooting into or within city limits (can be charged as class 6 felony at prosecutor's discretion), lying to LEO about possession of weapon if asked.				
Class 2 Misdemeanor	**4 mos.**	**$750**	**$10,000**	**1 Year**
Threatened assault, most hunting violations, any unclassified misdemeanor.				
Class 3 Misdemeanor	**30 days**	**$500**	**$2,000**	**1 Year**
Failure of medical personnel to report gunshot wound, physically provoking someone, criminal nuisance, bringing CCW firearm into a place that serves alcohol and has proper no-guns sign posted.				
Petty Offense	**None**	**$300**	**$1,000**	**1 Year**
Any offense not classified as a felony or misdemeanor.				

THE PROPER AUTHORITIES C

Arizona Citizens Defense League 623-594-8521; PO Box 86256, Tucson 85754; azcdl.org

Arizona Commission on Indian Affairs 602-542-4421, 1700 W. Washington Street Suite 156, Phoenix 85007; indianaffairs.state.az.us

Ak-Chin Reservation, Ak-Chin Indian Community 520-568-1000
42507 W. Peters & Nall Rds., Maricopa 85239; cba.nau.edu/caied/tribepages/AkChin.asp

Camp Verde Reservation, Yavapai-Apache Nation 928-567-3649
2400 W. Datsi Street, Camp Verde 86322; yavapai-apache.org

Cocopah Reservation, Cocopah Tribe 928-627-2102
County 15th & Avenue G, Somerton 85350; cba.nau.edu/caied/tribepages/Cocopah.asp

Colorado River Reservation, Colorado River Indian Tribes 928-669-9211
26600 Mohave Road, Parker 85344; crit-nsn.gov

Fort Apache Reservation, White Mountain Apache Tribe 928-338-4346
PO Box 700, Whiteriver 85941; wmat.nsn.us

Fort McDowell Indian Community, Mohave-Apache Tribe 480-789-7000
PO Box 17779, Fountain Hills 85269; ftmcdowell.org

Fort Mojave Reservation, Fort Mojave Tribe 760-629-4591
500 Merriman Avenue, Needles, CA 92363; fortmojave.com

Fort Yuma Reservation, Quechan Tribe 760-572-0213
PO Box 1899, Yuma 85366; itcaonline.com/tribes_quechan.html

Gila River Reservation, Gila River Indian Community 520-562-3311
PO Box 97, Sacaton 85147; gilariver.org

Havasupai Reservation, Havasupai Tribe 928-448-2731
PO Box 10, Supai 86435; havasupaitribe.com

Hopi Reservation, Hopi Tribe 520-734-2441 x441
PO Box 123, Kyakotsmovi 86039

Hualapai Reservation, Hualapai Tribe 928-769-2216
PO Box 179, Peach Springs 86434; hualapai-nsn.gov

Kaibab-Paiute Reservation, Kaibab-Paiute Tribe 928-643-7245
HC-65, Box 2, Fredonia 86022; kaibabpaiute-nsn.gov

Navajo Reservation, The Navajo Nation 928-871-6000
PO Box 9000, Window Rock 86515; navajo-nsn.gov

Pascua Yaqui Reservation, Pascua Yaqui Tribe 520-883-5000
7474 S. Camino de Oeste, Tucson 85746; pascuayaqui-nsn.gov

Salt River Reservation, Salt River Pima-Maricopa Indian Community 480-362-7400
10005 East Osborn Road, Scottsdale 85256; srpmic-nsn.gov

San Carlos Reservation, San Carlos Apache Tribe 928-475-2361
PO Box "O", San Carlos 85550; itcaonline.com/tribes_sancarl.html

Tohono O'Odham Reservation, Tohono O'Odham Tribe 520-383-2028
PO Box 837, Sells 85634; tonation-nsn.gov

Tonto Apache Reservation, Tonto Apache Tribe 928-474-5000
Reservation 30 Tonto Apache Reservation, Payson 85541

Yavapai-Prescott Reservation, Yavapai-Prescott Tribe 928-445-8790
530 E. Merritt Street, Prescott 86301; ypit.com

Arizona Game and Fish Department (AGFD) 602-942-3000 azgfd.gov
    5000 W. Carefree Highway, Phoenix 85086
        AGFD Region I 928-367-4281, 2878 E. White Mountain Boulevard, Pinetop 85935
        AGFD Region II 928-774-5045, 3500 S. Lake Mary Road, Flagstaff 86001
        AGFD Region III 928-692-7700, 5325 N. Stockton Hill Road, Kingman 86409
        AGFD Region IV 928-342-0091, 9140 E. 28th Street Yuma 85365
        AGFD Region V 520-628-5376, 555 N. Greasewood Road, Tucson 85745
        AGFD Region VI 480-981-9400, 7200 E. University, Mesa 85207
Arizona DPS Concealed Weapon Permit Unit
    602-256-6280, in Arizona only 1-800-256-6280, Fax 602-223-2928, PO Box 6488,
    Phoenix 85005; azdps.gov/Services/Concealed_Weapons
Arizona Legislative Council 602-926-4236, 1700 W. Washington St. #100, Phoenix 85007
    azleg.gov/az_leg_council/default.htm
Arizona State Land Department 602-542-4631, 1616 W. Adams, Phoenix 85007; land.state.az.us
Arizona State Parks 602-542-4174, 1300 W. Washington Street, Phoenix 85007; azstateparks.com
    Alamo Lake State Park 928-669-2088
        PO Box 38, Wenden 85357 38 mi. north of Wenden and US 60
    Boyce Thompson SW Arboretum 520-689-2811
        37615 US Hwy. 60, Superior 85273, 3 mi. west of Superior on US 60
    Buckskin Mountain State Park 928-667-3231
        5476 North US Hwy. 95, Parker 85344 11 mi. north of Parker on AZ 95
    Catalina State Park 520-628-5798
        11570 N. Oracle Rd, Tucson 85737 9 mi. north of Tucson on State Hwy. 77
    Cattail Cove State Park 928-855-1223, PO Box 1990
        Lake Havasu City 86405, 15 mi. south of Lake Havasu City
    Dead Horse Ranch State Park 928-634-5283, 675 Dead Horse Ranch Rd.,
        Cottonwood 86326, Across river from Cottonwood, Enter on north, 5th Street
    Fort Verde State Historic Park 928-567-3275
        PO Box 397, Camp Verde 86322 In Camp Verde, 3 mi. east of I-17
    Homolovi Ruins State Park 928-289-4106
        HCR-63, Box 5, Winslow 86047 5 mi. east of Winslow off Highway 87
    Jerome State Historic Park 928-634-5381
        PO Box D, Jerome 86331 In Jerome, off US 89A
    Kartchner Caverns State Park, PO Box 1849, Benson 85602 520-586-4100
    Lake Havasu State Park Windsor Beach 928-855-2784
        699 London Bridge Road, Lake Havasu City 86403 Off AZ 95, in Lake Havasu City
    Lost Dutchman State Park 480-982-4485, 6109 N. Apache Trail, Apache Junction 85119
        5 mi. northeast of Apache Junction on AZ 88
    Lyman Lake State Park 928-337-4441
        PO Box 1428, St. Johns 85936 11 mi. south of St. Johns, 1 mi. east of US 666
    McFarland Historical State Park 520-868-5216
        PO Box 109, Florence 85232 In Florence, off US 89 and AZ 287
    Oracle State Park 520-896-2425, 3820 Wildlife Drive, Oracle 85623
        1 mi. east of Oracle off the old Mt. Lemmon Rd.
    Patagonia Lake State Park 520-287-6965
        400 Patagonia Lake Road, Patagonia 85624 12 mi. northeast of Nogales on AZ 82
    Picacho Peak State Park 520-466-3183, P.O. Box 907, Eloy 85131
        Picacho, 40 mi. north of Tucson on I-10, Exit 219
    Red Rock State Park 928-282-6907, 4050 Red Rock Loop Rd.,
        Sedona 86336 South of Sedona, off Red Rock Loop Rd.
    Riordan Mansion State Historic Park 928-779-4395
        409 West Riordan Rd Flagstaff 86001 In Flagstaff, off Riordan Ranch St.
    Roper Lake State Park 928-428-6760, 101 E. Roper Lake Road, Safford 85546,
        6 mi. south of Safford, 1/2 mi. east of US 666
    Slide Rock State Park 928-282-3034
        6871 N. Highway 89A, Sedona 86336
        7 mi. north of Sedona on 89A

Tombstone Courthouse State Historic Park 520-457-3311
    PO Box 216, Tombstone 85638 In Tombstone, off US 80
Tubac Presidio State Historic Park 520-398-2252
    One Burruel Street, Tubac 85646 In Tubac. off 1-19
Yuma Quartermaster Depot Historic State Park, 928-329-0471, 201 N. 4th Ave. Yuma 85364
Yuma Territorial Prison State Historic Park 928-783-4771, 928-343-2500
    One Prison Hill Rd., Yuma 85364 In Yuma, off 1-8
Arizona State Rifle and Pistol Association, asrpa.com 623-687-4251
    PO Box 74424, New River, AZ 85087
Bureau of Alcohol, Tobacco, Firearms and Explosives 202-648-8500
    Office of Public and Governmental Affairs
    99 New York Ave. NE, Room 5N 540, Washington, DC 20226
Bureau of Alcohol, Tobacco, Firearms and Explosives, Arizona Office 602-776-5400
    201 East Washington Street, Suite 940, Phoenix, AZ 85004
Bureau of Indian Affairs 202-208-3710, 1849 C. Street, NW, MS-3658-MIB,
    Washington, DC 20240
Bureau of Indian Affairs Arizona Office 602-379-6600
    2600 N. Central Avenue, 4th Floor Mailroom, Phoenix 85004
Bureau of Land Management (BLM) 202-208-3801
    U.S. Dept. of Interior, 1849 C Street NW, Rm. 5637, Washington DC 20240
BLM Arizona State Office 602-417-9200, One North Central Ave., Phoenix 85004
       BLM Arizona Strip Dist. Office 435-688-3200
          345 E. Riverside Dr., St. George, UT 84790
       BLM Havasu Resource Area Office 928-505-1200
          2610 Sweetwater Blvd., Lake Havasu City 86406
       BLM Kingman Resource Field Office 928-718-3700
          2755 Mission Boulevard, Kingman 86401
       BLM Phoenix Field Office 623-580-5500, 21605 N. 7th Ave., Phoenix 85027
       BLM Safford Field Office 928-348-4400, 711 14th Ave., Safford 85546
       BLM Tucson Field Office 520-258-7200, 12661 E. Broadway Blvd., Tucson 85748
       BLM Yuma Field Office 928-317-3200, 2555 East Gila Ridge Rd., Yuma 85365
County Parks and Recreation Departments (P&RD)
       Coconino County P&RD 928-679-8000, HCR-39, Box 3A, Flagstaff 86001
       Maricopa County P&RD 602-506-2930, 234 N. Central Avenue Suite 6400, Phoenix 85004
       Mohave County P&RD 928-757-0915, 2251 Highway 68 Bullhead City,86429
       Navajo County P&RD 928-524-4250, 100 E Carter Ln. Holbrook 86025
       Pima County P&RD 520-877-6000, 3500 West River Road, Tucson 85741
       Yavapai County P&RD 928-771-3115, 840 Rodeo Drive, Prescott 86305
Director of Civilian Marksmanship 419-635-2141, PO Box 576, Port Clinton, OH 43452
Lawyer Referral 602-257-4434, 303 E. Palm Lane, Phoenix 85004
Lexis Nexis (Statute Publisher) 1-800-223-1940
National Park Service 602-640-5250
    3121 N. 3rd Ave., Park Central Mall #200, Phoenix 85013
       Canyon de Chelly National Monument 928-674-5500, PO Box 588, Chinle 86503
       Casa Grande Ruins National Monument 520-723-3172
          1100 West Ruins Drive, Coolidge 85228
       Chiracahua National Monument 520-824-3560 ext. 302 or 520-824-3460
          12856 E. Rhyolite Creek Road Wilcox 85643
       Glen Canyon National Recreation Area 928-608-6200, PO Box 1507, Page 86040
       Grand Canyon National Park 928-638-7888, PO Box 129, Grand Canyon 86023
       Lake Mead National Recreation Area 702-293-8990
          601 Nevada Way, Boulder City, NV 89005
       Montezuma Castle National Monument 928-567-3322
          PO Box 219, Camp Verde 86322
       Navajo National Monument 928-672-2700, HC-71, Box 3,Tonalea 86044

Organ Pipe Cactus National Monument 520-387-6849, 10 Organ Pipe Drive, Ajo 85321
Petrified Forest National Park 928-524-6228
   Petrified Forest National Park PO Box 2217, Petrified Forest 86028
Pipe Springs National Monument 801-772-3256, c/o Zion National Park,
   Springdale, UT 84767 or 928-643-7105, HC-65, Box 5, Fredonia 86022
Saguaro National Park 520-733-5100, 3693 S. Old Spanish Trail, Tucson 85730
Sunset Crater Volcano National Monument 928-526-1157
     6400 N. Hwy 89, Flagstaff 86004;
Tonto National Monument 928-467-2241, 26260 N Ariz Hwy 188 #2, Roosevelt 85545
Tumacacori National Historical Park 520-398-2341, PO Box 8067, Tumacacori 85640
Tuzigoot National Monument 928-634-5564, PO Box 219, Camp Verde, 86322
Walnut Canyon National Monument 928-526-3367
     6400 N. Hwy 89, Flagstaff 86004
Wupatki National Monument 928-679-2365, 6400 N. Hwy 89, Flagstaff 86004
National Rifle Association 800-672-3888
   11250 Waples Mill Rd., Fairfax, VA 22030
National Rifle Association, Arizona 480-664-9222
   PO Box 12965, Scottsdale, AZ 85267
Secretary of State (Arizona) 602-542-4285, Publications 602-542-4086
   Capitol West Wing, 1700 W. Washington, #103, Phoenix 85007
U.S. Forest Service, U.S. Dept. of. Agriculture 202-205-8333
   PO Box 96090, Washington, D.C. 20090
   Regional Forester, 333 Broadway SE, Albuquerque, NM 87102, 505-842-3292
   Apache-Sitgreaves National Forest 928-333-4301
     Hwy. 180, PO Box 640, Springerville 85938
   Coconino National Forest 928-527-3600
     1824 S. Thompson St., Flagstaff 86001
   Coronado National Forest 520-388-8300, Federal Bldg., 300 W. Congress, Tucson 85701
   Kaibab National Forest 928-635-8200, 800 S. 6th St., Williams 86046
   Prescott National Forest 928-443-8000 344 S. Cortez St., Prescott 86303
   Sitgreaves National Forest, Now consolidated with Apache National Forest
   Tonto National Forest 602-225-5200, 2324 E. McDowell. Phoenix 85006

APPENDIX D
THE ARIZONA GUN LAWS

On the following pages are **excerpts** from various titles of the *Arizona Revised Statutes,* downloaded from the official Arizona legislative website, and updated with the main new laws through Jan. 1, 2015. Although this has been prepared with great care, no assurance of accuracy or completeness is made or implied and **for any legal purpose official versions should be used**. If the official state website contained errors, they will be faithfully reproduced here. You can link to the official sites and laws from our website, **gunlaws.com**—*and check for new versions that may exist.*

The state statutes are broad, but **only gun laws for private citizens have been edited into this appendix.** Only those portions of the statutes that directly relate to the subject of this book are included. A complete copy of the statutes is available in libraries and online, and is highly recommended for serious study.

How State Law Is Arranged
Arizona's laws are covered under 46 separate "titles." Within each title, each piece of law is numbered, starting at 101, and going as high as necessary. Each numbered part is called a "section," represented by a "§" sign. This makes it easy to refer to any particular law—just call it by its title and section numbers. For instance, §13-3102 is the part about misconduct with weapons. You say it like this, "title thirteen, section thirty one oh two," or simply, "thirteen thirty one oh two."

Excerpt from the Constitution of the State of Arizona
Section 26. Bearing Arms. The right of the individual citizen to bear arms in defense of himself or the state shall not be impaired, but nothing in this section shall be construed as authorizing individuals or corporations to organize, maintain, or employ an armed body of men.

GROWTH OF ARIZONA GUN LAWS

These are the word counts for the law section, Appendix D, of this and previous editions of this book. The increases are caused by two factors—the discovery and inclusion of new sections of gun law (e.g., security guards, game and fish department, military affairs and emergency management, etc.), and the enactment of new laws by the state legislature, which has been occurring every year in recent times. Reductions, through amendments and repeals, also occur, but the net difference has been an increase since we began doing tracking. Gun laws are growing nationally, with no end in sight. Our gun laws here have tripled in 20 years. Politicians who claim they can't pass more gun laws are either ignorant or worse:

Year	Word Count	Edition	Words	Change
2014	45,556	26	+3,076	+7.2%
2012	42,480	25	+1,178	+2.9%
2010	41,302	24	+2,233	+5.7%
2009	39,069	24	+1,399	+3.7%
2008	37,670	24	+1,025	+2.8%
2006	36,645	23	+2,661	+7.8%
2005	33,984	22	+3,806	+12.6%
2004	30,178	21	+3,551	+13.3%
2002	26,627	20R	+405	+1.5%
2001	26,222	20	+5,646	+27.4%
1998	20,576	19	+703	+3.5%
1997	19,873	18	+2,837	+16.7%
1996	17,036	17	+1,252	+7.9%
1994	15,784	16	+5	0.0%
1994	15,779	15	–	–

EXCERPTS FROM THE ARIZONA REVISED STATUTES

<Editorial notes appear in pointed brackets and are not part of the law.>

TITLE 4 • ALCOHOLIC BEVERAGES

4-229. Licenses; handguns; posting of notice

A. A person with a permit issued pursuant to §13-3112 may carry a concealed handgun on the premises of a licensee who is an on-sale retailer unless the licensee posts a sign that clearly prohibits the possession of weapons on the licensed premises. The sign shall conform to the following requirements:

1. Be posted in a conspicuous location accessible to the general public and immediately adjacent to the liquor license posted on the licensed premises.

2. Contain a pictogram that shows a firearm within a red circle and a diagonal red line across the firearm.

3. Contain the words, "no firearms allowed pursuant to A.R.S. section 4-229".

B. A person shall not carry a firearm on the licensed premises of an on-sale retailer if the licensee has posted the notice prescribed in subsection A of this section.

C. It is an affirmative defense to a violation of subsection B of this section if:

1. The person was not informed of the notice prescribed in subsection A of this section before the violation.

2. Any one or more of the following apply:

(a) At the time of the violation the notice prescribed in subsection A of this section had fallen down.

(b) At the time of the violation the person was not a resident of this state.

(c) The licensee had posted the notice prescribed in subsection A of this section not more than thirty days before the violation.

D. The department of liquor licenses and control shall prepare the signs required by this section and make them available at no cost to licensees.

E. The signs required by this section shall be composed of block, capital letters printed in black on white laminated paper at a minimum weight of one hundred ten pound index. The lettering and pictogram shall consume a space at least six inches by nine inches. The letters comprising the words "No firearms allowed" shall be at least three-fourths of a vertical inch and all other letters shall be at least one-half of a vertical inch. Nothing shall prohibit a licensee from posting additional signs at one or more locations on the premises.

F. This section does not prohibit a person who possesses a handgun from entering the licensed premises for a limited time for the specific purpose of either:

1. Seeking emergency aid.

2. Determining whether a sign has been posted pursuant to subsection A of this section.

4-244. Unlawful acts

It is unlawful:

29. For any person other than a peace officer or a member of a sheriff's volunteer posse while on duty who has received firearms training that is approved by the Arizona peace officer standards and training board, the licensee or an employee of the licensee acting with the permission of the licensee to be in possession of a firearm while on the licensed premises of an on-sale retailer. This paragraph shall not be construed to include a situation in which a person is on licensed premises for a limited time in order to seek emergency aid and such person does not buy, receive, consume or possess spirituous liquor. This paragraph shall not apply to:

(a) Hotel or motel guest room accommodations.

(b) The exhibition or display of a firearm in conjunction with a meeting, show, class or similar event.

(c) A person with a permit issued pursuant to §13-3112 who carries a concealed handgun on the licensed premises of any on-sale retailer that has not posted a notice pursuant to §4-229

30. For a licensee or employee to knowingly permit a person in possession of a firearm other than a peace officer or a member of a sheriff's volunteer posse while on duty who has received firearms training that is approved by the Arizona peace officer standards and training board, the licensee or an employee of the licensee acting with the permission of the licensee to remain on the licensed premises or to serve, sell or furnish spirituous liquor to a person in possession of a firearm while on the licensed premises of an on-sale retailer. It shall be a defense to action under this paragraph if the licensee or employee requested assistance of a peace officer to remove such person. This paragraph shall not apply to:

(a) Hotel or motel guest room accommodations.

(b) The exhibition or display of a firearm in conjunction with a meeting, show, class or similar event.
(c) A person with a permit issued pursuant to §13-3112 who carries a concealed handgun on the licensed premises of any on-sale retailer that has not posted a notice pursuant to §4-229.
31. For any person in possession of a firearm while on the licensed premises of an on-sale retailer to consume spirituous liquor. This paragraph does not prohibit the consumption of small amounts of spirituous liquor by an undercover peace officer on assignment to investigate the licensed establishment.

4-246. Violation; classification
A. A person violating any provision of this title is guilty of a class 2 misdemeanor unless another classification is prescribed.
C. A person violating §§4-229, subsection B or 4-244, paragraph 31 is guilty of a class 3 misdemeanor.

TITLE 8 • CHILDREN

8-341. Disposition and commitment; definitions
R. If a juvenile is adjudicated delinquent for an offense that if committed by an adult would be a misdemeanor, the court may prohibit the juvenile from carrying or possessing a firearm while the juvenile is under the jurisdiction of the department of juvenile corrections or the juvenile court.

TITLE 9 • CITIES AND TOWNS

9-461.05. General plans; authority; scope
G. The land use element of a general plan of a city with a population of more than one million persons shall include protections from encroaching development for any shooting range that is owned by this state and that is located within or adjacent to the exterior municipal boundaries on or before January 1, 2004. The general plan shall establish land use categories within at least one-half mile from the exterior boundaries of the shooting range that are consistent with the continued existence of the shooting range and that exclude incompatible uses such as residences, schools, hotels, motels, hospitals or churches except that land zoned to permit these incompatible uses on August 25, 2004 are exempt from this exclusion. For the purposes of this subsection, "shooting range" means a permanently located and improved area that is designed and operated for the use of rifles, shotguns, pistols, silhouettes, skeet, trap, black powder or any other similar sport shooting in an outdoor environment. Shooting range does not include:
1. Any area for the exclusive use of archery or air guns.
2. An enclosed indoor facility that is designed to offer a totally controlled shooting environment and that includes impenetrable walls, floor and ceiling, adequate ventilation, lighting systems and acoustical treatment for sound attenuation suitable for the range's approved use.
3. A national guard facility located in a city or town with a population of more than one million persons.
4. A facility that was not owned by this state before January 1, 2002.

9-500.22. Prosecution diversion programs
A. The chief prosecuting officer of a city or town may establish a diversion program that provides for the dismissal of a criminal complaint on successful completion of the program's requirements. Diversion shall not be available to persons accused of a crime involving the discharge, use or threatening exhibition of a deadly weapon or dangerous instrument.
B. The prosecutor has sole discretion to decide whether to divert prosecution of an offender when the diversion occurs before a guilty plea or trial. The diversion program may be structured to require a guilty plea before entry into the program.

TITLE 11 • COUNTIES

11-812. Restriction on regulation; exceptions; aggregate mining regulation; definitions
A. Nothing contained in any ordinance authorized by this chapter shall:
4. Prevent, restrict or otherwise regulate the otherwise lawful discharge of a firearm or air gun or use of archery equipment on a private lot or parcel of land that is not open to the public on a commercial or membership basis.

TITLE 12 • COURTS AND CIVIL PROCEEDINGS

12-558. Actions related to the lawful discharge of a firearm; burden of proof; attorney fees and costs
A. Notwithstanding any other law, the otherwise lawful discharge of a firearm or air gun or the use of archery equipment may not be enjoined except by:
1. An action maintained by the attorney general to abate a public nuisance pursuant to §13-2917.
2. A private nuisance cause of action or an action based on negligence that is filed by a person who is occupying a permanent residence that is located within one-fourth mile of the location of the discharge or use.
B. The burden of proof is clear and convincing evidence in an action that is filed pursuant to subsection A of this section or in an action for damages that is based on negligence in the otherwise lawful discharge of a firearm or air gun or the use of archery equipment on a private lot or parcel of land that is not open to the public on a commercial or membership basis and that is filed by a person who was not lawfully present at the same private lot or parcel of land at the time that the alleged discharge occurred.
C. The prevailing party in an action filed pursuant to this section, except an officer or entity of this state, shall recover reasonable attorney fees and costs.
D. In an action alleging damages from the loss of property value due to the otherwise lawful discharge of a firearm or air

gun or the use of archery equipment on a private lot or parcel of land that belongs to another person, the lost value shall be proven by clear and convincing evidence.

12-714. Actions against firearm manufacturers; prohibition; findings; definitions

A. A political subdivision of this state shall not commence a qualified civil liability action in any Arizona court.

B. The legislature finds that:

1. The citizens of this state have the right, under the Second Amendment to the United States Constitution and article 2, section 26 of the Arizona Constitution, to keep and bear arms.
2. Lawsuits have been commenced against the manufacturers, distributors, dealers and importers of nondefective firearms for the harm caused by the misuse of firearms by third parties, including criminals.
3. Businesses in the United States that are engaged in the lawful sale to the public of firearms or ammunition are not, and should not be liable for the harm caused by those who unlawfully misuse firearms or ammunition.
4. The possibility of imposing liability on an entire industry for harm that is the sole responsibility of others is an abuse of the legal system, threatens the diminution of a basic constitutional right and constitutes an unreasonable burden on the free enterprise system.
5. The liability actions commenced by political subdivisions are based on theories without foundation in the common law and American jurisprudence. Such an expansion of liability would constitute a deprivation of the rights, privileges and immunities guaranteed to citizens of this state under both the Constitution of Arizona and the United States Constitution.

C. As used in this section:

1. "Manufacturer" means, with respect to a qualified product:
(a) A person who is engaged in a business to import, make, produce, create or assemble a qualified product and who designs or formulates, or has engaged another person to design or formulate, a qualified product.
(b) A seller of a qualified product, but only with respect to an aspect of the product that is made or affected when the seller makes, produces, creates or assembles and designs or formulates an aspect of the product made by another person.
(c) Any seller of a qualified product who represents to a user of a qualified product that the seller is a manufacturer of the qualified product.
2. "Qualified civil liability action" means a civil action brought by a political subdivision against a manufacturer or seller of a qualified product or a trade association, for damages resulting from the criminal or unlawful misuse of a qualified product by a third party. Qualified civil liability action does not include an action brought against a transferor convicted under 18 United States Code §924(h) or §13-3102, subsection A, paragraph 14, by a party directly harmed by the conduct of which the transferee is convicted.
3. "Qualified product" means a nondefective firearm as defined in 18 United States Code §921(a)(3) or nondefective ammunition as defined in 18 United States Code §921(a)(17), or a component part of a firearm or ammunition, that has been shipped or transported in interstate or foreign commerce.
4. "Seller" means, with respect to a qualified product, a person who either:
(a) In the course of a business conducted for that purpose sells, distributes, rents, leases, prepares, blends, packages, labels or otherwise is involved in placing a qualified product in the stream of commerce.
(b) Installs, repairs, refurbishes, reconditions or maintains an aspect of a qualified product that is alleged to have resulted in damages.
5. "Trade association" means any association or business organization, whether or not incorporated under federal or state law, two or more members of which are manufacturers or sellers of a qualified product.

12-716. Injury during criminal acts; civil actions; presumptions; definition

A. If the court finds by a preponderance of the evidence that a plaintiff is harmed while the plaintiff is attempting to commit, committing or fleeing after having committed or attempted to commit a felony criminal act, the following presumptions apply to any civil liability action or claim:

1. A victim or peace officer is presumed to be acting reasonably if the victim or peace officer threatens to use or uses physical force or deadly physical force to either:
(a) Protect himself against another person's use or attempted use of physical force or deadly physical force.
(b) Effect an arrest or prevent or assist in preventing a plaintiff's escape.
2. This state or a political subdivision of this state is presumed to have reasonably hired and trained its peace officers to use physical force or deadly physical force if a peace officer threatens to use or uses physical force or deadly physical force to either:
(a) Protect himself against another person's use or attempted use of physical force or deadly physical force.
(b) Effect an arrest or prevent or assist in preventing a plaintiff's escape.
3. The police tool product that caused the physical harm is presumed not to be defective and the manufacturer of police tools is presumed not to be negligent if, before the sale by the manufacturer, the product either:
(a) Conforms with the generally recognized state of the art applicable to the safety of the product at the time the product was designed, manufactured, packaged and labeled.
(b) Complies with any applicable code, standard, regulation or specification that is established, adopted, promulgated or approved by the United States or this state or any agency of the United States or this state.

B. For the purposes of this section, "police tool product" means any weapon, safety equipment or product that is used by law enforcement.

12-781. Transportation or storage of firearms; motor vehicles; applicability

A. A property owner, tenant, public or private employer or business entity shall not establish, maintain or enforce a policy or rule that prohibits a person from lawfully transporting or lawfully storing any firearm that is both:

1. In the person's locked and privately owned motor vehicle or in a locked compartment on the person's privately owned motorcycle.
2. Not visible from the outside of the motor vehicle or motorcycle.

B. Any policy or rule that is established or maintained or the attempted enforcement of any policy or rule that is in violation of subsection A is contrary to public policy, is null and void and does not have legal force or effect.

C. This section does not apply if:

1. The possession of the firearm is prohibited by federal or state law.
2. The motor vehicle is owned or leased by a public or private employer or business entity and is used by an employee in

the course of the employment, unless the employee is required to store or transport a firearm in the official discharge of the employee's duties or if the public or private employer or business entity consents to the transportation or storage of the firearm.

3. The property owner, tenant, public or private employer or business entity provides a parking lot, parking garage or other area designated for parking motor vehicles, that:
(a) Is secured by a fence or other physical barrier.
(b) Limits access by a guard or other security measure.
(c) Provides temporary and secure firearm storage. The storage shall be monitored and readily accessible on entry into the premises and allow for the immediate retrieval of the firearm on exit from the premises.

4. The property owner's, tenant's, public or private employer's or business entity's compliance with this section necessitates the violation of another applicable federal or state law or regulation.

5. The property owner, tenant, public or private employer or business entity is a nuclear generating station that provides a secured and gated or fenced parking lot, parking garage or other area designated for parking motor vehicles and provides temporary and secure firearm storage. The storage shall be readily accessible on entry into the premises and allow for the immediate retrieval of the firearm on exit from the premises.

6. The parking lot, parking garage or other area designated for parking motor vehicles is on an owner occupied single family detached residence or a tenant occupied single family detached residence.

7. The property owner, tenant, public or private employer or business entity is a current United States department of defense contractor and the property is located in whole or in part on a United States military base or a United States military installation. If any part of the property is not located on the United States military base or United States military installation, the property shall be contiguous with the base or installation.

8. The property owner, tenant, public or private employer or business entity provides alternative parking in a location reasonably proximate to the primary parking area for individuals who desire to transport or store a firearm in the individual's motor vehicle and does not charge an extra fee for such parking.

12-820.02. Qualified immunity

A. Unless a public employee acting within the scope of the public employee's employment intended to cause injury or was grossly negligent, neither a public entity nor a public employee is liable for:

1. The failure to make an arrest or the failure to retain an arrested person in custody.

2. An injury caused by an escaping or escaped prisoner or a youth committed to the department of juvenile corrections.

3. An injury resulting from the probation, community supervision or discharge of a prisoner or a youth committed to the department of juvenile corrections, from the terms and conditions of the prisoner's or youth's probation or community supervision or from the revocation of the prisoner's or youth's probation, community supervision or conditional release under the psychiatric security review board.

4. An injury caused by a prisoner to any other prisoner or an injury caused by a youth committed to the department of juvenile corrections to any other committed youth.

5. The issuance of or failure to revoke or suspend any permit, license, certificate, approval, order or similar authorization for which absolute immunity is not provided pursuant to §12-820.01.

6. The failure to discover violations of any provision of law when inspections are done of property other than property owned by the public entity in question.

7. An injury to the driver of a motor vehicle that is attributable to the violation by the driver of §28-693, 28-1381 or 28-1382.

8. The failure to prevent the sale or transfer of a handgun to a person whose receipt or possession of the handgun is unlawful under any federal law or any law of this state.

9. Preventing the sale or transfer of a handgun to a person who may lawfully receive or possess a handgun.

10. The failure to detain a juvenile taken into temporary custody or arrested for a criminal offense or delinquent or incorrigible act in the appropriate detention facility, jail or lockup described in §8-305.

B. The qualified immunity provided in this section applies to a public entity or public employee if the injury or damage was caused by a contractor's employee or a contractor of a public entity acting within the scope of the contract. The qualified immunity provided in this section does not apply to the contractor or the contractor's employee.

12-940. Definitions

In this article, unless the context otherwise requires:

1. "Dispose" means the transfer of property by its return to the owner, sale, conversion or destruction or by any other means of disposal.

2. "Evidence" means property that is held for possible presentation in a judicial or administrative proceeding to establish the truth or falsity of an alleged matter of fact.

3. "Found property" means recovered, lost, surrendered, abandoned or otherwise received property that is turned over to a public agency where the owner may or may not be known and that is not classified as evidence.

4. "Property" means any item, including currency, that is held for safekeeping or as evidence or found property or that has been abandoned, unclaimed or awarded by the court.

5. "Property value" means the reasonable value of the property in its present condition.

6. "Safekeeping" means storage of an asset or item of value by a public agency that is not classified as evidence and that belongs to a known individual.

12-941. Disposal of certain unclaimed property in the custody of a state, county, city or town agency

A. A state, county, city or town agency shall dispose of all property that was used as evidence and that remains unclaimed in the hands of the agency, after final disposition of the cause in which so used, or that was seized by a peace officer as being used unlawfully or for an unlawful purpose and that was held unclaimed from the date of seizure, or that came into the hands of the agency as unclaimed or contraband. A law enforcement agency may retain and use those items that have a useful value to that law enforcement agency.

B. Found property turned over to a state, county, city or town agency may be returned to the person who found and turned it over if all of the following conditions apply:

1. The property is not contraband or a firearm.

2. The property remains unclaimed for thirty days after reasonable efforts have been made to locate and notify the owner.

3. The person who found and turned over the property is not a public officer or employee of the federal, a state or a local

government who found the property in the course of performing the duties of the office or employment.

C. If United States currency is delivered to the proper agency pursuant to subsection A of this section, it shall be deposited in the general fund of the state, county, city or town, as the case may be.

D. A record of all transactions shall be maintained for at least twenty-four months.

12-943. Authorized dispositions

All property that is described in §12-941 and that is in the possession of a state, county, city or town agency may only be disposed of pursuant to this article.

12-944. Owner receipt; publication of property valued at more than one hundred fifty dollars

A. If an agency takes any property from a person, the agency shall provide the person with a detailed receipt for the property. The receipt shall contain a notice to the person on how to retrieve the property from the agency.

B. If the owner of found property that has a value of more than one hundred fifty dollars is not known, the agency holding the property shall publish or post a notice containing a description of the property before the final disposal of the property.

12-945. Sale of property

A. If after thirty days' notice has been given the owner or person entitled to the property has not taken it away, the property may be sold. The proceeds shall be paid to the general fund of the jurisdiction from which the unclaimed property was received.

B. Notwithstanding subsection A of this section, if the property is a firearm, the agency shall sell the firearm to any business that is authorized to receive and dispose of the firearm under federal and state law and that shall sell the firearm to the public according to federal and state law, unless the firearm is otherwise prohibited from being sold under federal and state law. A law enforcement agency may trade a firearm that it has retained to a federal firearms licensed business for ammunition, weapons, equipment or other materials to be exclusively used for law enforcement purposes.

12-2101. Judgments and orders that may be appealed

A. An appeal may be taken to the court of appeals from the superior court in the following instances:

5. From an order:

(d) Granting or denying a petition to restore a person's right to possess a firearm pursuant to §13-925.

TITLE 13 • CRIMINAL CODE

CHAPTER 1 · GENERAL PROVISIONS

13-101. Purposes

It is declared that the public policy of this state and the general purposes of the provisions of this title are:

1. To proscribe conduct that unjustifiably and inexcusably causes or threatens substantial harm to individual or public interests;

2. To give fair warning of the nature of the conduct proscribed and of the sentences authorized upon conviction;

3. To define the act or omission and the accompanying mental state which constitute each offense and limit the condemnation of conduct as criminal when it does not fall within the purposes set forth;

4. To differentiate on reasonable grounds between serious and minor offenses and to prescribe proportionate penalties for each;

5. To insure the public safety by preventing the commission of offenses through the deterrent influence of the sentences authorized; and

6. To impose just and deserved punishment on those whose conduct threatens the public peace; and

7. To promote truth and accountability in sentencing.

13-103. Abolition of common law offenses and affirmative defenses; definition

A. All common law offenses and affirmative defenses are abolished. No conduct or omission constitutes an offense or an affirmative defense unless it is an offense or an affirmative defense under this title or under another statute or ordinance.

B. For the purposes of this section, "affirmative defense" means a defense that is offered and that attempts to excuse the criminal actions of the accused or another person for whose actions the accused may be deemed to be accountable. Affirmative defense does not include any justification defense pursuant to chapter 4 of this title or any defense that either denies an element of the offense charged or denies responsibility, including alibi, misidentification or lack of intent.

13-105. Definitions

2. "Act" means a bodily movement.

6. "Conduct" means an act or omission and its accompanying culpable mental state.

7. "Crime" means a misdemeanor or a felony.

12. "Dangerous instrument" means anything that under the circumstances in which it is used, attempted to be used or threatened to be used is readily capable of causing death or serious physical injury.

13. "Dangerous offense" means an offense involving the discharge, use or threatening exhibition of a deadly weapon or dangerous instrument or the intentional or knowing infliction of serious physical injury on another person.

14. "Deadly physical force" means force that is used with the purpose of causing death or serious physical injury or in the

manner of its use or intended use is capable of creating a substantial risk of causing death or serious physical injury.
15. "Deadly weapon" means anything designed for lethal use, including a firearm.
19. "Firearm" means any loaded or unloaded handgun, pistol, revolver, rifle, shotgun or other weapon that will or is designed to or may readily be converted to expel a projectile by the action of expanding gases, except that it does not include a firearm in permanently inoperable condition.
22. "Historical prior felony conviction" means:
(a) Any prior felony conviction for which the offense of conviction either:
(ii) Involved in a dangerous offense.
(f) Any offense committed outside the jurisdiction of this state that involved the discharge, use or threatening exhibition of a deadly weapon or dangerous instrument or the intentional or knowing infliction of death or serious physical injury that was punishable by that jurisdiction as a felony. A person who has been convicted of a felony weapons possession violation in any court outside the jurisdiction of this state that would not be punishable as a felony under the laws of this state is not subject to this paragraph.
28. "Omission" means the failure to perform an act as to which a duty of performance is imposed by law.
32. "Physical force" means force used upon or directed toward the body of another person and includes confinement, but does not include deadly physical force.
33. "Physical injury" means the impairment of physical condition.
34. "Possess" means knowingly to have physical possession or otherwise to exercise dominion or control over property.
35. "Possession" means a voluntary act if the defendant knowingly exercised dominion or control over property.
39. "Serious physical injury" includes physical injury that creates a reasonable risk of death, or that causes serious and permanent disfigurement, serious impairment of health or loss or protracted impairment of the function on any bodily organ or limb.
40. "Unlawful" means contrary to law or, where the context so requires, not permitted by law.
42. "Voluntary act" means a bodily movement performed consciously and as a result of effort and determination.

13-107. Time limitations

A. A prosecution for any homicide, any offense that is listed in chapter 14 or 35.1 of this title and that is a class 2 felony, any violent sexual assault pursuant to §13-1423, any violation of §13-2308.01, any misuse of public monies or a felony involving falsification of public records or any attempt to commit an offense listed in this subsection may be commenced at any time.
B. Except as otherwise provided in this section and §28-672, prosecutions for other offenses must be commenced within the following periods after actual discovery by the state or the political subdivision having jurisdiction of the offense or discovery by the state or the political subdivision that should have occurred with the exercise of reasonable diligence, whichever first occurs:
1. For a class 2 through a class 6 felony, seven years.
2. For a misdemeanor, one year.
3. For a petty offense, six months.
C. For the purposes of subsection B of this section, a prosecution is commenced when an indictment, information or complaint is filed.
D. The period of limitation does not run during any time when the accused is absent from the state or has no reasonably ascertainable place of abode within the state.
E. The period of limitation does not run for a serious offense as defined in §13-706 during any time when the identity of the person who commits the offense or offenses is unknown.
F. The time limitation within which a prosecution of a class 6 felony shall commence shall be determined pursuant to subsection B, paragraph 1 of this section, irrespective of whether a court enters a judgment of conviction for or a prosecuting attorney designates the offense as a misdemeanor.
G. If a complaint, indictment or information filed before the period of limitation has expired is dismissed for any reason, a new prosecution may be commenced within six months after the dismissal becomes final even if the period of limitation has expired at the time of the dismissal or will expire within six months of the dismissal.

CHAPTER 2 · GENERAL PRINCIPLES OF CRIMINAL LIABILITY

13-205. Affirmative defenses; justification; burden of proof

A. Except as otherwise provided by law, a defendant shall prove any affirmative defense raised by a preponderance of the evidence. Justification defenses under chapter 4 of this title are not affirmative defenses. Justification defenses describe conduct that, if not justified, would constitute an offense but, if justified, does not constitute criminal or wrongful conduct. If evidence of justification pursuant to chapter 4 of this title is presented by the defendant, the state must prove beyond a reasonable doubt that the defendant did not act with justification.
B. This section does not affect the presumption contained in §13-411, subsection C and §13-503.

CHAPTER 4 · JUSTIFICATION

13-401. Unavailability of justification defense; justification as defense

A. Even though a person is justified under this chapter in threatening or using physical force or deadly physical force against another, if in doing so such person recklessly injures or kills an innocent third person, the justification afforded by this chapter is unavailable in a prosecution for the reckless injury or killing of the innocent third person.
B. Except as provided in subsection A, justification as defined in this chapter is a defense in any prosecution for an offense pursuant to this title.

13-402. Justification; execution of public duty

A. Unless inconsistent with the other sections of this chapter defining justifiable use of physical force or deadly physical force or with some other superseding provision of law, conduct which would otherwise constitute an offense is justifiable when it is required or authorized by law.
B. The justification afforded by subsection A also applies if:

1. A reasonable person would believe such conduct is required or authorized by the judgment or direction of a competent court or tribunal or in the lawful execution of legal process, notwithstanding lack of jurisdiction of the court or defect in the legal process; or
2. A reasonable person would believe such conduct is required or authorized to assist a peace officer in the performance of such officer's duties, notwithstanding that the officer exceeded the officer's legal authority.

13-403. Justification; use of physical force
The use of physical force upon another person which would otherwise constitute an offense is justifiable and not criminal under any of the following circumstances:
1. A parent or guardian and a teacher or other person entrusted with the care and supervision of a minor or incompetent person may use reasonable and appropriate physical force upon the minor or incompetent person when and to the extent reasonably necessary and appropriate to maintain discipline.
2. A superintendent or other entrusted official of a jail, prison or correctional institution may use physical force for the preservation of peace to maintain order or discipline, or to prevent the commission of any felony or misdemeanor.
3. A person responsible for the maintenance of order in a place where others are assembled or on a common motor carrier of passengers or a person acting under his direction, may use physical force if and to the extent that a reasonable person would believe it necessary to maintain order, but such person may use deadly physical force only if reasonably necessary to prevent death or serious physical injury.
4. A person acting under a reasonable belief that another person is about to commit suicide or to inflict serious physical injury upon himself may use physical force upon that person to the extent reasonably necessary to thwart the result.
5. A duly licensed physician or a registered nurse or a person acting under his direction, or any other person who renders emergency care at the scene of an emergency occurrence, may use reasonable physical force for the purpose of administering a recognized and lawful form of treatment which is reasonably adapted to promoting the physical or mental health of the patient if:
(a) The treatment is administered with the consent of the patient or, if the patient is a minor or an incompetent person, with the consent of his parent, guardian or other person entrusted with his care and supervision except as otherwise provided by law; or
(b) The treatment is administered in an emergency when the person administering such treatment reasonably believes that no one competent to consent can be consulted and that a reasonable person, wishing to safeguard the welfare of the patient, would consent.
6. A person may otherwise use physical force upon another person as further provided in this chapter.

13-404. Justification; self-defense
A. Except as provided in subsection B of this section, a person is justified in threatening or using physical force against another when and to the extent a reasonable person would believe that physical force is immediately necessary to protect himself against the other's use or attempted use of unlawful physical force.
B. The threat or use of physical force against another is not justified:
1. In response to verbal provocation alone; or
2. To resist an arrest that the person knows or should know is being made by a peace officer or by a person acting in a peace officer's presence and at his direction, whether the arrest is lawful or unlawful, unless the physical force used by the peace officer exceeds that allowed by law; or
3. If the person provoked the other's use or attempted use of unlawful physical force, unless:
(a) The person withdraws from the encounter or clearly communicates to the other his intent to do so reasonably believing he cannot safely withdraw from the encounter; and
(b) The other nevertheless continues or attempts to use unlawful physical force against the person.

13-405. Justification; use of deadly physical force
A person is justified in threatening or using deadly physical force against another:
1. If such person would be justified in threatening or using physical force against the other under §13-404, and
2. When and to the degree a reasonable person would believe that deadly physical force is immediately necessary to protect himself against the other's use or attempted use of unlawful deadly physical force.
B. A person has no duty to retreat before threatening or using deadly physical force pursuant to this section if the person is in a place where the person may legally be and is not engaged in an unlawful act.

13-406. Justification; defense of a third person
A person is justified in threatening or using physical force or deadly physical force against another to protect a third person if under the circumstances as a reasonable person would believe them to be, such person would be justified under §13-404 or 13-405 in threatening or using physical force or deadly physical force to protect himself against the unlawful physical force or deadly physical force a reasonable person would believe is threatening the third person he seeks to protect.

13-407. Justification; use of physical force in defense of premises
A. A person or his agent in lawful possession or control of premises is justified in threatening to use deadly physical force or in threatening or using physical force against another when and to the extent that a reasonable person would believe it immediately necessary to prevent or terminate the commission or attempted commission of a criminal trespass by the other person in or upon the premises.
B. A person may use deadly physical force under subsection A only in the defense of himself or third persons as described in sections 13-405 and 13-406.
C. In this section, "premises" means any real property and any structure, movable or immovable, permanent or temporary, adapted for both human residence and lodging whether occupied or not.

13-408. Justification; use of physical force in defense of property
A person is justified in using physical force against another when and to the extent that a reasonable person would believe it necessary to prevent what a reasonable person would believe is an attempt or commission by the other person of theft or criminal damage involving tangible movable property under his possession or control, but such person may use deadly physical force under these circumstances as provided in sections 13-405, 13-406 and 13-411.

13-409. Justification; use of physical force in law enforcement

A person is justified in threatening or using physical force against another if in making or assisting in making an arrest or detention or in preventing or assisting in preventing the escape after arrest or detention of that other person, such person uses or threatens to use physical force and all of the following exist:
1. A reasonable person would believe that such force is immediately necessary to effect the arrest or detention or prevent the escape.
2. Such person makes known the purpose of the arrest or detention or believes that it is otherwise known or cannot reasonably be made known to the person to be arrested or detained.
3. A reasonable person would believe the arrest or detention to be lawful.

13-410. Justification; use of deadly physical force in law enforcement

A. The threatened use of deadly physical force by a person against another is justified pursuant to §13-409 only if a reasonable person effecting the arrest or preventing the escape would believe the suspect or escapee is:
1. Actually resisting the discharge of a legal duty with deadly physical force or with the apparent capacity to use deadly physical force; or
2. A felon who has escaped from lawful confinement; or
3. A felon who is fleeing from justice or resisting arrest with physical force.
B. The use of deadly physical force by a person other than a peace officer against another is justified pursuant to §13-409 only if a reasonable person effecting the arrest or preventing the escape would believe the suspect or escapee is actually resisting the discharge of a legal duty with physical force or with the apparent capacity to use deadly physical force.
C. The use of deadly force by a peace officer against another is justified pursuant to §13-409 only when the peace officer reasonably believes that it is necessary:
1. To defend himself or a third person from what the peace officer reasonably believes to be the use or imminent use of deadly physical force.
2. To effect an arrest or prevent the escape from custody of a person whom the peace officer reasonably believes:
(a) Has committed, attempted to commit, is committing or is attempting to commit a felony involving the use or a threatened use of a deadly weapon.
(b) Is attempting to escape by use of a deadly weapon.
(c) Through past or present conduct of the person which is known by the peace officer that person is likely to endanger human life or inflict serious bodily injury to another unless apprehended without delay.
(d) Is necessary to lawfully suppress a riot if the person or another person participating in the riot is armed with a deadly weapon.
D. Not withstanding any other provisions of this chapter a peace officer is justified in threatening to use deadly physical force when and to the extent a reasonable officer believes it necessary to protect himself against another's potential use of physical force or deadly physical force.

13-411. Justification; use of force in crime prevention; applicability

A. A person is justified in threatening or using both physical force and deadly physical force against another if and to the extent the person reasonably believes that physical force or deadly physical force is immediately necessary to prevent the other's commission of arson of an occupied structure under §13-1704, burglary in the second or first degree under §13-1507 or 13-1508, kidnapping under §13-1304, manslaughter under §13-1103, second or first degree murder under §13-1104 or 13-1105, sexual conduct with a minor under §13-1405, sexual assault under §13-1406, child molestation under §13-1410, armed robbery under §13-1904 or aggravated assault under §13-1204, subsection A, paragraphs 1 and 2.
B. There is no duty to retreat before threatening or using physical force or deadly physical force justified by subsection A of this section.
C. A person is presumed to be acting reasonably for the purposes of this section if the person is acting to prevent what the person reasonably believes is the imminent or actual commission of any of the offenses listed in subsection A of this section.
D. This section includes the use or threatened use of physical force or deadly physical force in a person's home, residence, place of business, land the person owns or leases, conveyance of any kind, or any other place in this state where a person has a right to be.

13-412. Duress

A. Conduct which would otherwise constitute an offense is justified if a reasonable person would believe that he was compelled to engage in the proscribed conduct by the threat or use of immediate physical force against his person or the person of another which resulted or could result in serious physical injury which a reasonable person in the situation would not have resisted.
B. The defense provided by subsection A is unavailable if the person intentionally, knowingly or recklessly placed himself in a situation in which it was probable that he would be subjected to duress.
C. The defense provided by subsection A is unavailable for offenses involving homicide or serious physical injury.

13-413. No civil liability for justified conduct

No person in this state shall be subject to civil liability for engaging in conduct otherwise justified pursuant to the provisions of this chapter.

13-414. Justification; use of reasonable and necessary means

A correctional officer as defined in §41-1661 may use all reasonable and necessary means including deadly force to prevent the attempt of a prisoner sentenced to the custody of the state department of corrections to:
1. Escape from custody or from a correctional facility.
2. Take another person as a hostage.
3. Cause serious bodily harm to another person.

13-415. Justification; domestic violence

If there have been past acts of domestic violence as defined in §13-3601, subsection A against the defendant by the victim, the state of mind of a reasonable person under sections 13-404, 13-405 and 13-406 shall be determined from the perspective of a reasonable person who has been a victim of those past acts of domestic violence.

13-416. Justification; use of reasonable and necessary means; definition

A. A security officer who is employed by a private contractor may use all reasonable and necessary means, including deadly force, to prevent a prisoner in the custody of the private contractor from the following:

1. Escaping from the custody of a law enforcement officer, an authorized custodial agent or a correctional facility.
2. Taking another person as a hostage or causing death or serious bodily harm to another person.

B. Security officers who are described in subsection A and who are employed by private prisons in this state shall meet or exceed the standards established by the American correctional association.

C. For the purposes of this section, "private contractor" means a person that contracts with any governmental entity to provide detention or incarceration services for prisoners.

13-417. Necessity defense

A. Conduct that would otherwise constitute an offense is justified if a reasonable person was compelled to engage in the proscribed conduct and the person had no reasonable alternative to avoid imminent public or private injury greater than the injury that might reasonably result from the person's own conduct.

B. An accused person may not assert the defense under subsection A if the person intentionally, knowingly or recklessly placed himself in the situation in which it was probable that the person would have to engage in the proscribed conduct.

C. An accused person may not assert the defense under subsection A for offenses involving homicide or serious physical injury.

13-418. Justification; use of force in defense of residential structure or occupied vehicles; definitions

A. Notwithstanding any other provision of this chapter, a person is justified in threatening to use or using physical force or deadly physical force against another person if the person reasonably believes himself or another person to be in imminent peril of death or serious physical injury and the person against whom the physical force or deadly physical force is threatened or used was in the process of unlawfully or forcefully entering, or had unlawfully or forcefully entered, a residential structure or occupied vehicle, or had removed or was attempting to remove another person against the other person's will from the residential structure or occupied vehicle.

B. A person has no duty to retreat before threatening or using physical force or deadly physical force pursuant to this section.

C. For the purposes of this section:
1. "Residential structure" has the same meaning prescribed in §13-1501.
2. "Vehicle" means a conveyance of any kind, whether or not motorized, that is designed to transport persons or property.

13-419. Presumption; exceptions; definitions

A. A person is presumed to reasonably believe that the threat or use of physical force or deadly force is immediately necessary for the purposes of §§13-404 through 13-408, §13-418 and §13-421 if the person knows or has reason to believe that the person against whom physical force or deadly force is threatened or used is unlawfully or forcefully entering or has unlawfully or forcefully entered and is present in the person's residential structure or occupied vehicle.

B. For the purposes of §§13-404 through 13-408, §13-418 and §13-421, a person who is unlawfully or forcefully entering or who has unlawfully or forcefully entered and is present in a residential structure or occupied vehicle is presumed to pose an imminent threat of unlawful deadly harm to any person who is in the residential structure or occupied vehicle.

C. The presumptions in subsections A and b of this section do not apply if:
1. The person against whom physical force or deadly physical force was threatened or used has the right to be in or is a lawful resident of the residential structure or occupied vehicle, including an owner, lessee, invitee or titleholder, and an order of protection or injunction against harassment has not been filed against that person.
2. The person against whom physical force or deadly physical force was threatened or used is the parent or grandparent, or has legal custody or guardianship, of a child or grandchild sought to be removed from the residential structure or occupied vehicle.
3. The person who threatens or uses physical force or deadly physical force is engaged in an unlawful activity or is using the residential structure or occupied vehicle to further an unlawful activity.
4. The person against whom physical force or deadly physical force was threatened or used is a law enforcement officer who enters or attempts to enter a residential structure or occupied vehicle in the performance of official duties.

D. For the purposes of this section:
1. "Residential structure" has the same meaning prescribed in §13-1501.
2. "Vehicle" means a conveyance of any kind, whether or not motorized, that is designed to transport persons or property.

13-420. Attorney fees; costs

The court shall award reasonable attorney fees, costs, compensation for lost income and all expenses incurred by a defendant in the defense of any civil action based on conduct otherwise justified pursuant to this chapter if the defendant prevails in the civil action.

§13-421. Justification; defensive display of a firearm; definition

A. The defensive display of a firearm by a person against another is justified when and to the extent a reasonable person would believe that physical force is immediately necessary to protect himself against the use or attempted use of unlawful physical force or deadly physical force.

B. This section does not apply to a person who:
1. Intentionally provokes another person to use or attempt to use unlawful physical force.
2. Uses a firearm during the commission of a serious offense as defined in §13-706 or violent crime as defined in §13-901.03.

C. This section does not require the defensive display of a firearm before the use of physical force or the threat of physical force by a person who is otherwise justified in the use or threatened use of physical force.

D. For the purposes of this section, "defensive display of a firearm" includes:
1. Verbally informing another person that the person possesses or has available a firearm.
2. Exposing or displaying a firearm in a manner that a reasonable person would understand was meant to protect the

person against another's use or attempted use of unlawful physical force or deadly physical force.

3. Placing the person's hand on a firearm while the firearm is contained in a pocket, purse or other means of containment or transport.

CHAPTER 5 · RESPONSIBILITY

13-501. Persons under eighteen years of age; felony charging; definitions

A. The county attorney shall bring a criminal prosecution against a juvenile in the same manner as an adult if the juvenile is fifteen, sixteen or seventeen years of age at the time the alleged offense is committed and the juvenile is accused of any of the following offenses:

1. First degree murder in violation of §13-1105.
2. Second degree murder in violation of §13-1104.
3. Forcible sexual assault in violation of §13-1406.
4. Armed robbery in violation of §13-1904.
5. Any other violent felony offense.
6. Any felony offense committed by a chronic felony offender.
7. Any offense that is properly joined to an offense listed in this subsection.

B. Except as provided in subsection A of this section, the county attorney may bring a criminal prosecution against a juvenile in the same manner as an adult if the juvenile is at least fourteen years of age at the time the alleged offense is committed and the juvenile is accused of any of the following offenses:

1. A class 1 felony.
2. A class 2 felony.
3. A class 3 felony in violation of any offense in chapters 10 through 17 or chapter 19 or 23 of this title.
4. A class 3, 4, 5 or 6 felony involving a dangerous offense.
5. Any felony offense committed by a chronic felony offender.
6. Any offense that is properly joined to an offense listed in this subsection.

H. For the purposes of this section:

4. "Other violent felony offenses" means:

(a) Aggravated assault pursuant to §13-1204, subsection A, paragraph 1.
(b) Aggravated assault pursuant to §13-1204, subsection A, paragraph 2 involving the use of a deadly weapon.
(c) Drive by shooting pursuant to §13-1209.
(d) Discharging a firearm at a structure pursuant to §13-1211.

13-503 . Effect of alcohol or drug use

Temporary intoxication resulting from the voluntary ingestion, consumption, inhalation or injection of alcohol, an illegal substance under chapter 34 of this title or other psychoactive substances or the abuse of prescribed medications does not constitute insanity and is not a defense for any criminal act or requisite state of mind.

CHAPTER 6 · CLASSIFICATIONS OF OFFENSES AND AUTHORIZED DISPOSITIONS OF OFFENDERS

13-601. Classification of offenses

A. Felonies are classified, for the purpose of sentence, into the following six categories:

1. Class 1 felonies.
2. Class 2 felonies.
3. Class 3 felonies.
4. Class 4 felonies.
5. Class 5 felonies.
6. Class 6 felonies.

B. Misdemeanors are classified, for the purpose of sentence, into the following three categories:

1. Class 1 misdemeanors.
2. Class 2 misdemeanors.
3. Class 3 misdemeanors.

C. Petty offenses are not classified.

13-602. Designation of offenses

A. The particular classification of each felony defined in this title is expressly designated in the section or chapter defining it. Any offense defined outside this title which is declared by law to be a felony without either specification of the classification or of the penalty is a class 5 felony.

B. The particular classification of each misdemeanor defined in this title is expressly designated in the section or chapter defining it. Any offense defined outside this title which is declared by law to be a misdemeanor without either specification of the classification or of the penalty is a Class 2 misdemeanor.

C. Every petty offense in this title is expressly designated as such. Any offense defined outside this title without either designation as a felony or misdemeanor or specification of the classification or the penalty is a petty offense.

13-610. Deoxyribonucleic acid testing; exception

O. This section applies to persons who are:

3. Arrested for a violation of any offense in chapter 11 of this title, a violation of §13-1402, 13-1403, 13-1404, 13-1405, 13-1406, 13-1410, 13-1411, 13-1417, 13-1507, 13-1508, 13-3208, 13-3214, 13-3555 or 13-3608 or a violation of any serious offense as defined in §13-706 that is a dangerous offense.

CHAPTER 7 · IMPRISONMENT

13-701. Sentence of imprisonment for felony; presentence report; aggravating and mitigating factors; consecutive terms of imprisonment; definition

A. A sentence of imprisonment for a felony shall be a definite term of years and the person sentenced, unless otherwise provided by law or subsection J of this section applies, shall be committed to the custody of the state department of corrections.

C. The minimum or maximum term imposed pursuant to §13-702, 13-703, 13-704, 13-705, 13-708, 13-710, 13-1406, 13-3212 or 13-3419 may be imposed only if one or more of the circumstances alleged to be in aggravation of the crime are found to be true by the trier of fact beyond a reasonable doubt or are admitted by the defendant, except that an alleged aggravating circumstance under subsection D, paragraph 11 <priors> of this section shall be found to be true by the court, or in mitigation of the crime are found to be true by the court, on any evidence or information introduced or submitted to the court or the trier of fact before sentencing or any evidence presented at trial, and factual findings and reasons in support of such findings are set forth on the record at the time of sentencing.

D. For the purpose of determining the sentence pursuant to subsection C of this section, the trier of fact shall determine and the court shall consider the following aggravating circumstances, except that the court shall determine an aggravating circumstance under paragraph 11 of this subsection:

2. Use, threatened use or possession of a deadly weapon or dangerous instrument during the commission of the crime, except if this circumstance is an essential element of the offense of conviction or has been utilized to enhance the range of punishment under §13-704.

12. The defendant was wearing body armor as defined in §13-3116.

22. The defendant used a remote stun gun or an authorized remote stun gun in the commission of the offense. For the purposes of this paragraph:

(a) "Authorized remote stun gun" means a remote stun gun that has all of the following:

(i) An electrical discharge that is less than one hundred thousand volts and less than nine joules of energy per pulse.

(ii) A serial or identification number on all projectiles that are discharged from the remote stun gun.

(iii) An identification and tracking system that, on deployment of remote electrodes, disperses coded material that is traceable to the purchaser through records that are kept by the manufacturer on all remote stun guns and all individual cartridges sold.

(iv) A training program that is offered by the manufacturer.

(b) "Remote stun gun" means an electronic device that emits an electrical charge and that is designed and primarily employed to incapacitate a person or animal either through contact with electrodes on the device itself or remotely through wired probes that are attached to the device or through a spark, plasma, ionization or other conductive means emitting from the device.

13-702. First time felony offenders; sentencing; definition

A. Unless a specific sentence is otherwise provided, the term of imprisonment for a first felony offense shall be the presumptive sentence determined pursuant to subsection D of this section. Except for those felonies involving a dangerous offense or if a specific sentence is otherwise provided, the court may increase or reduce the presumptive sentence within the ranges set by subsection D of this section. Any reduction or increase shall be based on the aggravating and mitigating circumstances listed in §13-701, subsections D and E and shall be within the ranges prescribed in subsection D of this section.

D. The term of imprisonment for a presumptive, minimum, maximum, mitigated or aggravated sentence shall be within the range prescribed under this subsection. The terms are as follows:

Felony	Mitigated	Minimum	Presumptive	Maximum	Aggravated
Class 2	3 years	4 years	5 years	10 years	12.5 years
Class 3	2 years	2.5 years	3.5 years	7 years	8.75 years
Class 4	1 year	1.5 years	2.5 years	3 years	3.75 years
Class 5	.5 years	.75 years	1.5 years	2 years	2.5 years
Class 6	.33 years	.5 years	1 year	1.5 years	2 years

<Note: Sentencing was overhauled in 2008; see §13-703 for sentence ranges for repeat offences.>

13-704. Dangerous offenders; sentencing

A. Except as provided in §13-705, a person who is at least eighteen years of age or who has been tried as an adult and who stands convicted of a felony that is a dangerous offense shall be sentenced to a term of imprisonment as follows:

Felony	Minimum	Presumptive	Maximum
Class 2	7 years	10.5 years	21 years
Class 3	5 years	7.5 years	15 years
Class 4	4 years	6 years	8 years
Class 5	2 years	3 years	4 years
Class 6	1.5 years	2.25 years	3 years

K. A person who has been convicted in any court outside the jurisdiction of this state of an offense that was punishable by that jurisdiction as a felony is subject to subsection A, B, C, D or E of this section. A person who has been convicted of an offense punishable as a felony under the provisions of any prior code in this state or the jurisdiction in which the offense was committed is subject to subsection A, B, C, D or E of this section. A person who has been convicted of a felony weapons possession violation in any court outside the jurisdiction of this state that would not be punishable as a felony under the laws of this state is not subject to this section.

13-706. Serious, violent or aggravated offenders; sentencing; life imprisonment; definitions

F. For the purposes of this section:

1. "Serious offense" means any of the following offenses if committed in this state or any offense committed outside this state that if committed in this state would constitute one of the following offenses:

(d) Aggravated assault resulting in serious physical injury or involving the discharge, use or threatening exhibition of a deadly weapon or dangerous instrument.

(h) Armed robbery.

2. "Violent or aggravated felony" means any of the following offenses:
(c) Aggravated assault resulting in serious physical injury or involving the discharge, use or threatening exhibition of a deadly weapon or dangerous instrument.
(f) Drive by shooting.
(g) Discharging a firearm at a residential structure if the structure is occupied.
(n) Burglary in the first degree committed in a residential structure if the structure is occupied.
(q) Armed robbery.
(g) Discharging a firearm at a residential structure if the structure is occupied.

13-707. Sentence of imprisonment for misdemeanor
A. A sentence of imprisonment for a misdemeanor shall be for a definite term to be served other than a place within custody of the state department of corrections. The court shall fix the term of imprisonment within the following maximum limitations:
1. For a class 1 misdemeanor, six months.
2. For a class 2 misdemeanor, four months.
3. For a class 3 misdemeanor, thirty days.
E. The court may direct that a person who is sentenced pursuant to subsection A of this section shall not be released on any basis until the sentence imposed by the court has been served.

CHAPTER 7.1 · CAPITAL SENTENCING

13-751. Sentence of death or life imprisonment; aggravating and mitigating circumstances; definition
F. The trier of fact shall consider the following aggravating circumstances in determining whether to impose a sentence of death:
14. The defendant used a remote stun gun or an authorized remote stun gun in the commission of the offense.
J. For the purposes of this section, "serious offense" means any of the following offenses if committed in this state or any offense committed outside this state that if committed in this state would constitute one of the following offenses:
4. Aggravated assault resulting in serious physical injury or committed by the use, threatened use or exhibition of a deadly weapon or dangerous instrument.
9. Burglary in the first degree.

CHAPTER 8 · RESTITUTION AND FINES

13-801. Fines for felonies
A. A sentence to pay a fine for a felony shall be a sentence to pay an amount fixed by the court not more than one hundred fifty thousand dollars.
B. A judgment that the defendant shall pay a fine, with or without the alternative of imprisonment, shall constitute a lien in like manner as a judgment for money rendered in a civil action.
C. This section does not apply to an enterprise.

13-802. Fines for misdemeanors
A. A sentence to pay a fine for a class 1 misdemeanor shall be a sentence to pay an amount, fixed by the court, not more than two thousand five hundred dollars.
B. A sentence to pay a fine for a class 2 misdemeanor shall be a sentence to pay an amount, fixed by the court, not more than seven hundred fifty dollars.
C. A sentence to pay a fine for a class 3 misdemeanor shall be a sentence to pay an amount, fixed by the court, not more than five hundred dollars.
D. A sentence to pay a fine for a petty offense shall be a sentence to pay an amount, fixed by the court, of not more than three hundred dollars .
E. A judgment that the defendant shall pay a fine, with or without the alternative of imprisonment, shall constitute a lien in like manner as a judgment for money rendered in a civil action.
F. This section does not apply to an enterprise.

13-803. Fines against enterprises
A. A sentence to pay a fine, imposed on an enterprise for an offense defined in this title or for an offense defined outside this title for which no special enterprise fine is specified, shall be a sentence to pay an amount, fixed by the court, of not more than:
1. For a felony, one million dollars.
2. For a class 1 misdemeanor, twenty thousand dollars.
3. For a class 2 misdemeanor, ten thousand dollars.
4. For a class 3 misdemeanor, two thousand dollars.
5. For a petty offense, one thousand dollars.
B. A judgment that the enterprise shall pay a fine shall constitute a lien in like manner as a judgment for money rendered in a civil action.

CHAPTER 9 · PROBATION & RESTORATION OF CIVIL RIGHTS

13-901.03. Violent crimes; allegation; definition
B. For the purpose of this section, "violent crime" includes any criminal act that results in death or physical injury or any criminal use of a deadly weapon or dangerous instrument.

13-904. Suspension of civil rights and occupational disabilities
A. A conviction for a felony suspends the following civil rights of the person sentenced:
1. The right to vote.

2. The right to hold public office of trust or profit.
3. The right to serve as a juror.
4. During any period of imprisonment any other civil rights the suspension of which is reasonably necessary for the security of the institution in which the person sentenced is confined or for the reasonable protection of the public.
5. The right to possess a gun or firearm.
H. A person who is adjudicated delinquent under §8-341 for a felony does not have the right to carry or possess a gun or firearm.

13-905. Restoration of civil rights; persons completing probation

C. If the person was convicted of a dangerous offense under §13-704, the person may not file for the restoration of the right to possess or carry a gun or firearm. If the person was convicted of a serious offense as defined in §13-706 the person may not file for the restoration of the right to possess or carry a gun or firearm for ten years from the date of his discharge from probation. If the person was convicted of any other felony offense, the person may not file for the restoration of the right to possess or carry a gun or firearm for two years from the date of the person's discharge from probation.

13-906. Applications by persons discharged from prison

C. If the person was convicted of a dangerous offense under §13-704, the person may not file for the restoration of the right to possess or carry a gun or firearm. If the person was convicted of a serious offense as defined in §13-706, the person may not file for the restoration of the right to possess or carry a gun or firearm for ten years from the date of his absolute discharge from imprisonment. If the person was convicted of any other felony offense, the person may not file for the restoration of the right to possess or carry a gun or firearm for two years from the date of the person's absolute discharge from imprisonment.

13-909. Restoration of civil rights; persons completing probation for federal offense

C. If the person was convicted of an offense which would be a dangerous offense under §13-704, the person may not file for the restoration of the right to possess or carry a gun or firearm. If the person was convicted of an offense which would be a serious offense as defined in §13-706 the person may not file for the restoration of the right to possess or carry a gun or firearm for ten years from the date of the person's discharge from probation. If the person was convicted of any other felony offense, the person may not file for the restoration of his right to possess or carry a gun or firearm for two years from the date of his discharge from probation.

13-910. Applications by persons discharged from federal prison

C. If the person was convicted of an offense which would be a dangerous offense under section 13-704, the person may not file for the restoration of the right to possess or carry a gun or firearm. If the person was convicted of an offense which would be a serious offense as defined in section 13-706, the person may not file for the restoration of the right to possess or carry a gun or firearm for ten years from the date of the person's absolute discharge from imprisonment. If the person was convicted of any other felony offense, the person may not file for the restoration of the right to possess or carry a gun or firearm for two years from the date of the person's absolute discharge from imprisonment.

13-912. Restoration of civil rights; automatic for first offenders; persons excluded

A. Any person who has not previously been convicted of any other felony shall automatically be restored any civil rights that were lost or suspended by the conviction if the person both:
1. Completes a term of probation or receives an absolute discharge from imprisonment.
2. Pays any fine or restitution imposed.
B. This section does not apply to a person's right to possess weapons as defined in §13-3101 unless the person applies to a court pursuant to §13-905 or 13-906.
<NOTE: Chapter 9 contains extensive details for restoring civil rights not fully included here.>

13-912.01. Restoration of civil rights; persons adjudicated delinquent

C. If the person's adjudication was for a dangerous offense under §13-704, a serious offense as defined in §13-706, burglary in the first degree, burglary in the second degree or arson, the person may not file for the restoration of the right to possess or carry a gun or firearm until the person attains thirty years of age. If the person's adjudication was for any other felony offense, the person may not file for the restoration of the right to possess or carry a gun or firearm for two years from the date of the person's discharge.

13-924. Restoration of right to possess a firearm; mentally ill persons; application

A. On proper application, a person who was found to constitute a danger to himself or others or to be persistently or acutely disabled or gravely disabled and who was subject to a treatment order pursuant to §36-540 may request the court that entered the treatment order to restore the person's right to possess a firearm on a showing by clear and convincing evidence that the person no longer suffers from the mental disorder that led to the finding that the person constituted a danger to himself or others or was persistently or acutely disabled or gravely disabled. The person or the person's guardian or attorney may file the application.
B. On filing of the application the court shall set a hearing at which the applicant shall present psychological or psychiatric evidence in support of the application. The state may present evidence that the person remains a danger to himself or others or remains persistently or acutely disabled and should remain a prohibited possessor.
C. A finding that the person no longer suffers from the mental disorder pursuant to subsection a of this section only restores the person's right to possess a firearm and does not apply to and has no effect on any of the other rights or benefits the person receives.

13-925. Restoration of right to possess a firearm; mentally ill persons; petition

A. A person may petition the court that entered an order, finding or adjudication that resulted in the person being a prohibited possessor as defined in §13-3101, subsection A, paragraph 7, subdivision (a) or subject to 18 United States Code §922(d)(4) or (g)(4) to restore the person's right to possess a firearm.
B. The person or the person's guardian or attorney may file the petition. The petition shall be served on the attorney for the state who appeared in the underlying case.

C. On filing of the petition the court shall set a hearing. At the hearing, the person shall present psychological or psychiatric evidence in support of the petition. The state shall provide the court with the person's criminal history records, if any. The court shall receive evidence on and consider the following before granting or denying the petition:
1. The circumstances that resulted in the person being a prohibited possessor as defined in §13-3101, subsection A, paragraph 7, subdivision (a) or subject to 18 United States Code §922(d)(4) or (g)(4).
2. The person's record, including the person's mental health record and criminal history record, if any.
3. The person's reputation based on character witness statements, testimony or other character evidence.
4. Whether the person is a danger to self or others, is persistently, acutely or gravely disabled or whether the circumstances that led to the original order, adjudication or finding remain in effect.
5. Any change in the person's condition or circumstances that is relevant to the relief sought.
6. Any other evidence deemed admissible by the court.
D. The petitioner shall prove by Clear and convincing evidence both of the following:
1. The petitioner is not likely to act in a manner that is dangerous to public safety.
2. Granting the requested relief is not contrary to the public interest.
E. At the conclusion of the hearing, the court shall issue findings of fact and conclusions of law.
F. If the court grants the petition for relief, the original order, finding or adjudication is deemed not to have occurred for the purposes of applying §13-3101, subsection A, paragraph 7, subdivision (a), Public Law 110-180, §105(A) or 18 United States Code §922(d)(4) or (g)(4) to that person.
G. The granting of a petition under this section only restores the person's right to possess a firearm and does not apply to and has no affect on any other rights or benefits the person receives.
H. The court shall promptly notify the department of public safety of an order granting a petition under this section. As soon thereafter as practicable the department shall update, correct, modify or remove the person's record in any database that the department maintains and makes available to the national instant criminal background check system consistent with the rules pertaining to the database. Within ten business days after receiving the notification from the court, the department shall notify the united states attorney general that the person no longer falls within the provisions of §13-3101, subsection A, paragraph 7, subdivision (a) or 18 United States Code §922(d)(4) or (g)(4).

CHAPTER 11 · HOMICIDE

13-1101. Definitions
In this chapter, unless the context otherwise requires:
1. "Premeditation" means that the defendant acts with either the intention or the knowledge that he will kill another human being, when such intention or knowledge precedes the killing by any length of time to permit reflection. Proof of actual reflection is not required but an act is not done with premeditation if it is the instant effect of a sudden quarrel or heat of passion.
2. "Homicide" means first degree murder, second degree murder, manslaughter or negligent homicide.
3. "Person" means a human being.
4. "Adequate provocation" means conduct or circumstances sufficient to deprive a reasonable person of self-control.

13-1102. Negligent homicide; classification
A. A person commits negligent homicide if with criminal negligence the person causes the death of another person, including an unborn child.
C. Negligent homicide is a class 4 felony.

13-1103. Manslaughter; classification
A. A person commits manslaughter by:
1. Recklessly causing the death of another person, or
2. Committing second degree murder as defined in §13-1104, subsection A upon a sudden quarrel or heat of passion resulting from adequate provocation by the victim; or
3. Intentionally aiding another to commit suicide; or
4. Committing second degree murder as defined in §13-1104, subsection A, paragraph 3, while being coerced to do so by the use or threatened immediate use of unlawful deadly physical force upon such person or a third person which a reasonable person in his situation would have been unable to resist; or
5. Knowingly or recklessly causing the death of an unborn child by any physical injury to the mother.
C. Manslaughter is a class 2 felony.

13-1104. Second degree murder; classification
A. A person commits second degree murder if without premeditation:
1. The person intentionally causes the death of another person, including an unborn child or, as a result of intentionally causing the death of another person, causes the death of an unborn child; or
2. Knowing that the person's conduct will cause death or serious physical injury, the person causes the death of another person, including an unborn child or, as a result of knowingly causing the death of another person, causes the death of an unborn child; or
3. Under circumstances manifesting extreme indifference to human life, the person recklessly engages in conduct that creates a grave risk of death and thereby causes the death of another person, including an unborn child or, as a result of recklessly causing the death of another person, causes the death of an unborn child.
C. Second degree murder is a class 1 felony and is punishable as provided by §13-705 if the victim is under fifteen years of age or is an unborn child, §13-706, subsection A or §13-710.

13-1105. First degree murder; classification
A. A person commits first degree murder if:
1. Intending or knowing that his conduct will cause death, such person causes the death of another person, including an unborn child, with premeditation or, as a result of causing the death of another person with premeditation, causes the death of an unborn child.
2. Acting either alone or with one or more other persons such person commits or attempts to commit sexual conduct with a

minor under §13-1405, sexual assault under §13-1406, molestation of a child under §13-1410, terrorism under §13-2308.01, marijuana offenses under §13-3405, subsection A, paragraph 4, dangerous drug offenses under §13-3407, subsection A, paragraph 7, narcotics offenses under §13-3408, subsection A, paragraph 7 that equal or exceed the statutory threshold amount for each offense or combination of offenses, involving or using minors in drug offenses under §13-3409, kidnapping under §13-1304, burglary under §13-1506, 13-1507 or 13-1508, arson under §13-1704, robbery under §13-1902, 13-1903 or 13-1904, escape under §13-2503 or 13-2504, child abuse under §13-3623, subsection B, paragraph 1 or unlawful flight from a pursuing law enforcement vehicle under §28-622.01 and in the course of and in furtherance of such offense or immediate flight from such offense, such person or another person causes the death of any person.

B. Homicide, as defined in subsection A, paragraph 2 of this section, requires no specific mental state other than what is required for the commission of any of the enumerated felonies.

D. First degree murder is a class 1 felony and is punishable by death or life imprisonment as provided by §§13-751 and 13-752.

CHAPTER 12 · ASSAULT AND RELATED OFFENSES

13-1201. Endangerment; classification

A. A person commits endangerment by recklessly endangering another person with a substantial risk of imminent death or physical injury.

B. Endangerment involving a substantial risk of imminent death is a class 6 felony. In all other cases, it is a class 1 misdemeanor.

13-1202. Threatening or intimidating; classification

A. A person commits threatening or intimidating if the person threatens or intimidates by word or conduct:

1. To cause physical injury to another person or serious damage to the property of another; or

2. To cause, or in reckless disregard to causing, serious public inconvenience including, but not limited to, evacuation of a building, place of assembly or transportation facility; or

3. To cause physical injury to another person or damage to the property of another in order to promote, further or assist in the interests of or to cause, induce or solicit another person to participate in a criminal street gang, a criminal syndicate or a racketeering enterprise.

B. Threatening or intimidating pursuant to subsection A, paragraph 1 or 2 is a class 1 misdemeanor, except that it is a class 6 felony if:

1. The offense is committed in retaliation for a victim's either reporting criminal activity or being involved in an organization, other than a law enforcement agency, that is established for the purpose of reporting or preventing criminal activity.

2. The person is a criminal street gang member.

3. Threatening or intimidating pursuant to subsection A, paragraph 3 is a class 3 felony.

13-1203. Assault; classification

A. A person commits assault by:

1. Intentionally, knowingly or recklessly causing any physical injury to another person; or

2. Intentionally placing another person in reasonable apprehension of imminent physical injury; or

3. Knowingly touching another person with the intent to injure, insult or provoke such person.

B. Assault committed intentionally or knowingly pursuant to subsection A, paragraph 1 is a class 1 misdemeanor. Assault committed recklessly pursuant to subsection A, paragraph 1 or assault pursuant to subsection A, paragraph 2 is a class 2 misdemeanor. Assault committed pursuant to subsection A, paragraph 3 is a class 3 misdemeanor.

13-1204. Aggravated assault; classification; definition

A. A person commits aggravated assault if the person commits assault as prescribed by §13-1203 under any of the following circumstances:

1. If the person causes serious physical injury to another.

2. If the person uses a deadly weapon or dangerous instrument.

3. If the person commits the assault by any means of force that causes temporary but substantial disfigurement, temporary but substantial loss or impairment of any body organ or part or a fracture of any body part.

4. If the person commits the assault while the victim is bound or otherwise physically restrained or while the victim's capacity to resist is substantially impaired.

5. If the person commits the assault after entering the private home of another with the intent to commit the assault.

6. If the person is eighteen years of age or older and commits the assault on a minor under fifteen years of age.

7. If the person commits assault as prescribed by §13-1203, subsection A, paragraph 1 or 3 and the person is in violation of an order of protection issued against the person pursuant to §13-3602 or 13-3624.

8. If the person commits the assault knowing or having reason to know that the victim is any of the following:

(a) A peace officer, or a person summoned and directed by the officer while engaged in the execution of any official duties.

(b) A constable, or a person summoned and directed by the constable while engaged in the execution of any official duties.

(c) A firefighter, fire investigator, fire inspector, emergency medical technician or paramedic engaged in the execution of any official duties, or a person summoned and directed by such individual while engaged in the execution of any official duties.

(d) A teacher or other person employed by any school and the teacher or other employee is on the grounds of a school or grounds adjacent to the school or is in any part of a building or vehicle used for school purposes, any teacher or school nurse visiting a private home in the course of the teacher's or nurse's professional duties or any teacher engaged in any authorized and organized classroom activity held on other than school grounds.

(e) A health care practitioner who is certified or licensed pursuant to title 32, chapter 13, 15, 17 or 25, or a person summoned and directed by the licensed health care practitioner while engaged in the person's professional duties. This subdivision does not apply if the person who commits the assault is seriously mentally ill, as defined in §36-550, or is afflicted with alzheimer's disease or related dementia.

(f) A prosecutor.

(g) A code enforcement officer as defined in §39-123.

(h) A state or municipal park ranger.
(i) A public defender.
9. If the person knowingly takes or attempts to exercise control over any of the following:
(a) A peace officer's or other officer's firearm and the person knows or has reason to know that the victim is a peace officer or other officer employed by one of the agencies listed in paragraph 10, subdivision (a), item (i), (ii), (iii), (iv) or (v) of this subsection and is engaged in the execution of any official duties.
(b) Any weapon other than a firearm that is being used by a peace officer or other officer or that the officer is attempting to use, and the person knows or has reason to know that the victim is a peace officer or other officer employed by one of the agencies listed in paragraph 10, subdivision (a), item (i), (ii), (iii), (iv) or (v) of this subsection and is engaged in the execution of any official duties.
(c) Any implement that is being used by a peace officer or other officer or that the officer is attempting to use, and the person knows or has reason to know that the victim is a peace officer or other officer employed by one of the agencies listed in paragraph 10, subdivision (a), item (i), (ii), (iii), (iv) or (v) of this subsection and is engaged in the execution of any official duties. For the purposes of this subdivision, "implement" means an object that is designed for or that is capable of restraining or injuring an individual. Implement does not include handcuffs.
10. If the person meets both of the following conditions:
(a) Is imprisoned or otherwise subject to the custody of any of the following:
(i) The state department of corrections.
(ii) The department of juvenile corrections.
(iii) A law enforcement agency.
(iv) A county or city jail or an adult or juvenile detention facility of a city or county.
(v) Any other entity that is contracting with the state department of corrections, the department of juvenile corrections, a law enforcement agency, another state, any private correctional facility, a county, a city or the federal bureau of prisons or other federal agency that has responsibility for sentenced or unsentenced prisoners.
(b) Commits an assault knowing or having reason to know that the victim is acting in an official capacity as an employee of any of the entities listed in subdivision (a) of this paragraph.
B. A person commits aggravated assault if the person commits assault by either intentionally, knowingly or recklessly causing any physical injury to another person, intentionally placing another person in reasonable apprehension of imminent physical injury or knowingly touching another person with the intent to injure the person, and both of the following occur:
1. The person intentionally or knowingly impedes the normal breathing or circulation of blood of another person by applying pressure to the throat or neck or by obstructing the nose and mouth either manually or through the use of an instrument.
2. Any of the circumstances exists that are set forth in §13-3601, subsection a, paragraph 1, 2, 3, 4, 5 or 6.
C. A person who is convicted of intentionally or knowingly committing aggravated assault on a peace officer while the officer is engaged in the execution of any official duties pursuant to subsection A, paragraph 1 or 2 of this section shall be sentenced to imprisonment for not less than the presumptive sentence authorized under chapter 7 of this title and is not eligible for suspension of sentence, commutation or release on any basis until the sentence imposed is served.
D. Except pursuant to subsections E and FE of this section, aggravated assault pursuant to subsection A, paragraph 1 or 2 or paragraph 9, subdivision (a) of this section is a class 3 felony except if the victim is under fifteen years of age in which case it is a class 2 felony punishable pursuant to §13-705. Aggravated assault pursuant to subsection A, paragraph 3 or subsection B of this section is a class 4 felony. Aggravated assault pursuant to subsection A, paragraph 9, subdivision (b) or paragraph 10 of this section is a class 5 felony. Aggravated assault pursuant to subsection A, paragraph 4, 5, 6, 7 or 8, or paragraph 9, subdivision (c) of this section is a class 6 felony.
E. Aggravated assault pursuant to subsection A, paragraph 1 or 2 of this section committed on a peace officer while the officer is engaged in the execution of any official duties is a class 2 felony. Aggravated assault pursuant to subsection A, paragraph 3 of this section committed on a peace officer while the officer is engaged in the execution of any official duties is a class 3 felony. Aggravated assault pursuant to subsection A, paragraph 9, subdivision (a) of this section committed on a peace officer while the officer is engaged in the execution of any official duties is a class 5 felony unless the assault results in any physical injury to the peace officer while the officer is engaged in the execution of any official duties, in which case it is a class 4 felony.
F. Aggravated assault pursuant to:
1. Subsection A, paragraph 1 or 2 of this section is a class 2 felony if committed on a prosecutor.
2. Subsection A, paragraph 3 of this section is a class 3 felony if committed on a prosecutor.
3. Subsection A, paragraph 8, subdivision (e) of this section is a class 5 felony if the assault results in physical injury to a prosecutor.
G. For the purposes of this section, "prosecutor" means a county attorney, a municipal prosecutor or the attorney general and includes an assistant or deputy county attorney, municipal prosecutor or attorney general.

13-1209. Drive by shootings; driver's license revocation; classification; definitions
A. A person commits drive by shooting by intentionally discharging a weapon from a motor vehicle at a person, another occupied motor vehicle or an occupied structure.
D. Drive by shooting is a class 2 felony.
E. As used in this section:
1. "Motor vehicle" has the same meaning prescribed in §28-101.
2. "Occupied structure" has the same meaning prescribed in §13-3101.

13-1211. Discharging a firearm at a structure; classification; definitions
A. A person who knowingly discharges a firearm at a residential structure is guilty of a class 2 felony.
B. A person who knowingly discharges a firearm at a nonresidential structure is guilty of a class 3 felony.
C. For the purposes of this section:
1. "Nonresidential structure" means a structure other than a residential structure.
2. "Residential structure" means a movable or immovable or permanent or temporary structure that is adapted for both human residence or lodging.
3. "Structure" means any building, vehicle, railroad car or place with sides and a floor that is separately securable from any other structure attached to it and that is being used for lodging, business or transportation.

13-1213. Aiming a laser pointer at a peace officer; classification; definition
A. A person commits aiming a laser pointer at a peace officer if the person intentionally or knowingly directs the beam of light from an operating laser pointer at another person and the person knows or reasonably should know that the other person is a peace officer.
B. Aiming a laser pointer at a peace officer is a class 1 misdemeanor.
C. For the purposes of this section, "laser pointer" means any device that consists of a high or low powered visible light beam used for aiming, targeting or pointing out features.

CHAPTER 13 · KIDNAPPING AND RELATED OFFENSES

13-1304. Kidnapping; classification; consecutive sentence
A. A person commits kidnapping by knowingly restraining another person with the intent to:
1. Hold the victim for ransom, as a shield or hostage; or
2. Hold the victim for involuntary servitude; or
3. Inflict death, physical injury or a sexual offense on the victim, or to otherwise aid in the commission of a felony; or
4. Place the victim or a third person in reasonable apprehension of imminent physical injury to the victim or the third person; or
5. Interfere with the performance of a governmental or political function; or
6. Seize or exercise control over any airplane, train, bus, ship or other vehicle.
B. Kidnapping is a class 2 felony unless the victim is released voluntarily by the defendant without physical injury in a safe place before arrest and before accomplishing any of the further enumerated offenses in subsection A of this section in which case it is a class 4 felony. If the victim is released pursuant to an agreement with the state and without any physical injury, it is a class 3 felony. If the victim is under fifteen years of age kidnapping is a class 2 felony punishable pursuant to §13-705. The sentence for kidnapping of a victim under fifteen years of age shall run consecutively to any other sentence imposed on the defendant and to any undischarged term of imprisonment of the defendant.

CHAPTER 14 · SEXUAL OFFENSES

13-1405. Sexual conduct with a minor; classifications
A. A person commits sexual conduct with a minor by intentionally or knowingly engaging in sexual intercourse or oral sexual contact with any person who is under eighteen years of age.
B. Sexual conduct with a minor who is under fifteen years of age is a class 2 felony and is punishable pursuant to §13-705. Sexual conduct with a minor who is at least fifteen years of age is a class 6 felony. Sexual conduct with a minor who is at least fifteen years of age is a class 2 felony if the person is the minor's parent, stepparent, adoptive parent, legal guardian, foster parent or the minor's teacher or clergyman or priest and the convicted person is not eligible for suspension of sentence, probation, pardon or release from confinement on any basis except as specifically authorized by §31-233, subsection A or B until the sentence imposed has been served or commuted.

13-1406. Sexual assault; classification; increased punishment
A. A person commits sexual assault by intentionally or knowingly engaging in sexual intercourse or oral sexual contact with any person without consent of such person.
B. Sexual assault is a class 2 felony, and the person convicted shall be sentenced pursuant to this section and the person is not eligible for suspension of sentence, probation, pardon or release from confinement on any basis except as specifically authorized by §31-233, subsection A or B until the sentence imposed by the court has been served or commuted. If the victim is under fifteen years of age, sexual assault is punishable pursuant to §13-705. The presumptive term may be aggravated or mitigated within the range under this section pursuant to §13-701, subsections C, D and E. If the sexual assault involved the intentional or knowing administration of flunitrazepam, gamma hydroxy butyrate or ketamine hydrochloride without the victim's knowledge, the presumptive, minimum and maximum sentence for the offense shall be increased by three years. The additional sentence imposed pursuant to this subsection is in addition to any enhanced sentence that may be applicable. The term for a first offense is as follows <Note: repeat offenses carry greater penalties not shown here>:

Minimum	Presumptive	Maximum
5.25 years	7 years	14 years

13-1410. Molestation of child; classification
A person commits molestation of a child by intentionally or knowingly engaging in or causing a person to engage in sexual contact, except sexual contact with the female breast, with a child under fifteen years of age.
B. Molestation of a child is a class 2 felony that is punishable pursuant to §13-705.

CHAPTER 15 · CRIMINAL TRESPASS AND BURGLARY

13-1502. Criminal trespass in the third degree; classification
A. A person commits criminal trespass in the third degree by:
1. Knowingly entering or remaining unlawfully on any real property after a reasonable request to leave by a law enforcement officer, the owner or any other person having lawful control over such property, or reasonable notice prohibiting entry.
2. Knowingly entering or remaining unlawfully on the right-of-way for tracks, or the storage or switching yards or rolling stock of a railroad company.
B. Pursuant to subsection A, paragraph 1 of this section, a request to leave by a law enforcement officer acting at the request of the owner of the property or any other person having lawful control over the property has the same legal effect as a request made by the property owner or other person having lawful control of the property.
C. Criminal trespass in the third degree is a class 3 misdemeanor.

13-1503. Criminal trespass in the second degree; classification
A. A person commits criminal trespass in the second degree by knowingly entering or remaining unlawfully in or on any

nonresidential structure or in any fenced commercial yard.
B. Criminal trespass in the second degree is a class 2 misdemeanor.

13-1504. Criminal trespass in the first degree; classification
A. A person commits criminal trespass in the first degree by knowingly:
1. Entering or remaining unlawfully in or on a residential structure.
2. Entering or remaining unlawfully in a fenced residential yard.
3. Entering any residential yard and, without lawful authority, looking into the residential structure thereon in reckless disregard of infringing on the inhabitant's right of privacy.
4. Entering unlawfully on real property that is subject to a valid mineral claim or lease with the intent to hold, work, take or explore for minerals on the claim or lease.
5. Entering or remaining unlawfully on the property of another and burning, defacing, mutilating or otherwise desecrating a religious symbol or other religious property of another without the express permission of the owner of the property.
6. Entering or remaining unlawfully in or on a critical public service facility.
B. Criminal trespass in the first degree under subsection A, paragraph 1, 5 or 6 is a class 6 felony. Criminal trespass in the first degree under subsection A, paragraph 2, 3 or 4 is a class 1 misdemeanor.

13-1506. Burglary in the third degree; classification
A. A person commits burglary in the third degree by:
1. Entering or remaining unlawfully in or on a nonresidential structure or in a fenced commercial or residential yard with the intent to commit any theft or any felony therein.
2. Making entry into any part of a motor vehicle by means of a manipulation key or master key, with the intent to commit any theft or felony in the motor vehicle.
B. Burglary in the third degree is a class 4 felony.

13-1507. Burglary in the second degree; classification
A. A person commits burglary in the second degree by entering or remaining unlawfully in or on a residential structure with the intent to commit any theft or any felony therein.
B. Burglary in the second degree is a class 3 felony.

13- 1508 . Burglary in the first degree; classification
A. A person commits burglary in the first degree if such person or an accomplice violates the provisions of either §13-1506 or 13-1507 and knowingly possesses explosives, a deadly weapon or a dangerous instrument in the course of committing any theft or any felony.
B. Burglary in the first degree of a nonresidential structure or a fenced commercial or residential yard is a class 3 felony. It is a class 2 felony if committed in a residential structure.

CHAPTER 17 · ARSON

13-1704. Arson of an occupied structure; classification
A. A person commits arson of an occupied structure by knowingly and unlawfully damaging an occupied structure by knowingly causing a fire or explosion.
B. Arson of an occupied structure is a class 2 felony.

CHAPTER 19 · ROBBERY

13-1902. Robbery; classification
A. A person commits robbery if in the course of taking any property of another from his person or immediate presence and against his will, such person threatens or uses force against any person with intent either to coerce surrender of property or to prevent resistance to such person taking or retaining property.
B. Robbery is a class 4 felony.

13-1903. Aggravated robbery; classification
A. A person commits aggravated robbery if in the course of committing robbery as defined in §13-1902 such person is aided by one or more accomplices actually present.
B. Aggravated robbery is a class 3 felony.

13-1904. Armed robbery; classification
A. A person commits armed robbery if, in the course of committing robbery as defined in §13-1902, such person or an accomplice:
1. Is armed with a deadly weapon or a simulated deadly weapon; or
2. Uses or threatens to use a deadly weapon or dangerous instrument or a simulated deadly weapon.
B. Armed robbery is a class 2 felony.

CHAPTER 23 · ORGANIZED CRIME, FRAUD AND TERRORISM

13-2301. Definitions
C. For the purposes of this chapter:
8. "Explosive agent" means an explosive as defined in §13-3101 and flammable fuels or fire accelerants in amounts over fifty gallons but excludes:
(a) Fireworks as defined in §36-1601.
(b) Firearms.
(c) A propellant actuated device or propellant actuated industrial tool.
(d) A device that is commercially manufactured primarily for the purpose of illumination.
(e) A rocket having a propellant charge of less than four ounces.

9. "Material support or resources" includes money or other financial securities, financial services, lodging, sustenance, training, safehouses, false documentation or identification, communications equipment, facilities, weapons, lethal substances, explosives, personnel, transportation, disguises and other physical assets but does not include medical assistance, legal assistance or religious materials.

12. "Terrorism" means any felony, including any completed or preparatory offense, that involves the use of a deadly weapon or a weapon of mass destruction or the intentional or knowing infliction of serious physical injury with the intent to either:

(a) Influence the policy or affect the conduct of this state or any of the political subdivisions, agencies or instrumentalities of this state.

(b) Cause substantial damage to or substantial interruption of public communications, communication service providers, public transportation, common carriers, public utilities, public establishments or other public services.

13-2308.01. Terrorism; classification

A. It is unlawful for a person to intentionally or knowingly do any of the following:

1. Engage in an act of terrorism.

D. A violation of subsection A of this section is a class 2 felony, except that if the court finds that at least one of the aggravating circumstances listed in §13-701, subsection D applies, the court may impose a life sentence. If the court imposes a life sentence, the court may order that the defendant not be released on any basis for the remainder of the defendant's natural life. If the court does not sentence the defendant to natural life, the defendant shall not be released on any basis until the person has served twenty-five calendar years.

CHAPTER 24 · OBSTRUCTION OF PUBLIC ADMINISTRATION

13-2403. Refusing to aid a peace officer; classification

A. A person commits refusing to aid a peace officer if, upon a reasonable command by a person reasonably known to be a peace officer such person knowingly refuses or fails to aid such peace officer in:

1. Effectuating or securing an arrest; or

2. Preventing the commission by another of any offense.

B. A person who complies with this section by aiding a peace officer shall not be held liable to any person for damages resulting therefrom, provided such person acted reasonably under the circumstances known to him at the time.

C. Refusing to aid a peace officer is a class 1 misdemeanor.

13-2409. Obstructing criminal investigations or prosecutions; classification

A person who knowingly attempts by means of bribery, misrepresentation, intimidation or force or threats of force to obstruct, delay or prevent the communication of information or testimony relating to a violation of any criminal statute to a peace officer, magistrate, prosecutor or grand jury or who knowingly injures another in his person or property on account of the giving by the latter or by any other person of any such information or testimony to a peace officer, magistrate, prosecutor or grand jury is guilty of a class 5 felony, except that it is a class 3 felony if the person commits the offense with the intent to promote, further or assist a criminal street gang.

CHAPTER 25 · ESCAPE AND RELATED OFFENSES

13-2501. Definitions

In this chapter, unless the context otherwise requires:

1. "Contraband" means any dangerous drug, narcotic drug, marijuana, intoxicating liquor of any kind, deadly weapon, dangerous instrument, explosive, wireless communication device, multimedia storage device or other article whose use or possession would endanger the safety, security or preservation of order in a correctional facility or a juvenile secure care facility as defined in §41-2801, or of any person within a correctional or juvenile secure care facility.

13-2504. Escape in the first degree; classification

A. A person commits escape in the first degree by knowingly escaping or attempting to escape from custody or a juvenile secure care facility, juvenile detention facility or an adult correctional facility by:

1. Using or threatening the use of physical force against another person; or

2. Using or threatening to use a deadly weapon or dangerous instrument against another person.

B. Escape in the first degree is a class 4 felony and the sentence imposed for a violation of this section shall run consecutively to any sentence of imprisonment for which the person was confined or to any term of community supervision for the sentence including probation, parole, work furlough or any other release.

13-2505. Promoting prison contraband; classification; exceptions; x-radiation

A. A person, not otherwise authorized by law, commits promoting prison contraband:

1. By knowingly taking contraband into a correctional facility or the grounds of a correctional facility; or

2. By knowingly conveying contraband to any person confined in a correctional facility; or

3. By knowingly making, obtaining or possessing contraband while being confined in a correctional facility or while being lawfully transported or moved incident to correctional facility confinement.

B. Any person who has reasonable grounds to believe there has been a violation or attempted violation of this section shall immediately report the violation or attempted violation to the official in charge of the facility or to a peace officer.

F. Promoting prison contraband if the contraband is a deadly weapon, dangerous instrument or explosive is a class 2 felony. Promoting prison contraband if the contraband is a dangerous drug, narcotic drug or marijuana is a class 2 felony. In all other cases promoting prison contraband is a class 5 felony. Failure to report a violation or attempted violation of this section is a class 5 felony.

13-2508. Resisting arrest; classification

A. A person commits resisting arrest by intentionally preventing or attempting to prevent a person reasonably known to him to be a peace officer, acting under color of such peace officer's official authority, from effecting an arrest by:

1. Using or threatening to use physical force against the peace officer or another; or

2. Using any other means creating a substantial risk of causing physical injury to the peace officer or another.

B. Resisting arrest pursuant to subsection A, paragraph 1 or 2 of this section is a class 6 felony.

13-2510. Hindering prosecution; definition
For purposes of §13-2511 and §13-2512 a person renders assistance to another person by knowingly:
1. Harboring or concealing the other person; or
2. Warning the other person of impending discovery, apprehension prosecution or conviction. This does not apply to a warning given in connection with an effort to bring another into compliance with the law; or
3. Providing the other person with money, transportation, a weapon, a disguise or other similar means of avoiding discovery, apprehension, prosecution or conviction; or
4. Preventing or obstructing by means of force, deception or intimidation anyone from performing an act that might aid in the discovery, apprehension, prosecution or conviction of the other person; or
5. Suppressing by an act of concealment, alteration or destruction any physical evidence that might aid in the discovery, apprehension, prosecution or conviction of the other person; or
6. Concealing the identity of the other person.

13-2511. Hindering prosecution in the second degree; classification
A. A person commits hindering prosecution in the second degree if, with the intent to hinder the apprehension, prosecution, conviction or punishment of another for any misdemeanor or petty offense, such person renders assistance to such person.
B. Hindering prosecution in the second degree is a class 1 misdemeanor.

13-2512. Hindering prosecution in the first degree; classification
A. A person commits hindering prosecution in the first degree if, with the intent to hinder the apprehension, prosecution, conviction or punishment of another for any felony, the person renders assistance to the other person.
B. Hindering prosecution in the first degree is a class 5 felony, except that it is a class 3 felony if either:
1. The person knows or has reason to know that the offense involves terrorism or murder.
2. The person commits the offense with the intent to promote, further or assist a criminal street gang.

13-2514. Promoting secure care facility contraband; classifications
A. A person, not otherwise authorized by law, commits promoting secure care facility contraband by knowingly doing any of the following:
1. Taking contraband onto the grounds of or into a secure care facility under the jurisdiction of the department of juvenile corrections.
2. Conveying contraband to any person confined in a secure care facility under the jurisdiction of the department of juvenile corrections.
3. Making, obtaining or possessing contraband while being confined in a secure care facility under the jurisdiction of the department of juvenile corrections.
B. Except for information protected under attorney client privilege, any person who has reasonable grounds to believe there has been a violation or attempted violation of this section shall immediately report the violation or attempted violation to the official in charge of the facility or to a peace officer.
C. Promoting secure care facility contraband if the contraband is a deadly weapon, dangerous instrument or explosive is a class 2 felony. Promoting secure care facility contraband if the contraband is a dangerous drug, narcotic drug or marijuana is a class 2 felony. In all other cases promoting secure care facility contraband is a class 5 felony. Failure to report a violation or attempted violation of this section is a class 5 felony.
D. Notwithstanding any law to the contrary, any person convicted of a violation of this section shall be prohibited from employment by this state or any of its agencies or political subdivisions until the person's civil rights have been restored pursuant to chapter 9 of this title.

CHAPTER 27 · PERJURY AND RELATED OFFENSES

13-2702. Perjury; classification
A. A person commits perjury by making a false sworn statement in regard to a material issue, believing it to be false.
B. Perjury is a class 4 felony.

CHAPTER 28 · INTERFERENCE WITH JUDICIAL AND OTHER PROCEEDINGS

13-2809. Tampering with physical evidence; classification
A. A person commits tampering with physical evidence if, with intent that it be used, introduced, rejected or unavailable in an official proceeding which is then pending or which such person knows is about to be instituted, such person:
1. Destroys, mutilates, alters, conceals or removes physical evidence with the intent to impair its verity or availability; or
2. Knowingly makes, produces or offers any false physical evidence; or
3. Prevents the production of physical evidence by an act of force, intimidation or deception against any person.
B. Inadmissibility of the evidence in question is not a defense.
C. Tampering with physical evidence is a class 6 felony.

CHAPTER 29 · OFFENSES AGAINST PUBLIC ORDER

13-2904. Disorderly conduct; classification
A. A person commits disorderly conduct if, with intent to disturb the peace or quiet of a neighborhood, family or person, or with knowledge of doing so, such person:
1. Engages in fighting, violent or seriously disruptive behavior; or
2 Makes unreasonable noise; or
3. Uses abusive or offensive language or gestures to any person present in a manner likely to provoke immediate physical

retaliation by such person; or
4. Makes any protracted commotion, utterance or display with the intent to prevent the transaction of the business of a lawful meeting, gathering or procession; or
5. Refuses to obey a lawful order to disperse issued to maintain public safety in dangerous proximity to a fire, a hazard or any other emergency; or
6. Recklessly handles, displays or discharges a deadly weapon or dangerous instrument.
B. Disorderly conduct under subsection A, paragraph 6 is a class 6 felony. Disorderly conduct under subsection A, paragraph 1, 2, 3, 4 or 5 is a class 1 misdemeanor.

13-2908. Criminal nuisance; classification
A. A person commits criminal nuisance:
1. If, by conduct either unlawful in itself or unreasonable under the circumstances, such person recklessly creates or maintains a condition which endangers the safety or health of others.
2. By knowingly conducting or maintaining any premises, place or resort where persons gather for purposes of engaging in unlawful conduct.
Criminal nuisance is a class 3 misdemeanor.

13-2911. Interference with or disruption of an educational institution; violation; classification; definitions
A. A person commits interference with or disruption of an educational institution by doing any of the following:
1. Intentionally, knowingly or recklessly interfering with or disrupting the normal operations of an educational institution by either:
(a) Threatening to cause physical injury to any employee or student of an educational institution or any person on the property of an educational institution.
(b) Threatening to cause damage to any educational institution, the property of any educational institution or the property of any employee or student of an educational institution.
2. Intentionally or knowingly entering or remaining on the property of any educational institution for the purpose of interfering with the lawful use of the property or in any manner as to deny or interfere with the lawful use of the property by others.
3. Intentionally or knowingly refusing to obey a lawful order given pursuant to subsection C of this section.
B. To constitute a violation of this section, the acts that are prohibited by subsection A, paragraph 1 of this section are not required to be directed at a specific individual, a specific educational institution or any specific property of an educational institution.
C. The chief administrative officer of an educational institution or an officer or employee designated by the chief administrative officer to maintain order may order a person to leave the property of the educational institution if the officer or employee has reasonable grounds to believe either that:
1. Any person or persons are committing any act that interferes with or disrupts the lawful use of the property by others at the educational institution.
2. Any person has entered on the property of an educational institution for the purpose of committing any act that interferes with or disrupts the lawful use of the property by others at the educational institution.
D. The appropriate governing board of every educational institution shall adopt rules pursuant to title 41, chapter 6 for the maintenance of public order on all property of any educational institution under its jurisdiction that is used for educational purposes and shall provide a program for the enforcement of its rules. The rules shall govern the conduct of students, faculty and other staff and all members of the public while on the property of the educational institution. Penalties for violations of the rules shall be clearly set forth and enforced. Penalties shall include provisions for the ejection of a violator from the property and, in the case of a student, faculty member or other staff violator, the violator's suspension or expulsion or any other appropriate disciplinary action. A governing board shall amend its rules as necessary to ensure the maintenance of public order. Any deadly weapon, dangerous instrument or explosive that is used, displayed or possessed by a person in violation of a rule adopted pursuant to this subsection shall be forfeited and sold, destroyed or otherwise disposed of pursuant to chapter 39 of this title. This subsection does not do either of the following:
1. Preclude school districts from conducting approved gun safety programs on school campuses.
2. Apply to private universities, colleges, high schools or common schools or other private educational institutions.
E. An educational institution is not eligible to receive any state aid or assistance unless rules are adopted in accordance with this section.
F. This section does not prevent or limit the authority of the governing board of any educational institution to discharge any employee or expel, suspend or otherwise punish any student for any violation of its rules, even though the violation is unlawful under this chapter or is otherwise an offense.
G. This section may be enforced by any peace officer in this state wherever and whenever a violation occurs.
H. Restitution under §§8-341, 8-345 and 13-603 applies to any financial loss that is suffered by a person or educational institution as a result of a violation of this section.
I. Interference with or disruption of an educational institution pursuant to subsection A, paragraph 1 of this section is a class 6 felony. Interference with or disruption of an educational institution pursuant to subsection A, paragraph 2 or 3 of this section is a class 1 misdemeanor.
J. For the purposes of this section:
1. "Educational institution" means, except as otherwise provided, any university, college, community college, high school or common school in this state.
2. "Governing board" means the body, whether appointed or elected, that has responsibility for the maintenance and government of an educational institution.
3. "Interference with or disruption of" includes any act that might reasonably lead to the evacuation or closure of any property of the educational institution or the postponement, cancellation or suspension of any class or other school activity. For the purposes of this paragraph, an actual evacuation, closure, postponement, cancellation or suspension is not required for the act to be considered an interference or disruption.
4. "Property of an educational institution" means all land, buildings and other facilities that are owned, operated or controlled by the governing board of an educational institution and that are devoted to educational purposes.

CHAPTER 31 · WEAPONS AND EXPLOSIVES

13-3101. Definitions

A. In this chapter, unless the context otherwise requires:

1. "Deadly weapon" means anything that is designed for lethal use. The term includes a firearm.

2. "Deface" means to remove, alter or destroy the manufacturer's serial number.

3. "Explosive" means any dynamite, nitroglycerine, black powder, or other similar explosive material, including plastic explosives. Explosive does not include ammunition or ammunition components such as primers, percussion caps, smokeless powder, black powder and black powder substitutes used for hand loading purposes.

4. "Firearm" means any loaded or unloaded handgun, pistol, revolver, rifle, shotgun or other weapon that will expel, is designed to expel or may readily be converted to expel a projectile by the action of an explosive. Firearm does not include a firearm in permanently inoperable condition.

5. "Improvised explosive device" means a device that incorporates explosives or destructive, lethal, noxious, pyrotechnic or incendiary chemicals and that is designed to destroy, disfigure, terrify or harass.

6. "Occupied structure" means any building, object, vehicle, watercraft, aircraft or place with sides and a floor that is separately securable from any other structure attached to it, that is used for lodging, business, transportation, recreation or storage and in which one or more human beings either are or are likely to be present or so near as to be in equivalent danger at the time the discharge of a firearm occurs. Occupied structure includes any dwelling house, whether occupied, unoccupied or vacant.

7. "Prohibited possessor" means any person:

(a) Who has been found to constitute a danger to self or to others or to be persistently or acutely disabled or gravely disabled pursuant to court order under §36-540, and whose right to possess a firearm has not been restored pursuant to §13-924.

(b) Who has been convicted within or without this state of a felony or who has been adjudicated delinquent for a felony and whose civil right to possess or carry a gun or firearm has not been restored.

(c) Who is at the time of possession serving a term of imprisonment in any correctional or detention facility.

(d) Who is at the time of possession serving a term of probation pursuant to a conviction for a domestic violence offense as defined in §13-3601 or a felony offense, parole, community supervision, work furlough, home arrest or release on any other basis or who is serving a term of probation or parole pursuant to the interstate compact under title 31, chapter 3, article 4.1.

(e) Who is an undocumented alien or a nonimmigrant alien traveling with or without documentation in this state for business or pleasure or who is studying in this state and who maintains a foreign residence abroad. This subdivision does not apply to:

(i) Nonimmigrant aliens who possess a valid hunting license or permit that is lawfully issued by a state in the United States.

(ii) Nonimmigrant aliens who enter the United States to participate in a competitive target shooting event or to display firearms at a sports or hunting trade show that is sponsored by a national, state or local firearms trade organization devoted to the competitive use or other sporting use of firearms.

(iii) Certain diplomats.

(iv) Officials of foreign governments or distinguished foreign visitors who are designated by the United States department of state.

(v) Persons who have received a waiver from the United States attorney general.

8. "Prohibited weapon":

(a) Includes the following:

(i) An item that is a bomb, grenade, rocket having a propellant charge of more than four ounces or mine and that is explosive, incendiary or poison gas.

(ii) A device that is designed, made or adapted to muffle the report of a firearm.

(iii) A firearm that is capable of shooting more than one shot automatically, without manual reloading, by a single function of the trigger.

(iv) A rifle with a barrel length of less than sixteen inches, or shotgun with a barrel length of less than eighteen inches, or any firearm that is made from a rifle or shotgun and that, as modified, has an overall length of less than twenty-six inches.

(v) An instrument, including a nunchaku, that consists of two or more sticks, clubs, bars or rods to be used as handles, connected by a rope, cord, wire or chain, in the design of a weapon used in connection with the practice of a system of self-defense.

(vi) A breakable container that contains a flammable liquid with a flash point of one hundred fifty degrees Fahrenheit or less and that has a wick or similar device capable of being ignited.

(vii) A chemical or combination of chemicals, compounds or materials, including dry ice, that is possessed or manufactured for the purpose of generating a gas to cause a mechanical failure, rupture or bursting or an explosion or detonation of the chemical or combination of chemicals, compounds or materials.

(viii) An improvised explosive device.

(ix) Any combination of parts or materials that is designed and intended for use in making or converting a device into an item set forth in item (i), (vi) or (viii) of this subdivision.

(b) Does not include:

(i) Any fireworks that are imported, distributed or used in compliance with state laws or local ordinances.

(ii) Any propellant, propellant actuated devices or propellant actuated industrial tools that are manufactured, imported or distributed for their intended purposes.

(iii) A device that is commercially manufactured primarily for the purpose of illumination.

9. "Trafficking" means to sell, transfer, distribute, dispense or otherwise dispose of a weapon or explosive to another person, or to buy, receive, possess or obtain control of a weapon or explosive, with the intent to sell, transfer, distribute, dispense or otherwise dispose of the weapon or explosive to another person.

B. The items set forth in subsection A, paragraph 8, subdivision (a), items (i), (ii), (iii) and (iv) of this section do not include any firearms or devices that are registered in the national firearms registry and transfer records of the United States treasury department or any firearm that has been classified as a curio or relic by the United States treasury department.

13-3102. Misconduct involving weapons; defenses; classification; definitions

A. A person commits misconduct involving weapons by knowingly:

1. Carrying a deadly weapon except a pocket knife concealed on his person or within his immediate control in or on a means of transportation:

(a) In the furtherance of a serious offense as defined in §13-706, a violent crime as defined in §13-901.03 or any other felony offense; or

(b) When contacted by a law enforcement officer and failing to accurately answer the officer if the officer asks whether the person is carrying a concealed deadly weapon; or

2. Carrying a deadly weapon except a pocket knife concealed on his person or concealed within his immediate control in or on a means of transportation if the person is under twenty-one years of age; or

3. Manufacturing, possessing, transporting, selling or transferring a prohibited weapon, except that if the violation involves dry ice, a person commits misconduct involving weapons by knowingly possessing the dry ice with the intent to cause injury to or death of another person or to cause damage to the property of another person; or

4. Possessing a deadly weapon or prohibited weapon if such person is a prohibited possessor; or

5. Selling or transferring a deadly weapon to a prohibited possessor; or

6. Defacing a deadly weapon; or

7. Possessing a defaced deadly weapon knowing the deadly weapon was defaced; or

8. Using or possessing a deadly weapon during the commission of any felony offense included in chapter 34 of this title; or

9. Discharging a firearm at an occupied structure in order to assist, promote or further the interests of a criminal street gang, a criminal syndicate or a racketeering enterprise; or

10. Unless specifically authorized by law, entering any public establishment or attending any public event and carrying a deadly weapon on his person after a reasonable request by the operator of the establishment or the sponsor of the event or the sponsor's agent to remove his weapon and place it in the custody of the operator of the establishment or the sponsor of the event for temporary and secure storage of the weapon pursuant to §13-3102.01; or

11. Unless specifically authorized by law, entering an election polling place on the day of any election carrying a deadly weapon; or

12. Possessing a deadly weapon on school grounds; or

13. Unless specifically authorized by law, entering a nuclear or hydroelectric generating station carrying a deadly weapon on his person or within the immediate control of any person; or

14. Supplying, selling or giving possession or control of a firearm to another person if the person knows or has reason to know that the other person would use the firearm in the commission of any felony; or

15. Using, possessing or exercising control over a deadly weapon in furtherance of any act of terrorism as defined in §13-2301 or possessing or exercising control over a deadly weapon knowing or having reason to know that it will be used to facilitate any act of terrorism as defined in §13-2301; or

16. Trafficking in weapons or explosives for financial gain in order to assist, promote or further the interests of a criminal street gang, a criminal syndicate or a racketeering enterprise.

B. Subsection A, paragraph 2 of this section shall not apply to:

1. A person in his dwelling, on his business premises or on real property owned or leased by that person or that person's parent, grandparent or legal guardian.

2. A member of the sheriff's volunteer posse or reserve organization who has received and passed firearms training that is approved by the Arizona peace officer standards and training board and who is authorized by the sheriff to carry a concealed weapon pursuant to §11-441.

3. A firearm that is carried in:

(a) A manner where any portion of the firearm or holster in which the firearm is carried is visible.

(b) A holster that is wholly or partially visible.

(c) A scabbard or case designed for carrying weapons that is wholly or partially visible.

(d) Luggage.

(e) A case, holster, scabbard, pack or luggage that is carried within a means of transportation or within a storage compartment, map pocket, trunk or glove compartment of a means of transportation.

C. Subsection A, paragraphs 2, 3, 7, 10, 11, 12 and 13 of this section shall not apply to:

1. A peace officer or any person summoned by any peace officer to assist and while actually assisting in the performance of official duties; or

2. A member of the military forces of the United States or of any state of the United States in the performance of official duties; or

3. A warden, deputy warden, community correctional officer, detention officer, special investigator or correctional officer of the state department of corrections or the department of juvenile corrections; or

4. A person specifically licensed, authorized or permitted pursuant to a statute of this state or of the United States.

D. Subsection A, paragraph 10 of this section does not apply to an elected or appointed judicial officer in the court facility where the judicial officer works if the judicial officer has demonstrated competence with a firearm as prescribed in §13-3112, subsection N, except that the judicial officer shall comply with any rule or policy adopted by the presiding judge of the superior court while in the court facility. For the purposes of this subsection, appointed judicial officer does not include a hearing officer or a judicial officer pro-tempore that is not a full-time officer.

E. Subsection A, paragraphs 3 and 7 of this section shall not apply to:

1. The possessing, transporting, selling or transferring of weapons by a museum as a part of its collection or an educational institution for educational purposes or by an authorized employee of such museum or institution, if:

(a) Such museum or institution is operated by the United States or this state or a political subdivision of this state, or by an organization described in 26 United States Code §170(c) as a recipient of a charitable contribution; and

212   The ARIZONA Gun Owner's Guide

(b) Reasonable precautions are taken with respect to theft or misuse of such material.

2. The regular and lawful transporting as merchandise; or

3. Acquisition by a person by operation of law such as by gift, devise or descent or in a fiduciary capacity as a recipient of the property or former property of an insolvent, incapacitated or deceased person.

F. Subsection A, paragraph 3 of this section shall not apply to the merchandise of an authorized manufacturer of or dealer in prohibited weapons, when such material is intended to be manufactured, possessed, transported, sold or transferred solely for or to a dealer, a regularly constituted or appointed state, county or municipal police department or police officer, a detention facility, the military service of this or another state or the United States, a museum or educational institution or a person specifically licensed or permitted pursuant to federal or state law.

G. Subsection A, paragraph 10 of this section shall not apply to shooting ranges or shooting events, hunting areas or similar locations or activities.

H. Subsection A, paragraph 3 of this section shall not apply to a weapon described in §13-3101, subsection A, paragraph 8, subdivision (a), item (v), if such weapon is possessed for the purposes of preparing for, conducting or participating in lawful exhibitions, demonstrations, contests or athletic events involving the use of such weapon. Subsection A, paragraph 12 of this section shall not apply to a weapon if such weapon is possessed for the purposes of preparing for, conducting or participating in hunter or firearm safety courses.

I. Subsection A, paragraph 12 of this section shall not apply to the possession of a:

1. Firearm that is not loaded and that is carried within a means of transportation under the control of an adult provided that if the adult leaves the means of transportation the firearm shall not be visible from the outside of the means of transportation and the means of transportation shall be locked.

2. Firearm for use on the school grounds in a program approved by a school.

3. Firearm by a person who possesses a certificate of firearms proficiency pursuant to §13-3112, subsection T and who is authorized to carry a concealed firearm pursuant to the law enforcement officers safety act of 2004 (P.L. 108-277; 118 Stat. 865; 18 United States Code §§926B and 926C).

J. Subsection A, paragraphs 2, 3, 7 and 13 of this section shall not apply to commercial nuclear generating station armed nuclear security guards during the performance of official duties or during any security training exercises sponsored by the commercial nuclear generating station or local, state or federal authorities.

K. The operator of the establishment or the sponsor of the event or the employee of the operator or sponsor or the agent of the sponsor, including a public entity or public employee, is not liable for acts or omissions pursuant to subsection A, paragraph 10 of this section unless the operator, sponsor, employee or agent intended to cause injury or was grossly negligent.

L. If a law enforcement officer contacts a person who is in possession of a firearm, the law enforcement officer may take temporary custody of the firearm for the duration of that contact.

M. Misconduct involving weapons under subsection A, paragraph 15 of this section is a class 2 felony. Misconduct involving weapons under subsection A, paragraph 9 ,14 or 16 of this section is a class 3 felony. Misconduct involving weapons under subsection A, paragraph 3, 4, 8 or 13 of this section is a class 4 felony. Misconduct involving weapons under subsection A, paragraph 12 of this section is a class 1 misdemeanor unless the violation occurs in connection with conduct that violates §13-2308, subsection A, paragraph 5, §13-2312, subsection C, §13-3409 or §13-3411, in which case the offense is a class 6 felony. Misconduct involving weapons under subsection A, paragraph 1, subdivision (a) of this section or subsection A, paragraph 5, 6 or 7 of this section is a class 6 felony. Misconduct involving weapons under subsection A, paragraph 1, subdivision (b) of this section or subsection A, paragraph 10 or 11 of this section is a class 1 misdemeanor. Misconduct involving weapons under subsection A, paragraph 2 of this section is a class 3 misdemeanor.

N. For the purposes of this section:

1. "Contacted by a law enforcement officer" means a lawful traffic or criminal investigation, arrest or detention or an investigatory stop by a law enforcement officer that is based on reasonable suspicion that an offense has been or is about to be committed.

2. "Public establishment" means a structure, vehicle or craft that is owned, leased or operated by this state or a political subdivision of this state.

3. "Public event" means a specifically named or sponsored event of limited duration that is either conducted by a public entity or conducted by a private entity with a permit or license granted by a public entity. Public event does not include an unsponsored gathering of people in a public place.

4. "School" means a public or nonpublic kindergarten program, common school or high school.

5. "School grounds" means in, or on the grounds of, a school.

13-3102.01. Storage of deadly weapons; definitions

A. If an operator of a public establishment or a sponsor of a public event requests that a person carrying a deadly weapon remove the weapon, the operator or sponsor shall provide temporary and secure storage. The storage shall be readily accessible on entry into the establishment or event and allow for the immediate retrieval of the weapon on exit from the establishment or event.

B. This section does not apply to the licensed premises of any public establishment or public event with a license issued pursuant to title 4.

C. The operator of the establishment or the sponsor of the event or the employee of the operator or sponsor or the agent of the sponsor, including a public entity or public employee, is not liable for acts or omissions pursuant to this section unless the operator, sponsor, employee or agent intended to cause injury or was grossly negligent.

D. For the purposes of this section, "public establishment" and "public event" have the same meanings prescribed in §13-3102.

13-3103. Misconduct involving explosives; classification

A. A person commits misconduct involving explosives by knowingly:

1. Keeping or storing a greater quantity than fifty pounds of explosives in or upon any building or premises within a distance of one-half mile of the exterior limits of a city or town, except in vessels, railroad cars or vehicles receiving and keeping

them in the course of and for the purpose of transportation; or
2. Keeping or storing percussion caps or any blasting powder within two hundred feet of a building or premises where explosives are kept or stored; or
3. Selling, transporting or possessing explosives without having plainly marked, in a conspicuous place on the box or package containing the explosive, its name, explosive character and date of manufacture.
4. This section shall not apply to any person who legally keeps, stores or transports explosives, percussion caps or blasting powder as a part of their business.
B. Misconduct involving explosives is a class 1 misdemeanor.

13-3104. Depositing explosives; classification
A. A person commits depositing explosives if with the intent to physically endanger, injure, intimidate or terrify any person, such person knowingly deposits any explosive on, in or near any vehicle, building or place where persons inhabit, frequent or assemble.
B. Depositing explosives is a class 4 felony.

13-3105. Forfeiture of weapons and explosives
A. On the conviction of any person for a violation of any felony in this state in which a deadly weapon, dangerous instrument or explosive was used, displayed or unlawfully possessed by the person, the court shall order the article forfeited and sold within one year after its forfeiture to any business that is authorized to receive and dispose of the article under federal and state law and that shall sell the article to the public according to federal and state law, unless the article is otherwise prohibited from being sold under federal and state law, in which case it shall be destroyed or otherwise properly disposed.
B. On the conviction of any person for a violation of §13-2904, subsection A, paragraph 6 or §13-3102, subsection A, paragraph 1 or 8, the court may order the forfeiture of the deadly weapon or dangerous instrument involved in the offense.
C. If at any time the court finds pursuant to rule 11 of the Arizona rules of criminal procedure that a person who is charged with a violation of this title is incompetent, the court shall order that any deadly weapon, dangerous instrument or explosive used, displayed or unlawfully possessed by the person during the commission of the alleged offense be forfeited and sold within one year after its forfeiture to any business that is authorized to receive and dispose of the article under federal and state law and that shall sell the article to the public according to federal and state law, unless the article is otherwise prohibited from being sold under federal and state law, in which case it shall be destroyed or otherwise properly disposed.

13-3106. Firearm purchase in other states
A person residing in this state, or a corporation or other business entity maintaining a place of business in this state, may purchase or otherwise obtain firearms anywhere in the United States if such purchase or acquisition fully complies with the laws of this state and the state in which the purchase or acquisition is made and the purchaser and seller, prior to the sale or delivery for sale, have complied with all the requirements of the federal gun control act of 1968, public law 90-618, §922, subsection (c) and the code of federal regulations, volume 26, §178.96, subsection (c).

13-3107. Unlawful discharge of firearms; exceptions; classification; definitions
A. A person who with criminal negligence discharges a firearm within or into the limits of any municipality is guilty of a class 6 felony.
B. Notwithstanding the fact that the offense involves the discharge of a deadly weapon, unless a dangerous offense is alleged and proven pursuant to §13-704, subsection L, §13-604 applies to this offense.
C. This section does not apply if the firearm is discharged:
1. As allowed pursuant to chapter 4 of this title.
2. On a properly supervised range.
3. To lawfully take wildlife during an open season established by the Arizona game and fish commission and subject to the limitations prescribed by title 17 and Arizona game and fish commission rules and orders. This paragraph does not prevent a city, town or county from adopting an ordinance or rule restricting the discharge of a firearm within one-fourth mile of an occupied structure without the consent of the owner or occupant of the structure. For the purposes of this paragraph:
(a) "Occupied structure" means any building in which, at the time of the firearm's discharge, a reasonable person from the location where a firearm is discharged would expect a person to be present.
(b) "Take" has the same meaning prescribed in §17-101.
4. For the control of nuisance wildlife by permit from the Arizona game and fish department or the United States fish and wildlife service.
5. By special permit of the chief of police of the municipality.
6. As required by an animal control officer in the performance of duties as specified in §9-499.04.
7. Using blanks.
8. More than one mile from any occupied structure as defined in §13-3101.
9. In self-defense or defense of another person against an animal attack if a reasonable person would believe that deadly physical force against the animal is immediately necessary and reasonable under the circumstances to protect oneself or the other person.
D. For the purposes of this section:
1. "Municipality" means any city or town and includes any property that is fully enclosed within the city or town.
2. "Properly supervised range" means a range that is any of the following:
(a) Operated by a club affiliated with the national rifle association of America, the amateur trapshooting association, the national skeet association or any other nationally recognized shooting organization, or by any public or private school.
(b) Approved by any agency of the federal government, this state or a county or city within which the range is located.
(c) Operated with adult supervision for shooting air or carbon dioxide gas operated guns, or for shooting in underground ranges on private or public property.

13-3108. Firearms regulated by state; state preemption; violation; classification
A. Except as provided in subsection G of this section, a political subdivision of this state shall not enact any ordinance, rule

or tax relating to the transportation, possession, carrying, sale, transfer, purchase, acquisition, gift, devise, storage, licensing, registration, discharge or use of firearms or ammunition or any firearm or ammunition components or related accessories in this state.

B. A political subdivision of this state shall not require the licensing or registration of firearms or ammunition or any firearm or ammunition components or related accessories or prohibit the ownership, purchase, sale or transfer of firearms or ammunition or any firearm or ammunition components, or related accessories.

C. A political subdivision of this state shall not require or maintain a record in any form, whether permanent or temporary, including a list, log or database, of any of the following:

1. Any identifying information of a person who leaves a weapon in temporary storage at any public establishment or public event, except that the operator of the establishment or the sponsor of the event may require that a person provide a government issued identification or a reasonable copy of a government issued identification for the purpose of establishing ownership of the weapon. The operator or sponsor shall store any provided identification with the weapon and shall return the identification to the person when the weapon is retrieved. The operator or sponsor shall not retain records or copies of any identification provided pursuant to this paragraph after the weapon is retrieved.

2. Except in the course of a law enforcement investigation, any identifying information of a person who purchases, sells or transfers a firearm, unless the transaction involves a federally licensed firearms dealer.

3. The description, including the serial number, of a weapon that is left in temporary storage at any public establishment or public event.

D. A political subdivision of this state shall not enact any rule or ordinance that relates to firearms and is more prohibitive than or that has a penalty that is greater than any state law penalty. A political subdivision's rule or ordinance that relates to firearms and that is inconsistent with or more restrictive than state law, whether enacted before or after July 29, 2010, is null and void.

E. A political subdivision of this state shall not enact any ordinance, rule or regulation limiting the lawful taking of wildlife during an open season established by the Arizona game and fish commission unless the ordinance, rule or regulation is consistent with title 17 and rules and orders adopted by the Arizona game and fish commission. This subsection does not prevent a political subdivision from adopting an ordinance or rule restricting the discharge of a firearm within one-fourth mile of an occupied structure without the consent of the owner or occupant of the structure. For the purposes of this subsection:

1. "Occupied structure" means any building in which, at the time of the firearm's discharge, a reasonable person from the location where a firearm is discharged would expect a person to be present.

2. "Take" has the same meaning prescribed in §17-101.

F. This state, any agency or political subdivision of this state and any law enforcement agency in this state shall not facilitate the destruction of a firearm or purchase or otherwise acquire a firearm for the purpose of destroying the firearm except as authorized by §13-3105 or 17-240.

G. This section does not prohibit a political subdivision of this state from enacting and enforcing any ordinance or rule pursuant to state law or relating to any of the following:

1. Imposing any privilege or use tax on the retail sale, lease or rental of, or the gross proceeds or gross income from the sale, lease or rental of, firearms or ammunition or any firearm or ammunition components at a rate that applies generally to other items of tangible personal property.

2. Prohibiting a minor who is unaccompanied by a parent, grandparent or guardian or a certified hunter safety instructor or certified firearms safety instructor acting with the consent of the minor's parent, grandparent or guardian from knowingly possessing or carrying on the minor's person, within the minor's immediate control or in or on a means of transportation a firearm in any place that is open to the public or on any street or highway or on any private property except private property that is owned or leased by the minor or the minor's parent, grandparent or guardian. Any ordinance or rule that is adopted pursuant to this paragraph shall not apply to a minor who is fourteen, fifteen, sixteen or seventeen years of age and who is engaged in any of the following:

(a) Lawful hunting or shooting events or marksmanship practice at established ranges or other areas where the discharge of a firearm is not prohibited.

(b) Lawful transportation of an unloaded firearm for the purpose of lawful hunting.

(c) Lawful transportation of an unloaded firearm for the purpose of attending shooting events or marksmanship practice at established ranges or other areas where the discharge of a firearm is not prohibited.

(d) Any activity that is related to the production of crops, livestock, poultry, livestock products, poultry products or ratites or storage of agricultural commodities.

3. The regulation of commercial land and structures, including a business relating to firearms or ammunition or their components or a commercial shooting range in the same manner as other commercial businesses. Notwithstanding any other law, this paragraph does not:

(a) authorize a political subdivision to regulate the sale or transfer of firearms on property it owns, leases, operates or controls in a manner that is different than or inconsistent with state law. For the purposes of this subdivision, a use permit or other contract that provides for the use of property owned, leased, operated or controlled by a political subdivision shall not be considered a sale, conveyance or disposition of property.

(b) Authorize a political subdivision through a zoning ordinance to prohibit or otherwise regulate the otherwise lawful discharge of a firearm or maintenance or improvements directly related to the discharge, on a private lot or parcel of land that is not open to the public on a commercial or membership basis.

(c) Authorize a political subdivision to regulate the otherwise lawful discharge of a firearm or maintenance or improvements directly related to the discharge, on land that is used for agriculture or other non-commercial purposes.

4. Regulating employees or independent contractors of the political subdivision who are acting within the course and scope of their employment or contract.

5. Limiting or prohibiting the discharge of firearms in parks and preserves except:

(a) As allowed pursuant to chapter 4 of this title.

(b) On a properly supervised range as defined in §13-3107.

(c) In an area approved as a hunting area by the Arizona game and fish department. Any such area may be closed when deemed unsafe by the director of the Arizona game and fish department.

(d) To control nuisance wildlife by permit from the Arizona game and fish department or the United States fish and wildlife service.

(e) By special permit of the chief law enforcement officer of the political subdivision.

(f) As required by an animal control officer in performing duties specified in §9-499.04 and title 11, chapter 7, article 6.

(g) In self-defense or defense of another person against an animal attack if a reasonable person would believe that deadly physical force against the animal is immediately necessary and reasonable under the circumstances to protect oneself or the other person.

H. A violation of any ordinance established pursuant to subsection F, paragraph 5 of this section is a class 2 misdemeanor unless the political subdivision designates a lesser classification by ordinance.

I. For the purposes of this section, "political subdivision" includes a political subdivision acting in any capacity, including under police power, in a proprietary capacity or otherwise.

13-3109. Sale or gift of firearm to minor; classification

A. Except as provided in subsection C of this section, a person who sells or gives to a minor, without written consent of the minor's parent or legal guardian, a firearm, ammunition or a toy pistol by which dangerous and explosive substances may be discharged is guilty of a class 6 felony.

B. Nothing in this section shall be construed to require reporting sales of firearms, nor shall registration of firearms or firearms sales be required.

C. The temporary transfer of firearms and ammunition by firearms safety instructors, hunter safety instructors, competition coaches or their assistants shall be allowed if the minor's parent or guardian has given consent for the minor to participate in activities such as firearms or hunting safety courses, firearms competition or training. With the consent of the minor's parent or guardian, the temporary transfer of firearms and ammunition by an adult accompanying minors engaged in hunting or formal or informal target shooting activities shall be allowed for those purposes.

13-3110. Misconduct involving simulated explosive devices; classification; definition

A. A person commits misconduct involving simulated explosive devices by intentionally giving or sending to another person or placing in a private or public place a simulated explosive device with the intent to terrify, intimidate, threaten or harass.

B. The placing or sending of a simulated explosive device without written notice attached to the device in a conspicuous place that the device has been rendered inert and is possessed for the purpose of curio or relic collection, display or other similar purpose is prima facie evidence of intent to terrify, intimidate, threaten or harass.

C. Misconduct involving simulated explosive devices is a class 5 felony.

D. For the purposes of this section "simulated explosive device" means a simulation of a prohibited weapon described in §13-3101, subsection A, paragraph 8, subdivision (a), item (i), (vi) or (viii) that a reasonable person would believe is such a prohibited weapon.

13-3111. Minors prohibited from carrying or possessing firearms; exceptions; seizure and forfeiture; penalties; classification

A. Except as provided in subsection B, an unemancipated person who is under eighteen years of age and who is unaccompanied by a parent, grandparent or guardian, or a certified hunter safety instructor or certified firearms safety instructor acting with the consent of the unemancipated person's parent or guardian, shall not knowingly carry or possess on his person, within his immediate control, or in or on a means of transportation a firearm in any place that is open to the public or on any street or highway or on any private property except private property owned or leased by the minor or the minor's parent, grandparent or guardian.

B. This section does not apply to a person who is fourteen, fifteen, sixteen or seventeen years of age and who is any of the following:

1. Engaged in lawful hunting or shooting events or marksmanship practice at established ranges or other areas where the discharge of a firearm is not prohibited.

2. Engaged in lawful transportation of an unloaded firearm for the purpose of lawful hunting.

3. Engaged in lawful transportation of an unloaded firearm between the hours of 5:00 a.m. and 10:00 p.m. for the purpose of shooting events or marksmanship practice at established ranges or other areas where the discharge of a firearm is not prohibited.

4. Engaged in activities requiring the use of a firearm that are related to the production of crops, livestock, poultry, livestock products, poultry products, or ratites or in the production or storage of agricultural commodities.

C. If the minor is not exempt under subsection B and is in possession of a firearm, a peace officer shall seize the firearm at the time the violation occurs.

D. In addition to any other penalty provided by law, a person who violates subsection A shall be subject to the following penalties:

1. If adjudicated a delinquent juvenile for an offense involving an unloaded firearm, a fine of not more than two hundred fifty dollars, and the court may order the suspension or revocation of the person's driver license until the person reaches eighteen years of age. If the person does not have a driver license at the time of the adjudication, the court may direct that the department of transportation not issue a driver license to the person until the person reaches eighteen years of age.

2. If adjudicated a delinquent juvenile for an offense involving a loaded firearm, a fine of not more than five hundred dollars, and the court may order the suspension or revocation of the person's driver license until the person reaches eighteen years of age. If the person does not have a driver license at the time of the adjudication, the court may direct that the department of transportation not issue a driver license to the person until the person reaches eighteen years of age.

3. If adjudicated a delinquent juvenile for an offense involving a loaded or unloaded firearm, if the person possessed the firearm while the person was the driver or an occupant of a motor vehicle, a fine of not more than five hundred dollars and the court shall order the suspension or revocation of the person's driver license until the person reaches eighteen years of age. If the person does not have a driver license at the time of adjudication, the court shall direct that the department of transportation not issue a driver license to the person until the person reaches eighteen years of age. If the court finds that no other means of transportation is available, the driving privileges of the child may be restricted to travel between the child's home, school and place of employment during specified periods of time according to the child's school and employment schedule.

E. Firearms seized pursuant to subsection C shall be held by the law enforcement agency responsible for the seizure until the charges have been adjudicated or disposed of otherwise or the person is convicted. Upon adjudication or conviction of a person for a violation of this section, the court shall order the firearm forfeited. However, the law enforcement agency shall return the firearm to the lawful owner if the identity of that person is known.

F. If the court finds that the parent or guardian of a minor found responsible for violating this section knew or reasonably should have known of the minor's unlawful conduct and made no effort to prohibit it, the parent or guardian is jointly and severally responsible for any fine imposed pursuant to this section or for any civil actual damages resulting from the unlawful use of the firearm by the minor.

G. This section is supplemental to any other law imposing a criminal penalty for the use or exhibition of a deadly weapon. A minor who violates this section may be prosecuted and adjudicated delinquent for any other criminal conduct involving the use or exhibition of the deadly weapon.

H. A person who violates subsection A is guilty of a class 6 felony.

13-3112. Concealed weapons; qualification; application; permit to carry; certificate of firearms proficiency; training program; program instructors; report; applicability; violation; classification

A. The department of public safety shall issue a permit to carry a concealed weapon to a person who is qualified under this section. The person shall carry the permit at all times when the person is in actual possession of the concealed weapon and is required by §4-229 or 4-244 to carry the permit. If the person is in actual possession of the concealed weapon and is required by §4-229 or 4-244 to carry the permit, the person shall present the permit for inspection to any law enforcement officer on request.

B. The permit of a person who is arrested or indicted for an offense that would make the person unqualified under §13-3101, subsection A, paragraph 7 or this section shall be immediately suspended and seized. The permit of a person who becomes unqualified on conviction of that offense shall be revoked. The permit shall be restored on presentation of documentation from the court if the permittee is found not guilty or the charges are dismissed. The permit shall be restored on presentation of documentation from the county attorney that the charges against the permittee were dropped or dismissed.

C. A permittee who carries a concealed weapon, who is required by §4-229 or 4-244 to carry a permit and who fails to present the permit for inspection on the request of a law enforcement officer commits a violation of this subsection and is subject to a civil penalty of not more than three hundred dollars. The department of public safety shall be notified of all violations of this subsection and shall immediately suspend the permit. A permittee shall not be convicted of a violation of this subsection if the permittee produces to the court a legible permit that is issued to the permittee and that was valid at the time the permittee failed to present the permit for inspection.

D. A law enforcement officer shall not confiscate or forfeit a weapon that is otherwise lawfully possessed by a permittee whose permit is suspended pursuant to subsection C of this section, except that a law enforcement officer may take temporary custody of a firearm during an investigatory stop of the permittee.

E. The department of public safety shall issue a permit to an applicant who meets all of the following conditions:

1. Is a resident of this state or a United States citizen.

2. Is twenty-one years of age or older or is at least nineteen years of age and provides evidence of current military service or proof of honorable discharge or general discharge under honorable conditions from the United States armed forces, United States armed forces reserve or a state national guard.

3. Is not under indictment for and has not been convicted in any jurisdiction of a felony unless that conviction has been expunged, set aside or vacated or the applicant's rights have been restored and the applicant is currently not a prohibited possessor under state or federal law.

4. Does not suffer from mental illness and has not been adjudicated mentally incompetent or committed to a mental institution.

5. Is not unlawfully present in the United States.

6. Has ever demonstrated competence with a firearm as prescribed by subsection N of this section and provides adequate documentation that the person has satisfactorily completed a training program or demonstrated competence with a firearm in any state or political subdivision in the United States. For the purposes of this paragraph, "adequate documentation" means:

(a) A current or expired permit issued by the department of public safety pursuant to this section.

(b) An original or copy of a certificate, card or document that shows the applicant has ever completed any course or class prescribed by subsection N of this section or an affidavit from the instructor, school, club or organization that conducted or taught the course or class attesting to the applicant's completion of the course or class.

(c) An original or a copy of a United States department of defense form 214 (DD-214) indicating an honorable discharge or general discharge under honorable conditions, a certificate of completion of basic training or any other document demonstrating proof of the applicant's current or former service in the United States armed forces as prescribed by subsection N, paragraph 5 of this section.

(d) An original or a copy of a concealed weapon, firearm or handgun permit or a license as prescribed by subsection N, paragraph 6 of this section.

F. The application shall be completed on a form prescribed by the department of public safety. The form shall not require the applicant to disclose the type of firearm for which a permit is sought. The applicant shall attest under penalty of perjury that all of the statements made by the applicant are true, that the applicant has been furnished a copy of this chapter and chapter 4 of this title and that the applicant is knowledgeable about the provisions contained in those chapters. The applicant shall submit the application to the department with any documentation prescribed by subsection E of this section, two sets of fingerprints and a reasonable fee determined by the director of the department.

G. On receipt of a concealed weapon permit application, the department of public safety shall conduct a check of the applicant's criminal history record pursuant to §41-1750. The department of public safety may exchange fingerprint card information with the federal bureau of investigation for federal criminal history record checks.

H. The department of public safety shall complete all of the required qualification checks within sixty days after receipt of the application and shall issue a permit within fifteen working days after completing the qualification checks if the applicant meets all of the conditions specified in subsection E of this section. If a permit is denied, the department of public safety shall notify the applicant in writing within fifteen working days after the completion of all of the required qualification checks and shall state the reasons why the application was denied. On receipt of the notification of the denial, the applicant has twenty days to submit any additional documentation to the department. On receipt of the additional documentation, the department shall reconsider its decision and inform the applicant within twenty days of the result of the reconsideration. If denied, the applicant shall be informed that the applicant may request a hearing pursuant to title 41, chapter 6, article 10. For the purposes of this subsection, "receipt of the application" means the first day that the department has physical control of the application and that is presumed to be on the date of delivery as evidenced by proof of delivery by the United States postal service or a written receipt, which shall be provided by the department on request of the applicant.

I. On issuance, a permit is valid for five years, except a permit that is held by a member of the United States armed forces, including a member of the Arizona national guard or a member of the reserves of any military establishment of the United States, who is on federal active duty and who is deployed overseas shall be extended until ninety days after the end of the member's overseas deployment.

J. The department of public safety shall maintain a computerized permit record system that is accessible to criminal justice agencies for the purpose of confirming the permit status of any person who is contacted by a law enforcement officer and who claims to hold a valid permit issued by this state. This information and any other records that are maintained regarding applicants, permit holders or instructors shall not be available to any other person or entity except on an order from a state or federal court. A criminal justice agency shall not use the computerized permit record system to conduct inquiries on whether a person is a concealed weapons permit holder unless the criminal justice agency has reasonable suspicion to believe the person is carrying a concealed weapon and the person is subject to a lawful criminal investigation, arrest, detention or an investigatory stop.

K. A permit issued pursuant to this section is renewable every five years. Before a permit may be renewed, a criminal history records check shall be conducted pursuant to §41-1750 within sixty days after receipt of the application for renewal. For the purposes of permit renewal, the permit holder is not required to submit additional fingerprints.

L. Applications for renewal shall be accompanied by a fee determined by the director of the department of public safety.

M. The department of public safety shall suspend or revoke a permit issued under this section if the permit holder becomes ineligible pursuant to subsection E of this section. The department of public safety shall notify the permit holder in writing within fifteen working days after the revocation or suspension and shall state the reasons for the revocation or suspension.

N. An applicant shall demonstrate competence with a firearm through any of the following:

1. Completion of any firearms safety or training course or class that is available to the general public, that is offered by a law enforcement agency, a junior college, a college or a private or public institution, academy, organization or firearms training school and that is approved by the department of public safety or that uses instructors who are certified by the national rifle association.

2. Completion of any hunter education or hunter safety course approved by the Arizona game and fish department or a similar agency of another state.

3. Completion of any national rifle association firearms safety or training course.

4. Completion of any law enforcement firearms safety or training course or class that is offered for security guards, investigators, special deputies or other divisions or subdivisions of law enforcement or security enforcement and that is approved by the department of public safety.

5. Evidence of current military service or proof of honorable discharge or general discharge under honorable conditions from the United States armed forces.

6. A valid current or expired concealed weapon, firearm or handgun permit or license that is issued by another state or a political subdivision of another state and that has a training or testing requirement for initial issuance.

7. Completion of any governmental police agency firearms training course and qualification to carry a firearm in the course of normal police duties.

8. Completion of any other firearms safety or training course or class that is conducted by a department of public safety approved or national rifle association certified firearms instructor.

O. The department of public safety shall maintain information comparing the number of permits requested, the number of permits issued and the number of permits denied. The department shall annually report this information to the governor and the legislature.

P. The director of the department of public safety shall adopt rules for the purpose of implementing and administering this section including fees relating to permits that are issued pursuant to this section.

Q. This state and any political subdivision of this state shall recognize a concealed weapon, firearm or handgun permit or license that is issued by another state or a political subdivision of another state if both:

1. The permit or license is recognized as valid in the issuing state.

2. The permit or license holder is all of the following:

(a) Legally present in this state.

(b) Not legally prohibited from possessing a firearm in this state.

R. For the purpose of establishing mutual permit or license recognition with other states, the department of public safety shall enter into a written agreement if another state requires a written agreement.

S. Notwithstanding the provisions of this section, a person with a concealed weapons permit from another state may not carry a concealed weapon in this state if the person is under twenty-one years of age or is under indictment for, or has been convicted of, a felony offense in any jurisdiction, unless that conviction is expunged, set aside or vacated or the person's rights have been restored and the person is currently not a prohibited possessor under state or federal law.

T. The department of public safety may issue certificates of firearms proficiency according to the Arizona peace officer standards and training board firearms qualification for the purposes of implementing the law enforcement officers safety act of 2004 (P.L. 108-277; 118 Stat. 865; 18 United States Code §§926B and 926C). A law enforcement agency shall issue to a law enforcement officer who has honorably retired a photographic identification that states that the officer has honorably retired from the agency. The chief law enforcement officer shall determine whether an officer has honorably retired and the determination is not subject to review. A law enforcement agency has no obligation to revoke, alter or modify the honorable discharge photographic identification based on conduct that the agency becomes aware of or that occurs after the officer has separated from the agency.

13-3113. Adjudicated delinquents; firearm possession; violation; classification

A person who was previously adjudicated delinquent for an offense that would be a felony if committed by an adult and who possesses, uses or carries a firearm within ten years from the date of his adjudication or his release or escape from custody is guilty of a class 5 felony for a first offense and a class 4 felony for a second or subsequent offense if the

person was previously adjudicated for an offense that if committed as an adult would constitute:
1. Burglary in the first degree.
2. Burglary in the second degree.
3. Arson.
4. Any felony offense involving the use or threatening exhibition of a deadly weapon or dangerous instrument.
5. A serious offense as defined in §13-706.

Firearms clearance center; definition <Repealed>
If the Brady Handgun Violence Protection Act (P.L. 103-159) is repealed or if there is a final determination by a court of competent jurisdiction that the Brady Handgun Violence Protection Act is unconstitutional, this section <13-3114> is repealed. <NOTE: The correct name is Brady Handgun Violence Prevention Act> <NOTE: This section was repealed in 2002 for budgetary reasons, and its language has been removed here; the state's dealers now go directly to the federal Brady law NICS system to conduct background checks.>
From HB 2708, 2002: The director of the department of public safety shall notify the director of the federal bureau of investigation that the responsibility to perform background checks to determine whether purchases, sales or transfers of firearms to any person violate any federal law or any law of this state prohibiting the possession of firearms is transferred to the federal bureau of investigation on the effective date of this act.

13-3114. Arizona manufactured firearms; regulation; definitions
A. Beginning October 1, 2010, a personal firearm, a firearm accessory or ammunition that is manufactured commercially or privately in this state and that remains within the borders of this state is not subject to federal law or federal regulation, including registration, under the authority of Congress to regulate interstate commerce and is not considered to have traveled in interstate commerce.
B. This section applies to a firearm, a firearm accessory or ammunition that is manufactured in this state from basic materials and that can be manufactured without the inclusion of any significant parts imported from another state.
C. The importation into this state of a firearm accessory, any generic or insignificant part that has other manufacturing or consumer product applications or any basic materials, including unmachined steel and unshaped wood that is incorporated into, attached to or used in conjunction with a firearm, firearm accessory or ammunition manufactured in this state, does not subject the firearm, firearm accessory or ammunition to federal regulation.
D. This section does not apply to:
1. A firearm that cannot be carried and used by one person.
2. A firearm that has a bore diameter of more than one and one-half inches and that uses smokeless powder as a propellant.
3. Ammunition with a projectile that explodes using an explosion of chemical energy after the projectile leaves the firearm.
4. A firearm that discharges two or more projectiles with one activation of the trigger or other firing device.
E. A firearm that is manufactured and sold in this state pursuant to this section shall have the words "made in Arizona" clearly stamped on a central metallic part such as the receiver or frame.
F. For the purposes of this section:
1. "Firearm accessory" means an item that is used in conjunction with or mounted on a firearm but that is not essential to the basic function of a firearm, including telescopic or laser sights, magazines, flash suppressors, folding or aftermarket stocks and grips, speedloaders, ammunition carriers and lights for target illumination.
2. "Generic or insignificant part" includes springs, screws, nuts and pins.
3. "Manufactured" means that a firearm, a firearm accessory or ammunition has been created from basic materials for functional usefulness, including forging, casting, machining or other processes for working materials.
Sec. 2. Legislative findings. The Legislature finds:
1. The tenth amendment to the United States constitution guarantees to the states and their people all powers not granted to the federal government elsewhere in the constitution and reserves to the state and people of Arizona certain powers as they were understood at the time that Arizona was admitted to statehood in 1912. The guaranty of those powers is a matter of contract between the state and people of Arizona and the United States as of the time that the compact with the United States was agreed on and adopted by Arizona and the United States in 1912.
2. The ninth amendment to the United States constitution guarantees to the people rights not granted in the constitution and reserves to the people of Arizona certain rights as they were understood at the time that Arizona was admitted to statehood in 1912. The guaranty of those rights is a matter of contract between the state and people of Arizona and the United States as of the time that the compact with the United States was agreed on and adopted by Arizona and the United States in 1912.
3. The regulation of intrastate commerce is vested in the states under the ninth and tenth amendments to the United States constitution, particularly if not expressly preempted by federal law. Congress has not expressly preempted state regulation of intrastate commerce pertaining to the manufacture on an intrastate basis of firearms, firearms accessories and ammunition.
4. The second amendment to the United States constitution reserves to the people the right to keep and bear arms as that right was understood at the time that Arizona was admitted to statehood in 1912, and the guaranty of the right is a matter of contract between the state and people of Arizona and the United States as of the time that the compact with the United States was agreed on and adopted by Arizona and the United States in 1912.
5. Article II, section 26, Constitution of Arizona, clearly secures to Arizona citizens, and prohibits government interference with, the right of individual Arizona citizens to keep and bear arms. This constitutional protection is unchanged from the 1912 Arizona Constitution, which was approved by Congress and the people of Arizona, and the right exists as it was understood at the time that the compact with the United States was agreed on and adopted by Arizona and the United States in 1912.

13-3115. Forensics firearms identification system
The department of public safety is authorized to establish and maintain a forensics firearms identification system designed to provide investigative information on criminal street gangs and the unlawful use of firearms.

13-3116 . Misconduct involving body armor; classification; definition
A. A person commits misconduct involving body armor by knowingly wearing or otherwise using body armor during the

commission of any felony offense.
B. Misconduct involving body armor is a class 4 felony.
C. For purposes of this section, "body armor" means any clothing or equipment designed in whole or in part to minimize the risk of injury from a deadly weapon.

13-3117. Remote stun guns; sales records; use; classification; definitions

A. It is unlawful for a person or entity to do any of the following:
1. Sell an authorized remote stun gun without keeping an accurate sales record as to the identity of the purchaser with the manufacturer of the authorized remote stun gun. The identification that is required by this paragraph shall be verified with a government issued identification. This requirement does not apply to secondary sales.
2. Knowingly use or threaten to use a remote stun gun or an authorized remote stun gun against a law enforcement officer who is engaged in the performance of the officer's official duties.
B. This section does not:
1. Preclude the prosecution of any person for the use of a remote stun gun or an authorized remote stun gun during the commission of any criminal offense.
2. Preclude any justification defense under chapter 4 of this title.
C. The regulation of remote stun guns and authorized remote stun guns is a matter of statewide concern.
D. A violation of:
1. Subsection A, paragraph 1 is a petty offense.
2. Subsection A, paragraph 2 is a class 4 felony.
E. For the purposes of this section:
1. "Authorized remote stun gun" means a remote stun gun that has all of the following:
(a) An electrical discharge that is less than one hundred thousand volts and less than nine joules of energy per pulse.
(b) A serial or identification number on all projectiles that are discharged from the remote stun gun.
(c) An identification and tracking system that, on deployment of remote electrodes, disperses coded material that is traceable to the purchaser through records that are kept by the manufacturer on all remote stun guns and all individual cartridges sold.
(d) A training program that is offered by the manufacturer.
2. "Remote stun gun" means an electronic device that emits an electrical charge and that is designed and primarily employed to incapacitate a person or animal either through contact with electrodes on the device itself or remotely through wired probes that are attached to the device or through a spark, plasma, ionization or other conductive means emitting from the device.

13-3118. Possession or storage of firearms; restrictions prohibited; exceptions

A. Except for the legislature, this state and any agency or political subdivision of this state shall not enact or implement any law, rule or ordinance relating to the possession or storage of firearms other than as provided in statute.
B. This section does not prohibit:
1. A state, county or municipal judicial department, law enforcement agency or prosecutorial agency from prohibiting a deadly weapon pursuant to §13-3102, subsection A, paragraph 10.
2. A political subdivision of this state from enacting any rule or ordinance requiring a business that obtains a secondhand firearm by purchase, trade or consignment to retain the firearm for a period of not more than ten days at its place of business or another storage location that is approved by the applicable law enforcement agency.

13-3119. Misconduct involving weapons in a secured area of an airport; classification; definitions

A. A person commits misconduct involving weapons by intentionally carrying, possessing or exercising control over a deadly weapon in a secured area of an airport.
B. This section does not apply to:
1. A peace officer or a federally sworn officer while in the actual performance of the officer's duties.
2. A member of the military forces of the United States or of any state of the United States in the actual performance of the member's official duties.
3. An individual who is authorized by a federal agency in the actual performance of the individual's official duties.
4. General aviation areas not included in the security identification display area or sterile area as defined in the airport security program approved by the transportation security administration.
5. The lawful transportation of deadly weapons in accordance with state and federal law.
C. A violation of this section is a class 1 misdemeanor.
D. For the purposes of this section:
1. "Deadly weapon" has the same meaning prescribed in §13-105.
2. "Secured area of an airport" means any area of an airport specified in an airport security program that is authorized and approved by the United States transportation security administration pursuant to 49 United States Code §44903(h)(7)(F) and defined in 49 Code of Federal Regulations §1540.5.

13-3120. Knives regulated by state; state preemption; definitions

A. Except as provided in subsections C and D, a political subdivision of this state shall not enact any ordinance, rule or tax relating to the transportation, possession, carrying, sale, transfer, purchase, gift, devise, licensing, registration or use of a knife or knife making components in this state.
B. A political subdivision of this state shall not enact any rule or ordinance that relates to the manufacture of a knife and that is more prohibitive than or that has a penalty that is greater than any rule or ordinance that is related to the manufacture of any other commercial goods.
C. This section does not prohibit a political subdivision of this state from enacting and enforcing any ordinance or rule pursuant to state law, to implement or enforce state law or relating to imposing any privilege or use tax on the retail sale, lease or rental of, or the gross proceeds or gross income from the sale, lease or rental of, a knife or any knife components at a rate that applies generally to other items of tangible personal property.
D. This section does not prohibit a political subdivision of this state from regulating employees or independent contractors of the political subdivision who are acting within the course and scope of their employment or contract.
E. A political subdivision's rule or ordinance that relates to knives and that is inconsistent with or more restrictive than state

law, whether enacted before or after the effective date of this amendment to this section, is null and void.
F. For the purposes of this section:
1. "Knife" means a cutting instrument and includes a sharpened or pointed blade.
2. "Political subdivision" includes any county, city, including a charter city, town, municipal corporation or special district, any board, commission or agency of a county, city, including a charter city, town, municipal corporation or special district or any other local public agency.
Sec. 3. Legislative intent. It is the intent of the legislature to preempt the regulation of knives in this state. Knife regulation is of statewide concern. Therefore, the legislature intends to limit the ability of any political subdivision of this state to regulate knives. This act applies to any ordinance enacted before or after the effective date of this act. <SB1153, 2010>

13-3121. Firearm transfers; chief law enforcement officer certification; notification; definitions

A. If a chief law enforcement officer's certification is required by federal law or regulation for the transfer of a firearm, the chief law enforcement officer, within sixty days after receipt of a request for certification by an applicant, shall provide the certification if the applicant is not prohibited by law from receiving the firearm or is not the subject of a proceeding that could result in the applicant being prohibited by law from receiving the firearm. If the chief law enforcement officer is unable to provide a certification as required by this section, the chief law enforcement officer shall notify the applicant, in writing, of the denial and the reason for this determination.
B. The chief law enforcement officer of a law enforcement agency that has fifteen peace officers or fewer may refer an applicant who is requesting a certification pursuant to this section to the county sheriff. A county sheriff who receives a request for certification from a referred applicant shall provide the certification required by this section.
C. §12-820.02 applies to a chief law enforcement officer who provides a certification pursuant to this section.
D. This section does not apply to a county attorney or a tribal agency. This subsection does not prohibit a county attorney or a tribal agency from providing an applicant with a certification.
E. A chief law enforcement officer is not required to provide a certification pursuant to this section that the officer knows is untrue but may not refuse to provide a certification that is based on a generalized objection to private persons or entities making, possessing or receiving firearms or any certain type of firearm the possession of which is not prohibited by law.
F. For the purposes of this section:
1. "Certification" means the participation and assent that is required by federal law for the approval of an application to transfer or make a firearm.
2. "Chief law enforcement officer" means any official that the bureau of alcohol, tobacco, firearms and explosives, or any successor agency, identifies by regulation or otherwise as eligible to provide any required certification to make or transfer a firearm.
3. "Firearm" has the same meaning prescribed in 26 United States Code §5845(a).
4. "Proceeding" includes an ongoing criminal investigation that could result in the applicant being prohibited by law from receiving a firearm.

CHAPTER 36 · FAMILY OFFENSES

13-3601. Domestic violence; definition; classification; sentencing option; arrest and procedure for violation; weapon seizure; notice; report; diversion

A. "Domestic violence" means any act that is a dangerous crime against children as defined in §13-705 or an offense prescribed in §13-1102, 13-1103, 13-1104, 13-1105, 13-1201, 13-1202, 13-1203, 13-1204, 13-1302, 13-1303, 13-1304, 13-1406, 13-1502, 13-1503, 13-1504, 13-1602 or 13-2810, §13-2904, subsection A, paragraph 1, 2, 3 or 6, §13-2910, subsection a, paragraph 8 or 9, §13-2915, subsection a, paragraph 3 or §13-2916, 13-2921, 13-2921.01, 13-2923, 13-3019, 13-3601.02 or 13-3623, if any of the following applies:
1. The relationship between the victim and the defendant is one of marriage or former marriage or of persons residing or having resided in the same household.
2. The victim and the defendant have a child in common.
3. The victim or the defendant is pregnant by the other party.
4. The victim is related to the defendant or the defendant's spouse by blood or court order as a parent, grandparent, child, grandchild, brother or sister or by marriage as a parent-in-law, grandparent-in-law, stepparent, step-grandparent, stepchild, step-grandchild, brother-in-law or sister-in-law.
5. The victim is a child who resides or has resided in the same household as the defendant and is related by blood to a former spouse of the defendant or to a person who resides or who has resided in the same household as the defendant.
6. The relationship between the victim and the defendant is currently or was previously a romantic or sexual relationship. The following factors may be considered in determining whether the relationship between the victim and the defendant is currently or was previously a romantic or sexual relationship:
(a) The type of relationship.
(b) The length of the relationship.
(c) The frequency of the interaction between the victim and the defendant.
(d) If the relationship has terminated, the length of time since the termination.
B. A peace officer, with or without a warrant, may arrest a person if the officer has probable cause to believe that domestic violence has been committed and the officer has probable cause to believe that the person to be arrested has committed the offense, whether the offense is a felony or a misdemeanor and whether the offense was committed within or without the presence of the peace officer. In cases of domestic violence involving the infliction of physical injury or involving the discharge, use or threatening exhibition of a deadly weapon or dangerous instrument, the peace officer shall arrest a person, with or without a warrant, if the officer has probable cause to believe that the offense has been committed and the officer has probable cause to believe that the person to be arrested has committed the offense, whether the offense was committed within or without the presence of the peace officer, unless the officer has reasonable grounds to believe that the circumstances at the time are such that the victim will be protected from further injury. Failure to make an arrest does not give rise to civil liability except pursuant to §12-820.02. In order to arrest both parties, the peace officer shall have probable cause to believe that both parties independently have committed an act of domestic violence. An act of self-defense that is justified under chapter 4 of this title is not deemed to be an act of domestic violence. The release procedures available under §13-3883, subsection A, paragraph 4 and §13-3903 are not

applicable to arrests made pursuant to this subsection.

C. A peace officer may question the persons who are present to determine if a firearm is present on the premises. On learning or observing that a firearm is present on the premises, the peace officer may temporarily seize the firearm if the firearm is in plain view or was found pursuant to a consent to search and if the officer reasonably believes that the firearm would expose the victim or another person in the household to a risk of serious bodily injury or death. A firearm that is owned or possessed by the victim shall not be seized unless there is probable cause to believe that both parties independently have committed an act of domestic violence.

D. If a firearm is seized pursuant to subsection C of this section, the peace officer shall give the owner or possessor of the firearm a receipt for each seized firearm. The receipt shall indicate the identification or serial number or other identifying characteristic of each seized firearm. Each seized firearm shall be held for at least seventy-two hours by the law enforcement agency that seized the firearm.

E. If a firearm is seized pursuant to subsection C of this section, the victim shall be notified by a peace officer before the firearm is released from temporary custody.

F. If there is reasonable cause to believe that returning a firearm to the owner or possessor may endanger the victim, the person who reported the assault or threat or another person in the household, the prosecutor shall file a notice of intent to retain the firearm in the appropriate superior, justice or municipal court. The prosecutor shall serve notice on the owner or possessor of the firearm by certified mail. The notice shall state that the firearm will be retained for not more than six months following the date of seizure. On receipt of the notice, the owner or possessor may request a hearing for the return of the firearm, to dispute the grounds for seizure or to request an earlier return date. The court shall hold the hearing within ten days after receiving the owner's or possessor's request for a hearing. At the hearing, unless the court determines that the return of the firearm may endanger the victim, the person who reported the assault or threat or another person in the household, the court shall order the return of the firearm to the owner or possessor.

G. A peace officer is not liable for any act or omission in the good faith exercise of the officer's duties under subsections C, D, E and F of this section.

13-3602. Order of protection; procedure; contents; arrest for violation; penalty; protection order from another jurisdiction

G. If a court issues an order of protection, the court may do any of the following:

4. If the court finds that the defendant is a credible threat to the physical safety of the plaintiff or other specifically designated persons, prohibit the defendant from possessing or purchasing a firearm for the duration of the order. If the court prohibits the defendant from possessing a firearm, the court shall also order the defendant to transfer any firearm owned or possessed by the defendant immediately after service of the order to the appropriate law enforcement agency for the duration of the order. If the defendant does not immediately transfer the firearm, the defendant shall transfer the firearm within twenty-four hours after service of the order.

CHAPTER 38 • MISCELLANEOUS

13-3801. Preventing offenses; aiding officer

A. Public offenses may be prevented by intervention of peace officers as follows:

1. By requiring security to keep the peace.
2. Forming a police detail in cities and towns and requiring their attendance in exposed places.
3. Suppressing riots.

B. When peace officers are authorized to act in preventing public offenses, other persons, who, by their command, act in their aid, are justified in so doing.

13-3802. Right to command aid for execution of process; punishment for resisting process

A. When a sheriff or other public officer authorized to execute process finds, or has reason to believe that resistance will be made to execution of the process, such officer may command as many inhabitants of the county as the officer deems proper to assist in overcoming such resistance.

B. The officer shall certify to the court from which the process issued the names of those persons resisting, and they may be proceeded against for contempt of court.

13-3803. Preserving peace at public meetings

The mayor or other officer having direction of the police of a city or town shall order a force, sufficient to preserve the peace, to attend any public meeting when apprehensive of a breach of the peace.

13-3804. Duty of officers to disperse unlawful assembly

A. Where any number of persons, whether armed or not, are unlawfully or riotously assembled, the sheriff and his deputies, officials governing the city or town, or justice of the peace and constables, or any of them, shall go among the persons assembled, or as near to them as possible, and command them, in the name of the state, immediately to disperse.

B. If the people assembled do not immediately disperse, the magistrate and officers shall arrest them, and for that purpose may command the aid of all persons present or within the county.

13-3806. Duty of physician or attendant upon treating certain wounds; classification

A. A physician, surgeon, nurse or hospital attendant called upon to treat any person for gunshot wounds, knife wounds or other material injury which may have resulted from a fight, brawl, robbery or other illegal or unlawful act, shall immediately notify the chief of police or the city marshal, if in an incorporated city or town, or the sheriff, or the nearest police officer, of the circumstances, together with the name and description of the patient, the character of the wound and other facts which may be of assistance to the police authorities in the event the condition of the patient may be due to any illegal transaction or circumstances.

B. Any violation of the provisions of this section by a physician, surgeon, nurse or hospital attendant, is a class 3 misdemeanor.

13-3884. Arrest by private person

A private person may make an arrest:

1. When the person to be arrested has in his presence committed a misdemeanor amounting to a breach of the peace, or a

felony.
2. When a felony has been in fact committed and he has reasonable ground to believe that the person to be arrested has committed it.

13-3889. Method of arrest by private person
A private person when making an arrest shall inform the person to be arrested of the intention to arrest him and the cause of the arrest, unless he is then engaged in the commission of an offense, or is pursued immediately after its commission or after an escape, or flees or forcibly resists before the person making the arrest has opportunity so to inform him, or when the giving of such information will imperil the arrest.

13-3892. Right of private person to break into building
A private person, in order to make an arrest where a felony was committed in his presence, as authorized in §13-3884, may break open a door or window of any building in which the person to be arrested is or is reasonably believed to be, if he is refused admittance after he has announced his purpose.

13-3893. Right to break door or window to effect release
When an officer or private person has entered a building in accordance with the provisions of §13-3891 or 13-3892, he may break open a door or window of the building, if detained therein, when necessary for the purpose of liberating himself.

13-3894. Right to break into building in order to effect release of person making arrest detained therein
A peace officer or a private person may break open a door or window of any building when necessary for the purpose of liberating a person who entered the building in accordance with the provisions of §13-3891 or 13-3892 and is detained therein.

13-3895. Weapons to be taken from person arrested
Any person making a lawful arrest may take from the person arrested all weapons which he may have about his person and shall deliver them to the magistrate before whom he is taken.

13-3900. Duty of private person after making arrest
A private person who has made an arrest shall without unnecessary delay take the person arrested before the nearest or most accessible magistrate in the county in which the arrest was made, or deliver him to a peace officer, who shall without unnecessary delay take him before such magistrate. The private person or officer so taking the person arrested before the magistrate shall make before the magistrate a complaint, which shall set forth the facts showing the offense for which the person was arrested. If, however, the officer cannot make the complaint, the private person who delivered the person arrested to the officer shall accompany the officer before the magistrate and shall make to the magistrate the complaint against the person arrested.

13-3967. Release on bailable offenses before trial; definition
D. After providing notice to the victim pursuant to §13-4406, a judicial officer may impose any of the following conditions on a person who is released on his own recognizance or on bail:
4. Prohibit the person from possessing any dangerous weapon or engaging in certain described activities or indulging in intoxicating liquors or certain drugs.

CHAPTER 39 · FORFEITURE

13-4305. Seizure of property
A. Property subject to forfeiture under this chapter may be seized for forfeiture by a peace officer:
1. On process issued pursuant to the rules of civil procedure or the provisions of this title including a seizure warrant.
2. By making a seizure for forfeiture on property seized on process issued pursuant to law, including sections 13-3911 through 13-3915.
3. By making a seizure for forfeiture without court process if any of the following is true:
(a) The seizure for forfeiture is of property seized incident to an arrest or search.
(b) The property subject to seizure for forfeiture has been the subject of a prior judgment in favor of this state or any other state or the federal government in a forfeiture proceeding.
(c) The peace officer has probable cause to believe that the property is subject to forfeiture.

CHAPTER 40 · CRIME VICTIMS' RIGHTS

13-4441. Right to be heard on a petition to restore the right to possess a firearm; notice
A. A victim has the right to be present and be heard at any proceeding in which the defendant has filed a petition pursuant to §13-925 to restore the defendant's right to possess a firearm.
B. If the victim has made a request for postconviction notice, the attorney for the state shall provide notice to the victim at least five days before the hearing.

CHAPTER 45 · COMMERCIAL NUCLEAR GENERATING STATION SECURITY

13-4901. Definitions
In this chapter, unless the context otherwise requires:
1. "Armed nuclear security guard" means a security guard who works at a commercial nuclear generating station, who is employed as part of the security plan approved by the nuclear regulatory commission and who meets the requirements mandated by the nuclear regulatory commission for carrying a firearm.
2. "Commercial nuclear generating station" means an electric power generating facility that is owned by a public service corporation, a municipal corporation or a consortium of public service corporations or municipal corporations and that produces electricity by means of a nuclear reactor and includes the property on which the facility is located.

3. "Enter" means the intrusion of any part of any instrument or any part of a person's body inside of a commercial nuclear generating station or a structure or fenced yard of a commercial nuclear generating station.
4. "Entering or remaining unlawfully" means an act by a person who enters or remains in or on a commercial nuclear generating station or a structure or fenced yard of a commercial nuclear generating station if that person's intent for entering or remaining is not licensed, authorized or otherwise privileged.
5. "Structure or fenced yard" means any structure, fenced yard, wall, building or other similar barrier or any combination of structures, fenced yards, walls, buildings or other barriers that surrounds a commercial nuclear generating station and that is posted with signage indicating it is a felony to trespass.

13-4902. Criminal trespass on commercial nuclear generating station; classification
A. A person commits criminal trespass on a commercial nuclear generating station by knowingly either:
1. Entering or remaining unlawfully in or on a commercial nuclear generating station.
2. Entering or remaining unlawfully within a structure or fenced yard of a commercial nuclear generating station.
B. Criminal trespass on a commercial nuclear generating station is a class 4 felony.

13-4903. Use of force; armed nuclear security guards
A. An armed nuclear security guard is justified in using physical force against another person at a commercial nuclear generating station or structure or fenced yard of a commercial nuclear generating station if the armed nuclear security guard reasonably believes that such force is necessary to prevent or terminate the commission or attempted commission of criminal damage under § 13-1602, subsection A, paragraph 3 and subsection B, paragraph 1, misconduct involving weapons under §13-3102, subsection A, paragraph 13 or criminal trespass on a commercial nuclear generating station under §13-4902.
B. Notwithstanding sections 13-403, 13-404, 13-405, 13-406, 13-408, 13-409, 13-410 and 13-411, an armed nuclear security guard is justified in using physical force up to and including deadly physical force against another person at a commercial nuclear generating station or structure or fenced yard of a commercial nuclear generating station if the armed nuclear security guard reasonably believes that such force is necessary to:
1. Prevent the commission of manslaughter under §13-1103, second or first degree murder under §13-1104 or 13-1105, aggravated assault under §13-1204, subsection A, paragraph 1 or 2, kidnapping under §13-1304, burglary in the second or first degree under §13-1507 or 13-1508, arson of a structure or property under §13-1703, arson of an occupied structure under §13-1704, armed robbery under §13-1904 or an act of terrorism under §13-2308.01.
2. Defend oneself or a third person from the use or imminent use of deadly physical force.
C. Notwithstanding any other provision of this chapter, an armed nuclear security guard is justified in threatening to use physical or deadly physical force if and to the extent a reasonable armed nuclear security guard believes it necessary to protect oneself or others against another person's potential use of physical force or deadly physical force.
D. An armed nuclear security guard is not subject to civil liability for engaging in conduct that is otherwise justified pursuant to this chapter.

13-4904. Detention authority; armed nuclear security guards
A. An armed nuclear security guard, with reasonable belief, may detain in or on a commercial nuclear generating station or a structure or fenced yard of a commercial nuclear generating station in a reasonable manner and for a reasonable time any person who is suspected of or attempting to commit manslaughter under §13-1103, second or first degree murder under §13-1104 or 13-1105, aggravated assault under §13-1204, subsection A, paragraph 1 or 2, kidnapping under §13-1304, burglary in the second or first degree under §13-1507 or 13-1508, criminal damage under §13-1602, subsection A, paragraph 3 and subsection B, paragraph 1, arson of a structure or property under §13-1703, arson of an occupied structure under §13-1704, armed robbery under §13-1904, an act of terrorism under §13-2308.01, misconduct involving weapons under §13-3102, subsection A, paragraph 13 or criminal trespass on a commercial nuclear generating station under §13-4902 for the purpose of summoning a law enforcement officer.
B. Reasonable belief of an armed nuclear security guard is a defense to a civil or criminal action against an armed nuclear security guard for false arrest, false or unlawful imprisonment or wrongful detention.

TITLE 15 • EDUCATION

15-341. General powers and duties; immunity; delegation
A. The governing board shall:
23. Notwithstanding §§13-3108 and 13-3120, prescribe and enforce policies and procedures that prohibit a person from carrying or possessing a weapon on school grounds unless the person is a peace officer or has obtained specific authorization from the school administrator.
31. Report to local law enforcement agencies any suspected crime against a person or property that is a serious offense as defined by §13-706 or that involves a deadly weapon or dangerous instrument or serious physical injury and any conduct that poses a threat of death or serious physical injury to employees, students or anyone on the property of the school. This paragraph does not limit or preclude the reporting by a school district or an employee of a school district of suspected crimes other than those required to be reported by this paragraph. For the purposes of this paragraph, "dangerous instrument", "deadly weapon" and "serious physical injury" have the same meanings prescribed in §13-105.

15-515. Duty to report violations occurring on school premises
All school personnel who observe a violation of §13-3102, subsection A, paragraph 12 or §13-3111 on school premises shall immediately report the violation to the school administrator. The administrator shall immediately report the violation to a peace officer. The peace officer shall report this violation to the department of public safety for inclusion in the statewide and federal uniform crime reports prescribed in §41-1750, subsection A, paragraph 2.

15-713. Training in use of bows or firearms; instruction materials; certification of instructors; cooperating agencies
A. The Arizona game and fish department may provide training in the safe handling and use of bows or firearms and safe hunting practices, in conjunction with the common schools and high schools of the state when the schools request the

training.
B. The Arizona game and fish department pay prescribe courses of study, approve instruction materials, certify instructors for training programs conducted by private organizations or public agencies and issue certificates of completion of the required course of study.
C. To carry out the purposes of the training program authorized by this section and §15-714, the Arizona game and fish department may cooperate with other agencies and private organizations.

15-714. Eligibility for training in use of bows or firearms
A. Training courses may be offered on a voluntary basis pursuant to §17-245.
B. The courses held for students in the common schools and high schools shall be elective only, and attendance in such classes shall not be considered in computing a school district's student count.

15-714.01. Arizona gun safety program course
A. In addition to the voluntary training in the use of bows and firearms prescribed in §§15-713 and 15-714, any school district or charter school may offer as an elective course a one semester, one credit course in firearm marksmanship that shall be designated as the Arizona gun safety program course.
B. A pupil shall be deemed to have satisfactorily completed the Arizona gun safety program course by demonstrating that the pupil has the ability to safely discharge a firearm as defined in §13-3101.
C. The course of instruction prescribed in this section shall be jointly developed by the Arizona game and fish commission, the department of public safety and private firearms organizations and may include materials provided by private youth organizations. At a minimum, the Arizona gun safety program course shall include each of the following:
1. Instruction on the rules of firearm safety.
2. Instruction on the basic operation of firearms.
3. Instruction on the history of firearms and marksmanship.
4. Instruction on the role of firearms in preserving peace and freedom.
5. Instruction on the constitutional roots of the right to keep and bear arms.
6. Instruction on the use of clay targets.
7. Practice time at a shooting range.
8. Actual demonstration by the pupil of competence with a firearm as defined in §13-3101 by safely discharging the firearm at one or more targets.
D. School districts and charter schools shall arrange for adequate use of shooting range time by pupils in the Arizona gun safety program course at any established shooting range.
E. Pupils who satisfactorily complete the Arizona gun safety program course shall receive a certificate of accomplishment.
F. A person who is currently certified as a firearms safety instructor by the Arizona game and fish department, the national rifle association, a federal, state or local law enforcement agency, a branch of the United States military, a federal agency, the reserve officer training corps, the junior reserve officer training corps or the civilian marksmanship program is qualified to teach the Arizona gun safety program course.
G. Nothing in this section shall be construed to limit or expand the liability of any person under other provisions of law.

15-841. Responsibilities of pupils; expulsion; alternative education programs; community service; placement review committee
B. A pupil may be expelled for continued open defiance of authority, continued disruptive or disorderly behavior, violent behavior that includes use or display of a dangerous instrument or a deadly weapon as defined in §13-105, use or possession of a gun, or excessive absenteeism. A pupil may be expelled for excessive absenteeism only if the pupil has reached the age or completed the grade after which school attendance is not required as prescribed in §15-802. A school district may expel pupils for actions other than those listed in this subsection as the school district deems appropriate.
G. A school district or charter school shall expel from school for a period of not less than one year a pupil who is determined to have brought a firearm to a school within the jurisdiction of the school district or the charter school, except that the school district or charter school may modify this expulsion requirement for a pupil on a case by case basis. This subsection shall be construed consistently with the requirements of the individuals with disabilities education act (20 United States Code sections 1400 through 1420). For the purposes of this subsection:
2. "Firearm" means a firearm as defined in 18 United States Code §921.

TITLE 17 • GAME AND FISH

17-101. Definitions
A. In this title, unless the context otherwise requires:
6. "Device" means any net, trap, snare, salt lick, scaffold, deadfall, pit, explosive, poison or stupefying substance, crossbow, firearm, bow and arrow, or other implement used for taking wildlife. Device does not include a raptor or any equipment used in the sport of falconry.

17-231. General powers and duties of the commission
A. The commission shall:
1. Adopt rules and establish services it deems necessary to carry out the provisions and purposes of this title.
3. Establish hunting, trapping and fishing rules and prescribe the manner and methods that may be used in taking wildlife, but the commission shall not limit or restrict the magazine capacity of any authorized firearm.
B. The commission may:
4. Expend funds to provide training in the safe handling and use of firearms and safe hunting practices.
13. Adopt rules relating to range operations at public shooting ranges operated by and under the jurisdiction of the commission, including the hours of operation, the fees for the use of the range, the regulation of groups and events, the operation of related range facilities, the type of firearms and ammunition that may be used at the range, the safe handling of firearms at the range, the required safety equipment for a person using the range, the sale of firearms, ammunition and shooting supplies at the range, and the authority of range officers to enforce these rules, to remove

violators from the premises and to refuse entry for repeat violations.

17-240. Disposition of wildlife; devices; unlawful devices; notice of intention to destroy; waiting period; destruction; jurisdiction of recovery actions; disposition of unclaimed property

C. Devices other than those referred to in subsection B <referring to devices that cannot be lawfully used to take wildlife but were so used when seized>, including firearms seized under this title shall, after final disposition of the case, be returned to the person from whom the device was seized. If the person from whom the device was seized cannot be located or ascertained, the device seized shall be retained by the department at least ninety days after final disposition of the case, and all devices so held by the department may be:

1. Sold annually.

2. Destroyed only if considered a prohibited or defaced weapon as defined in §13-3101, except that any seized firearm registered in the national firearms registry and transfer records of the United States treasury department or has been classified as a curio or relic by the United States treasury department, shall not be destroyed.

D. If no complaint is filed pursuant to this title, the device shall be returned to the person from whom seized within thirty days from the date seized.

E. A complete report of all wildlife and devices seized by the department showing a description of the items, the person from whom it was seized, if known, and a record of the disposition shall be kept by the department. The money derived from the sale of any devices shall be deposited in the game and fish fund.

17-245. Training courses

The commission may:

1. Offer training courses on a voluntary basis to all persons as prescribed by rule.

2. Require any person whose hunting, fishing or guide license has been revoked or suspended to show a certificate of completion of a training course as a condition to issuance or renewal of a hunting, fishing or guide license.

17-273. Firearms safety and ranges fund; uses; criteria

A. The firearms safety and ranges fund is established consisting of monies transferred to the fund pursuant to §42-5029, subsection D, paragraph 4, subdivision (c) item (iii) and revenues derived from the sale or lease of real property owned by the commission and acquired for or used for the purpose of providing public shooting ranges and monies received from the sale of goods and services from commissioned-owned shooting ranges except for program income associated with federal grants. The Arizona game and fish commission shall administer the fund which is continuously appropriated. Monies in the fund are exempt from the provisions of §35-190 relating to lapsing of appropriations. Interest earned on monies in the fund shall be credited to the fund.

B. The Arizona game and fish commission shall use monies in the fund on shooting ranges open to the public and operated by government or nonprofit entities for the following purposes:

1. Shooting range engineering and studies.

2. Noise abatement.

3. Safety enhancement.

4. Shooting range design.

5. New shooting range sites and construction.

6. Shooting range relocation.

7. Shooting sports programs.

8. Inventory for sale at ranges.

9. Other projects or expenses that are necessary to operate and maintain a shooting range under good practices and management.

C. The director of the Arizona game and fish department shall consult with the state land commissioner to identify eligible state trust land suitable for the location or relocation of shooting ranges.

D. The Arizona game and fish commission may accept and spend private grants, gifts and contributions to assist in carrying out this section.

17-301. Times when wildlife may be taken; exceptions; methods of taking

A. A person may take wildlife, except aquatic wildlife, only during daylight hours unless otherwise prescribed by the commission. A person shall not take any species of wildlife by the aid or with the use of a jacklight, other artificial light, or illegal device, except as provided by the commission.

B. A person shall not take wildlife, except aquatic wildlife, or discharge a firearm or shoot any other device from a motor vehicle, including an automobile, aircraft, train or powerboat, or from a sailboat, boat under sail, or a floating object towed by powerboat or sailboat except as expressly permitted by the commission. No person may knowingly discharge any firearm or shoot any other device upon, from, across or into a road or railway.

17-304. Prohibition by landowner upon hunting; posting; exception

A. Landowners or lessees of private land who desire to prohibit hunting, fishing or trapping on their lands without their written permission shall post such lands closed to hunting, fishing or trapping using notices or signboards.

B. State or federal lands including those under lease may not be posted except by consent of the commission.

C. The notices or signboards shall meet all of the following criteria:

1. Be not less than eight inches by eleven inches with plainly legible wording in capital and bold-faced lettering at least one inch high.

2. Contain the words "no hunting", "no trapping" or "no fishing" either as a single phrase or in any combination.

3. Be conspicuously placed on a structure or post at least four feet above ground level at all points of vehicular access, at all property or fence corners and at intervals of not more than one-quarter mile along the property boundary, except that a post with one hundred square inches or more of orange paint may serve as the interval notices between property or fence corners and points of vehicular access. The orange paint shall be clearly visible and shall cover the entire aboveground surface of the post facing outward and on both lateral sides from the closed area.

D. The entry of any person for the taking of wildlife shall not be grounds for an action for criminal trespassing pursuant to §13-1502 unless either:

1. The land has been posted pursuant to this section and the notices and signboards also contain the words "no trespassing".

2. The person knowingly remains unlawfully on any real property after a reasonable request to leave by a law enforcement officer acting at the request of the owner, the owner or any other person having lawful control over the property or the person knowingly disregards reasonable notice prohibiting entry to any real property.

17-305. Carrying firearms or game-taking devices in closed areas; exceptions; permits

A. The possession of legal weapons, devices, ammunition or magazines, which are not authorized to take wildlife, is not prohibited while hunting if the weapon or device is not used to take wildlife.

B. Taking wildlife by using a weapon, device, ammunition or magazine that is not authorized to take wildlife is a class 1 misdemeanor.

17-309. Violations; classification

A. Unless otherwise prescribed by this title, it is unlawful for a person to:

4. Discharge a firearm while taking wildlife within one-fourth mile of an occupied farmhouse or other residence, cabin, lodge or building without permission of the owner or resident.

6. Take a game bird, game mammal or game fish and knowingly permit an edible portion thereof to go to waste, except as provided in §17-302.

B. Unless a different or other penalty or punishment is specifically prescribed a person who violates any provision of this title, or who violates or fails to comply with a lawful order or rule of the commission, is guilty of a class 2 misdemeanor.

17-311. Duty to report shooting accident resulting in injury or death; duty to give assistance; authority of officers

A. Any person who, while taking wildlife, is involved in a shooting accident resulting in injury to another person shall render every possible assistance to the injured person, and if the accident if fatal, he shall immediately report the accident to the nearest law enforcement officer available and render such assistance as may be required.

B. Such person shall within ten days file with the department a full and complete written report of such accident.

17-312. Misuse of firearms

A. It is unlawful for any person while taking wildlife, or while in any hunting area, to handle or discharge any firearm while intoxicated or in a careless or reckless manner or with wanton disregard for the safety of human life or property.

B. Nothing in this section shall be construed in any way to limit the right of the state to prosecute any person who injures or kills another.

17-316. Interference with rights of hunters; classification; civil action; exceptions

A. It is a class 2 misdemeanor for a person while in a hunting area to intentionally interfere with, prevent or disrupt the lawful taking of wildlife by:

1. Harassing, driving or disturbing any wildlife.

2. Blocking, obstructing or impeding, or attempting to block, obstruct or impede, a person lawfully taking wildlife.

3. Erecting a barrier without the consent of the landowner or lessee with the intent to deny ingress to or egress from areas where wildlife may be lawfully taken.

4. Making or attempting to make physical contact, without permission, with a person lawfully taking wildlife.

5. Engaging in, or attempting to engage in, theft, vandalism or destruction of real or personal property.

6. Disturbing or altering, or attempting to disturb or alter, the condition or authorized placement of real or personal property intended for use in the lawful taking of wildlife.

7. Making or attempting to make loud noises or gestures, set out or attempt to set out animal baits, scents or lures or human scent, use any natural or artificial visual, aural, olfactory or physical stimuli, or engage in or attempt to engage in any other similar action or activity, in order to disturb, alarm, drive, attract or affect the behavior of wildlife or disturb, alarm, disrupt or annoy a person lawfully taking wildlife.

8. Interjecting oneself into the line of fire of a person lawfully taking wildlife.

B. It is a class 3 misdemeanor for a person to enter or remain on a designated hunting on any public or private lands or waters or state lands including state trust lands with the intent to interfere with, prevent or disrupt the lawful taking of wildlife.

C. The commission or any person properly licensed to take wildlife who is directly affected by a violation of this section may bring an action to restrain conduct declared unlawful in this section and to recover damages.

D. A peace officer who reasonably believes that a person has violated this section may order the person to desist or to leave the area or arrest such person upon refusal to desist or leave.

E. The conduct declared unlawful in this section does not:

1. Include any incidental interference arising from lawful activity by public land users, including ranchers, miners or recreationists.

2. Apply to landowners, permittees, lessees or their agents or contractors engaged in animal husbandry practices or agricultural operations.

17-362. Guides; appointment; licenses; duties; reports; carrying firearms

A. No person shall act as a guide without first satisfying the director of the person's qualifications and without having procured a guide license. No person under eighteen years of age shall be issued a guide license. If a licensed guide fails to comply with the provisions of this title or is convicted of violating any provision of this title, his license may, after public hearing, be revoked by the commission and he shall be liable to punishment as for a violation of this title.

D. No person acting as guide shall carry firearms other than a revolver or pistol.

17-601. Definition of outdoor shooting range

In this article, unless the context otherwise requires, "outdoor shooting range" or "range" means a permanently located and improved area that is designed and operated for the use of rifles, shotguns, pistols, silhouettes, skeet, trap, black powder or any other similar sport shooting in an outdoor environment. Outdoor shooting range does not include:

1. Any area for the exclusive use of archery or air guns.

2. A totally enclosed facility that is designed to offer a totally controlled shooting environment that includes impenetrable walls, floor and ceiling, adequate ventilation, lighting systems and acoustical treatment for sound attenuation suitable for the range's approved use.

3. Any area that is used for shooting on a private lot or parcel of land that is not open to the public on a commercial or membership basis.

17-602. State outdoor shooting range noise standards; preemption; measurement; definitions

A. The legislature finds that outdoor shooting range noise standards are a matter of statewide concern. City, town, county and any other state noise standards are preempted as applied to outdoor shooting ranges.

B. Each outdoor shooting range in this state shall measure the noise emitted from the range pursuant to subsection E at least once. In addition, the range shall measure the noise it emits if the range expands the area designed and operated for the use of firearms or explosives by more than twenty per cent in size than at the time of its initial noise measurement or if the range introduces the use of a type of firearm or explosive device that will increase noise production. The range shall pay for the measurement and shall keep the results of the measurement at the range at all times. Any person may review the noise measurement during the range's business hours. Ranges that are located at least one mile from areas that are zoned for residences, schools, hotels, motels, hospitals or churches are exempt from this subsection.

C. Any person, at the person's expense, may measure the noise emitted from an outdoor shooting range pursuant to subsection E.

D. The noise emitted from an outdoor shooting range shall not exceed an Leq(h) of sixty-four dBA.

E. In measuring the noise emitted from an outdoor shooting range:

1. If a range performs the measurement of noise pursuant to subsection B, sound pressure measurements shall be taken twenty feet from the nearest occupied residence, school, hotel, motel, hospital or church, or from the nearest proposed location of a residence, school, hotel, motel, hospital or church if the property is zoned for such a structure but is currently unimproved. If a person performs the measurement of noise pursuant to subsection C, sound pressure measurements shall be taken twenty feet from the person's residence, school, hotel, motel, hospital or church, or twenty feet from the proposed residence, school, hotel, motel, hospital or church if the property is zoned for such a structure but is currently unimproved.

2. Sound pressure measurements shall be made in a location directly between the range and the nearest existing or proposed residence, school, hotel, motel, hospital or church. If there are natural or artificial obstructions that prevent an accurate noise measurement, the measurement may be taken within an additional twenty feet radius from the initial measurement location.

3. Sound pressure measurements shall be made on the A-weighted fast response mode scale. Measurements shall be taken during the noisiest hour of peak use during the operation of the range. Measurements shall be taken according to American national standards institute's standard methods ANSI S1.2-1962 (R1976) American national standard method for physical measurement of sound and ANSI S1.2-1971 (R1976) American national standard method for measuring sound pressure levels. Measurements shall be taken using a type 1 sound meter meeting the requirements of ANSI S1.4L-1971. Any part of the measurements conducted on a range shall comply with the range safety rules.

F. Outdoor shooting ranges in operation on July 1, 2002 shall comply with the provisions of this section before July 1, 2003. Ranges not in operation on July 1, 2002 shall comply with the provisions of this section when they begin operation.

G. Subsection B does not apply to an outdoor shooting range that is built for military or armed nuclear security guard training and that is not open to the general public.

H. For the purposes of this section:

1. "A-weighted" means a frequency weighting network used to account for changes in sensitivity as a function of frequency.

2. "DBA" means A-weighted decibels, taking into account human response to sound energy in different frequency bands.

3. "Decibel" means the unit of measure for sound pressure denoting the ratio between two quantities that are proportional to power. The number of decibels is ten times the base ten logarithm of this ratio.

4. "Leq(h)" means the equivalent energy level that is the steady state level that contains the same amount of sound energy as a time varying sound level for a sixty minute time period.

17-603. Preexisting outdoor shooting ranges; noise buffering or attenuation

A. If an outdoor shooting range was constructed before July 1, 2002 in compliance with existing applicable county or municipal ordinances and zoning requirements and if property located within one mile of the exterior property boundary of the range is rezoned after July 1, 2002 for residential use or any other use that includes a school, hotel, motel, hospital or church, the zoning authority must provide for noise buffers or attenuation devices that are either:

1. Within the new development as a condition for developing the property or as supplied by the zoning authority.

2. Supplied or funded by the zoning authority for location in the range.

B. Property owners, developers, zoning authorities and ranges may negotiate and provide for noise buffers or attenuation devices located on or off the range.

C. Any noise buffering or attenuation under this section must comply with the state noise standards prescribed by section 17-602.

17-604. Nighttime outdoor shooting range operations

A. Outdoor shooting ranges that are located in areas that are zoned for residential use or any other use that includes a school, hotel, motel, hospital or church shall not operate from 10:00 p.m. through 7:00 a.m.

B. This section does not apply to any outdoor shooting range while it is providing law enforcement or military training. These ranges must provide adequate public notice including posting in four public locations within one mile of the exterior boundaries of the range each calendar quarter of the schedule of when the range will operate from 10:00 p.m. through 7:00 a.m. and the purpose for those nighttime operations. Nighttime operations under this subsection must comply with the nighttime noise standards prescribed by section 17-602.

17-605. Noise pollution; nuisance; defense; costs

A. It is an affirmative defense to any civil liability or claim for equitable relief arising from any allegation regarding noise or noise pollution that results from owning, operating or using an outdoor shooting range if the entity or individual owning, operating or using the range complies with this article.

B. In any action where a defense has been raised pursuant to subsection A, the court shall award the prevailing party its costs and all expenses, including the party's costs incurred in measuring noise emitted from the range and reasonable attorney fees.

17-621. Recording proximity to shooting range; definition

A. A city with a population of more than one million persons shall execute and record in the office of the county recorder a document relating to real property located within one-half mile of the exterior boundaries of any shooting range that is owned by this state and that is located within or adjacent to the exterior municipal boundaries on or before January 1, 2004. The city attorney shall prepare the document in recordable form. The document must be on eight and one-half inch by eleven inch paper containing the following information in twelve point type:

1. A legal description of the property within one-half mile of the exterior boundaries of the shooting range. To assist in identifying that property, the game and fish commission shall submit the legal description of the shooting range to the city attorney.

2. The following disclosure: This property is located within one-half mile of the exterior boundaries of a shooting range and may be subject to:

1. Increased noise.

2. Restrictions on the use of the property under the city's general plan and zoning ordinances.

B. The game and fish commission shall not close a shooting range described in this section unless all of the following occur:

1. The director of the department recommends the closure in writing.

2. The commission issues a report detailing the basis for the recommendation.

3. The commission unanimously approves the closure after public hearings have been held to discuss the closure in the three counties with the highest population.

4. The joint committee on capital review reviews the closure recommendation.

5. The governor approves the closure in an executive order.

C. For the purposes of this section, "shooting range" means a permanently located and improved area that is designed and operated for the use of rifles, shotguns, pistols, silhouettes, skeet, trap, black powder or any other similar sport shooting in an outdoor environment. Shooting range does not include:

1. Any area for the exclusive use of archery or air guns.

2. An enclosed indoor facility that is designed to offer a totally controlled shooting environment and that includes impenetrable walls, floor and ceiling, adequate ventilation, lighting systems and acoustical treatment for sound attenuation suitable for the range's approved use.

3. A national guard facility located in a city or town with a population of more than one million persons.

4. A facility that was not owned by this state before January 1, 2002.

TITLE 26 •MILITARY AFFAIRS AND EMERGENCY MANAGEMENT

26-178. Illegal possession of equipment; classification

A. A person having in his possession a uniform, arms, equipment, supplies or other military property of the state or United States, who secretes, disposes of, offers for sale or in any manner pledges, retains or refuses to deliver to an officer entitled to demand possession of the property, or who, being a member of the national guard, wears, when not on duty, such uniform or equipment without permission of his commanding officer, is, if the property is of a value more than fifty dollars, guilty of a class 5 felony, and if the value is less than fifty dollars, guilty of a class 2 misdemeanor.

B. Possession of such military equipment or accoutrements of the state, or the United States, by any person not a member of the military forces of the state or the United States, shall be presumptive evidence of unlawful barter, exchange, pledge, loan or gift thereof. A person not a member of the military forces of the United States, or a duly authorized officer or agent thereof, having possession of such articles which have been subjects of unlawful disposition, shall have no right, title or interest therein, and the property may be seized and taken wherever found by an officer of the state, civil or military, and shall thereupon be delivered to any commanding officer or other officer authorized to receive the property who shall make an immediate report thereof to the adjutant general.

26-303. Emergency powers of governor; termination; authorization for adjutant general; limitation

A. During a state of war emergency, the governor may:

2. Commandeer and utilize any property, except for firearms or ammunition or firearms or ammunition components or personnel deemed necessary in carrying out the responsibilities vested in the office of the governor by this chapter as chief executive of the state and thereafter the state shall pay reasonable compensation therefor as follows:

J. Pursuant to the second amendment of the United States Constitution and article II, §26, Constitution of Arizona, and notwithstanding any other law, the emergency powers of the governor, the adjutant general or any other official or person shall not be construed to allow the imposition of additional restrictions on the lawful possession, transfer, sale, transportation, carrying, storage, display or use of firearms or ammunition or firearms or ammunition components.

K. Nothing in this section shall be construed to prohibit the governor, the adjutant general or other officials responding to an emergency from ordering the reasonable movement of stores of ammunition out of the way of dangerous conditions.

TITLE 28 • TRANSPORTATION

28-627. Powers of local authorities

E. In addition to the appointment of peace officers, a local authority may provide by ordinance for the appointment of:

1. Unarmed police aides or municipally approved private contractors who are employed or contracted by the police department and who are empowered to commence an action or proceeding before a court or judge for a violation of the local authority's ordinances regulating the standing or parking of vehicles. A municipally approved private contractor shall not include a relative of an employee or of an elected official of the municipality. The authority of the unarmed police aide or municipally approved private contractor as authorized in this section is limited to the enforcement of the ordinances of local authorities regulating the standing or parking of vehicles. Pursuant to rules established by the

supreme court, an unarmed police aide appointed pursuant to this paragraph may serve any process originating out of a municipal court in the municipality in which the unarmed police aide is employed. Service of process under this paragraph shall only be made during the hours the municipal court is open for the transaction of business and only on court premises. This paragraph does not grant to unarmed police aides or municipally approved private contractors other powers or benefits to which peace officers of this state are entitled.

2. Traffic investigators who may:

(a) Investigate traffic accidents within the jurisdiction of the local authority.

F. A traffic investigator appointed pursuant to this section shall:

1. Be unarmed at all times during the course of the traffic investigator's duties.

G. Notwithstanding subsection E of this section, an unarmed police aide, a municipally approved private contractor or a traffic investigator shall not serve any process resulting from a citation issued for a violation of §28-701 or 28-644 or of a city or town ordinance for excessive speed or failure to obey a traffic control device that is obtained using automated enforcement technology.

28-8429. Misconduct involving weapons in a secured area of an airport; classification; definitions

A. A person commits misconduct involving weapons by intentionally carrying, possessing or exercising control over a deadly weapon in a secured area of an airport.

B. This section does not apply to:

1. A peace officer or a federally sworn officer while in the actual performance of the officer's duties.

2. A member of the military forces of the United States or of any state of the United States in the actual performance of the member's official duties.

3. An individual who is authorized by a federal agency in the actual performance of the individual's official duties.

4. General aviation areas not included in the security identification display area or sterile area as defined in the airport security program approved by the transportation security administration.

5. The lawful transportation of deadly weapons in accordance with state and federal law.

C. A violation of this section is a class 1 misdemeanor.

D. For the purposes of this section:

1. "deadly weapon" has the same meaning prescribed in §13-105.

2. "secured area of an airport" means any area of an airport specified in an airport security program that is authorized and approved by the United States transportation security administration pursuant to 49 United States Code §44903(h)(7)(f) and defined in 49 Code of Federal Regulations §1540.5.

TITLE 32 • PROFESSIONS AND OCCUPATIONS

32-2422. Qualification of applicant for agency license; substantiation of work experience

A. An applicant as a qualifying party for an agency license under this chapter shall:

4. Within the five years immediately preceding the application for an agency license, not have been convicted of any misdemeanor act involving:

(b) Misconduct involving a deadly weapon as provided in §13-3102.

32-2441. Qualification of applicant for associate or employee registration

An applicant for an associate or employee registration certificate shall:

4. Within the five years immediately preceding the application for an associate or employee registration certificate, not have been convicted of any misdemeanor act involving:

(b) Misconduct involving a deadly weapon as provided in §13-3102.

32-2457. Grounds for disciplinary action; emergency summary suspension; judicial review

A. The following constitute grounds for which disciplinary action specified in subsection B of this section may be taken against a licensee or registrant or, if the licensee is other than an individual, against the licensee's qualifying party or any of its associates, directors or managers:

8. Conviction of any act involving a weapon pursuant to §13-3102.

32-2601. Definitions

4. "Armed security guard" means a registered security guard who wears, carries, possesses or has access to a firearm at any time during the course of employment.

32-2606. Exceptions

This chapter does not apply to:

3. A company that employs security guards solely for use of and service to itself and not for others and that complies with the following requirements:

(a) If the company's security guards are armed, each guard must complete sixteen hours of firearms training initially and complete an additional eight hours of refresher training each year thereafter.

4. The Arizona Rangers organization as identified in §41-4201, or authorized persons performing official Arizona Ranger duties when in the service of a nonprofit organization recognized under §501(c)(3) of the internal revenue code.

32-2612. Qualifications of applicant for agency license

A. Each applicant, if an individual, or each associate, director or manager, if the applicant is other than an individual, for an agency license to be issued pursuant to this chapter shall:

4. Within the five years immediately preceding the application for an agency license, not have been convicted of any misdemeanor act involving:

b. Misconduct involving a deadly weapon as provided in §13-3102.

32-2621. Necessity of security guard registration

A. No person, except a regularly commissioned peace officer, shall act, attempt to act or represent himself as a security guard unless such person is registered as a guard pursuant to this chapter and acting within the scope of his employment for an agency licensed pursuant to article 2 of this chapter.

32-2622. Qualifications of applicant for security guard or armed security guard registration certificate

A. An applicant for an associate or a security guard registration certificate issued pursuant to this article shall:

1. Be at least eighteen years of age.
2. Be a citizen or legal resident of the United States who is authorized to seek employment in the United States.
3. Not have been convicted of any felony or currently be under indictment for a felony.
4. Within the five years immediately preceding the application for an associate, security guard or armed security guard registration certificate, not have been convicted of any misdemeanor act involving:
(a) Personal violence or force against another person or threatening to commit any act of personal violence or force against another person.
(b) Misconduct involving a deadly weapon as provided in §13-3102.
(c) Dishonesty or fraud.
(d) Arson.
(e) Theft.
(f) Domestic violence.
(g) A violation of title 13, chapter 34 or 34.1 or an offense that has the same elements as an offense listed in title 13, chapter 34 or 34.1.
(h) Sexual misconduct.
5. Not be on parole, on community supervision, on work furlough, on home arrest, on release on any other basis or named in an outstanding arrest warrant.
6. Not be serving a term of probation pursuant to a conviction for any act of personal violence or domestic violence, as defined in §13-3601, or an offense that has the same elements as an offense listed in §13-3601.
7. Not be either of the following:
(a) Adjudicated mentally incompetent.
(b) Found to constitute a danger to self or others pursuant to §36-540.
8. Not have a disability as defined in §41-1461, unless that person is a qualified individual as defined in §41-1461.
9. Not have been convicted of acting or attempting to act as an associate security guard or armed security guard without a license if a license was required.
10. Not be a registered sex offender.
B. An applicant for an armed security guard registration certificate issued pursuant to this chapter shall:
1. Meet the requirements of subsection A of this section.
2. Successfully complete all background screening and training requirements.
3. Not be a prohibited possessor as defined in §13-3101 or as described in 18 United States Code §922.
4. Not have been discharged from the armed services of the United States under other than honorable conditions.
5. Not have been convicted of any crime involving domestic violence as defined in §13-3601.

32-2623. Application for employee registration certificate

A. Every application for an employee registration certificate must set forth verified information to assist the department in determining the applicant's ability to meet the requirements set forth in this chapter, as follows:

1. The full name and address of the applicant.
2. Fingerprints of the applicant of a quality and number prescribed by the department for the purpose of obtaining state and federal criminal records checks pursuant to section 41-1750 and Public Law 92-544. The department may exchange this fingerprint data with the federal bureau of investigation. The department may conduct periodic state criminal history checks to ensure continued qualification under this chapter.
3. Photographs of the applicant of a number and type prescribed by the department.
4. Such other information, evidence, statements or documents as may reasonably be required by the department.
B. An application for an original or renewal security guard or armed security guard registration certificate shall be accompanied by:
1. The fees prescribed pursuant to section 32-2607.
2. A statement from the applicant's employer requesting and authorizing armed security guard registration status for the applicant.
C. If an application is incomplete, the department shall notify the applicant pursuant to section 41-1074. If the department requires additional information to make a decision on registration, the department shall notify the applicant pursuant to section 41-1075. The department shall send notices issued under this subsection to the applicant's last known residential address and shall include sufficient information to assist the applicant to complete the application process. The applicant has forty-five calendar days from the date of notification to provide the additional documentation. If the applicant fails to respond within forty-five calendar days, the application and any certificates issued are automatically suspended until the department receives the necessary documentation to approve or deny the application.

32-2624. Issuance of security guard provisional certificate, registration certificate and identification card

A. After investigation, the department shall issue a security guard registration certificate or armed security guard registration certificate under this chapter to any applicant who satisfactorily complies with this chapter. Each security guard registration certificate shall contain the name and address of the registrant and the number of the certificate and shall be issued for two years.
B. When a security guard registration certificate is issued, an identification card as described in §32-2633 shall be issued to the registrant. The identification card is evidence that the person is a duly registered security guard. An employee must obtain an armed security guard registration certificate and identification card for each sponsoring agency licensee.
C. A security guard employee may not possess or carry a firearm while on official duty unless the employee is currently registered as an armed security guard and is authorized by the person's employer to possess or carry the firearm.

32-2632. Duty of licensee to provide training of security guards; records; firearms training

A. An agency licensee shall provide eight hours of preassignment training of all persons employed as security guards before the employee acts in the capacity of a security guard. The required training curriculum shall be established by the department.

B. All renewal applicants shall complete eight hours of refresher training within ninety days before submitting a renewal application. The department shall establish the required training curriculum.
C. Every agency licensee shall keep an accurate and current record of pertinent information on all persons employed as security guards, which shall be made available to the department in the event of an alleged violation of this chapter.
D. At least sixteen hours of initial firearms instruction and eight hours annual continuing firearms instruction in the use of the weapon used by the security guard is required if a firearm is used within the scope of employment. All firearms training and qualifications shall be conducted by a firearms instructor certified by the department and shall be completed before the security guard is assigned to any position requiring the carrying of a firearm. The licensee shall provide a monthly report to the department identifying all armed security guards employed by the agency.
E. The department shall adopt rules for both of the following:
1. Certification of firearms instructors who provide the firearms training required by subsection D.
2. A firearms training curriculum.

32-2635. Uniform and insignia
A. The particular type of uniform and insignia for a security guard or an armed security guard shall be subject to approval by the director and shall be such that it will not deceive or confuse the public or be identical with that of any law enforcement officer of the federal government, the state or any political subdivision thereof. Shoulder identification patches shall be worn on all uniform jackets, coats and shirts and shall include the name of the agency licensee. Shoulder identification patches or emblems shall not be less than two inches by three inches in size.
B. No badge or shield shall be worn or carried by a security guard, an armed security guard or an employee or registrant of any patrol service agency or private security guard agency, unless previously approved by the director.

32-2636. Grounds for disciplinary action; emergency summary suspension; judicial review
A. The following constitute grounds for disciplinary action against a licensee or registrant, or if the licensee is other than an individual, against its qualifying party or any of its associates, directors or managers:
7. Committing an act of misconduct involving a weapon pursuant to section 13-3102.

32-2637. Violations; classification
Any person who violates any of the provisions of this chapter is guilty of a class 1 misdemeanor.

32-2640. Grounds for refusal to issue an agency license
A. Except as provided in subsection E of this section the department may deny an agency license if the individual applicant, or if the applicant is other than an individual, any qualifying party:
1. Does not meet the requirements prescribed in §32-2612.
D. If an applicant is denied an agency license, the applicant may petition the board for a good cause exception.
E. If the board granted a licensee a good cause exception pursuant to §32-2609, the department may not deny the licensee's renewal application based on factors already reviewed by the board when granting the good cause exception.

32-2641. Grounds for refusal to issue a security guard provisional certificate or registration certificate; judicial review; good cause exceptions
A. Except as provided in subsection F of this section the department may deny a security guard provisional certificate, a security guard registration certificate or an armed security guard registration certificate if the applicant:
1. Does not meet the requirements prescribed in §32-2622 for the appropriate type of certificate.
2. Has committed any act which would be grounds for the suspension or revocation of a security guard registration pursuant to this chapter.
3. Has knowingly made any statement which is false in his application.
B. If the director determines that an applicant's criminal history contains open arrest information, the director shall:
1. Issue a notice to the applicant allowing forty-five days for the applicant to provide documentation concerning the disposition of the arrest or arrests.
2. Send to the applicant at the applicant's last known residential address sufficient information to assist the applicant in complying with the director's request under paragraph 1 of this subsection.
C. If the applicant fails to respond within forty-five days to the director's request under subsection B, paragraph 1, the applicant's certificate is automatically suspended until the department receives the necessary documentation to approve or deny the application.
D. The denial of the issuance of a provisional or registration certificate under this article shall be in writing and shall describe the basis for the denial. The denial shall inform the applicant that if the applicant desires a hearing by the private investigator and security guard hearing board to contest the denial, the applicant shall submit his request in writing to the director within thirty days of service of the denial. Service is complete on the mailing of the denial to the address listed on the application.
E. If an applicant is denied a registration certificate, the applicant may petition the board for a good cause exception.
F. If the board granted an applicant for a security guard registration certificate or an armed security guard registration certificate a good cause exception pursuant to §32-2609, the department may not deny the person's renewal application based on factors already reviewed by the board when granting the good cause exception.

TITLE 33 • PROPERTY

33-1125. Personal items
The following property of a debtor used primarily for personal, family or household purposes shall be exempt from process:
7. One typewriter, one bicycle, one sewing machine, a family bible, a lot in any burial ground, one shotgun or one rifle or one pistol, not in excess of an aggregate fair market value of five hundred dollars.

33-1315. Prohibited provisions in rental agreements
A. A rental agreement shall not provide that the tenant does any of the following:

1. Agrees to waive or to forego rights or remedies under this chapter.

33-1368. Noncompliance with rental agreement by tenant; failure to pay rent; utility discontinuation; liability for guests; definition

2. ... If there is a breach that is both material and irreparable and that occurs on the premises, including but not limited to an illegal discharge of a weapon, homicide as defined in sections 13-1102 through 13-1105, prostitution as defined in §13-3211, criminal street gang activity as prescribed in §13-105, activity as prohibited in §13-2308, the unlawful manufacturing, selling, transferring, possessing, using or storing of a controlled substance as defined in §13-3451, threatening or intimidating as prohibited in §13-1202, assault as prohibited in §13-1203, acts that have been found to constitute a nuisance pursuant to §12-991 or a breach of the lease agreement that otherwise jeopardizes the health, safety and welfare of the landlord, the landlord's agent or another tenant or involving imminent or actual serious property damage, the landlord may deliver a written notice for immediate termination of the rental agreement and shall proceed under §33-1377.

TITLE 36 • PUBLIC SAFETY

36-1601. Definitions
In this article, unless the context otherwise requires:
1. "Consumer firework" means small firework devices that contain restricted amounts of pyrotechnic composition designed primarily to produce visible or audible effects by combustion and that comply with the construction, chemical composition and labeling regulations prescribed in 49 Code of Federal Regulations part 172 and 173, regulations of the United States consumer product safety commission as prescribed in 16 Code of Federal Regulations parts 1500 and 1507 and the American pyrotechnics association standard 87-1, standard for construction and approval for transportation of fireworks, novelties and theatrical pyrotechnics, December 1, 2001 version.
2. "Display firework" means large firework devices that are explosive materials intended for use in fireworks displays and designed to produce visible or audible effects by combustion, deflagration or detonation as prescribed by 49 Code of Federal Regulations part 172, regulations of the United States consumer product safety commission as prescribed in 16 Code of Federal Regulations parts 1500 and 1507 and the American pyrotechnics association standard 87-1, standard for construction and approval for transportation of fireworks, novelties and theatrical pyrotechnics, December 1, 2001 version.
3. "Fireworks":
(a) Means any combustible or explosive composition, substance or combination of substances, or any article prepared for the purpose of producing a visible or audible effect by combustion, explosion, deflagration or detonation, that is a consumer firework or display firework.
(b) Does not include:
(i) Toy pistols, toy canes, toy guns or other devices in which paper caps containing not more than twenty-five hundredths grains of explosive compound are used if constructed so that the hand cannot come in contact with the cap when in place for the explosion.
(ii) Toy pistol paper caps that contain less than twenty-hundredths grains of explosive mixture, or fixed ammunition or primers therefor.
(iii) Federally deregulated novelty items that are known as snappers, snap caps, party poppers, glow worms, snakes, toy smoke devices and sparklers.
4. "Governing body" means the board of supervisors of a county as to the area within the county but without the corporate limits of an incorporated city or town and means the governing body of an incorporated city or town as to the area within its corporate limits.
5. "Permissible consumer fireworks":
(a) Means the following types of consumer fireworks as defined by the American pyrotechnics association standard 87-1, standard for construction and approval for transportation of fireworks, novelties and theatrical pyrotechnics, December 1, 2001 version:
(i) Ground and handheld sparkling devices.
(ii) Cylindrical fountains.
(iii) Cone fountains.
(iv) Illuminating torches.
(v) Wheels.
(vi) Ground spinners.
(vii) Flitter sparklers.
(viii) Toy smoke devices.
(ix) Wire sparklers or dipped sticks.
(x) Multiple tube fireworks devices and pyrotechnic articles.
(b) Does not include anything that is designed or intended to rise into the air and explode or to detonate in the air or to fly above the ground, including, for example, firework items commonly known as bottle rockets, sky rockets, missile-type rockets, helicopters, torpedoes, roman candles and jumping jacks.
6. "Person" includes an individual, partnership, firm or corporation.

36-1602. Fireworks prohibited
A. Except as otherwise provided by this article, it is unlawful to sell, offer or expose for sale, use, explode or possess any fireworks.
B. This section shall not be construed to prohibit or restrict the manufacture or possession, by a qualified pyrotechnic expert, of aerial set pieces designed for use in pyrotechnical displays, or the display of such set pieces in accordance with the terms of this article. The governing body as defined by §36-1601 shall determine if the expert is qualified.

36-1603. Permit for public display

A. Each governing body may adopt reasonable rules and regulations for granting permits for supervised public displays of fireworks within its jurisdiction, by municipalities, fair associations, amusement parks and other organizations and groups.

B. Application for a permit shall be made in writing not less than five days prior to the date of the display. Every display shall be handled by a competent operator, and shall be of a character and located, discharged and fired so that it will not be hazardous to property or endanger any person. Before a permit is granted, the operator, location and handling of the display shall be approved, after investigation, by the fire chief of the city or town or the sheriff of the county as is appropriate. After a permit is granted, the sale, possession, use and distribution of fireworks for the display shall be lawful for that purpose only. No permit is transferable or assignable.

C. If a community, organization or group authorized under this article to obtain a permit for a public display of fireworks desires a permit for a locality more than fifty miles from the county seat and not within the limits of an incorporated city or town, application may be made to the justice of the peace of the precinct in which that locality is situated. The justice may issue the permit, subject to the conditions prescribed by this article, in the same manner as the board of supervisors. The constable shall make the prescribed investigation. The justice of the peace shall promptly report to the board of supervisors any permit issued by him pursuant to this subsection, and shall transmit the bond of the permittee to the board.

36-1604. Bond of permittee

The governing body shall require each permittee to give a satisfactory bond in a principal amount not less than five hundred dollars, conditioned upon payment of all damages which may be caused to persons or property by reason of the display.

36-1605. Permitted uses

This article does not prohibit:

1. The sale at wholesale by a resident wholesaler, dealer or jobber of fireworks that are not prohibited by this article.
2. The sale of fireworks that are to be and are shipped directly out of the state.
3. The use of fireworks by railroads or other transportation agencies for signal purposes or illumination.
4. The sale or use of explosives for blasting or other legitimate industrial purposes.
5. The use of fireworks or explosives, or both, by farmers, ranchers and their employees, and by state and federal employees who manage wildlife resources, to rally, drive or otherwise disperse concentrations of wildlife for the purpose of protecting property or wildlife.
6. The sale of permissible consumer fireworks by a retail establishment if the retail establishment complies with the rules adopted pursuant to §36-1609.
7. The use of permissible consumer fireworks by the general public, unless the use is prohibited by a governing body of an incorporated city or town.

36-1606. Consumer fireworks regulation; state preemption; further regulation of fireworks by local jurisdiction

A. The sale and use of permissible consumer fireworks are of statewide concern. The regulation of permissible consumer fireworks pursuant to this article and their use is not subject to further regulation by a governing body, except that an incorporated city or town in a county with a population of less than five hundred thousand persons may regulate the use and sale of permissible consumer fireworks within its corporate limits and a county with a population of less than five hundred thousand persons may regulate the use and sale of permissible consumer fireworks within the unincorporated areas of the county when a federal or state agency implements stage one fire restrictions in any portion of the county.

B. In a county with a population of more than five hundred thousand persons, an incorporated city or town may regulate the use and sale of permissible consumer fireworks within its corporate limits and the county may regulate the use and sale of permissible consumer fireworks within the unincorporated areas of the county.

C. Except as provided in § 36-1608 and notwithstanding subsection B of this section:

1. The sale of permissible consumer fireworks shall be allowed from May 20 through July 6 and December 10 through January 3 each year.
2. The use of permissible consumer fireworks shall be allowed from June 24 through July 6 and December 24 through January 3 each year.

D. This article does not prohibit the imposition by ordinance of further regulations and prohibitions on the sale, use and possession of fireworks other than permissible consumer fireworks by a governing body. A governing body shall not permit or authorize the sale, use or possession of any fireworks in violation of this article.

36-1607. Seizure

The Arizona highway patrol or any sheriff or other peace officer shall seize, remove or cause to be removed, at the expense of the owner, all fireworks or combustibles offered or exposed for sale, stored or possessed in violation of this article.

36-1608. Violation; classification

A. A person violating a provision of this article is subject to a civil penalty of one thousand dollars.

B. A person who uses fireworks or permissible consumer fireworks on preservation lands owned by a city or town that has purchased more than fifteen thousand acres of land for preservation purposes is guilty of a class 1 misdemeanor and shall pay a fine of at least one thousand dollars.

36-1609. State fire marshal; adoption of code; sale of permissible consumer fireworks

A. The state fire marshal shall adopt rules pursuant to title 41, chapter 6 to carry out this article, including a rule that adopts the national fire protection association code for the manufacture, transportation, storage and retail sales of fireworks and pyrotechnic articles, 2013 edition as published in August, 2012. A person who sells permissible consumer fireworks to the public shall comply with those rules relating to the storage of consumer fireworks and relating to the retail sales of consumer fireworks before selling permissible consumer fireworks to the public.

B. A person shall not sell or permit or authorize the sale of permissible consumer fireworks to a person who is under sixteen years of age.

36-1610. Prohibited use of fireworks on state land; civil penalty

A. The state fire marshal may impose a civil penalty of one thousand dollars for each incident of prohibited use of fireworks

on state land in violation of this article.
B. The state fire marshal shall deposit, pursuant to §§35-146 and 35-147, civil penalties collected pursuant to this section in the fire suppression revolving fund established by §37-623.02.

TITLE 38 • PUBLIC OFFICERS AND EMPLOYEES

38-1102. Carrying of firearms by peace officers; exceptions; definitions

A. Notwithstanding any other law and except as provided pursuant to subsection C of this section, a peace officer shall not be prohibited from carrying a firearm if the peace officer is in compliance with the firearm requirements prescribed by the Arizona peace officer standards and training board.
B. Notwithstanding any other law and except as provided pursuant to subsection C, paragraphs 1, 2, 4, 5, 6, 7 and 8 of this section, a retired peace officer shall not be prohibited from carrying a firearm.
C. A peace officer or retired peace officer may be prohibited from carrying a firearm as follows:
1. In a jail, correctional facility or juvenile detention facility.
2. Except for peace officers acting in their official capacity and carrying official peace officer identification, by order of:
(a) The presiding judge or justice when attending any court that is established pursuant to the constitution of this state or title 12, except if the peace officer or retired peace officer is providing court security or responding to an emergency.
(b) A justice court when attending the justice court, except if the peace officer or retired peace officer is providing court security or responding to an emergency.
(c) A municipal court when attending the municipal court, except if the peace officer or retired peace officer is providing court security or responding to an emergency.
3. When the peace officer is relieved of duty and is under a criminal or administrative investigation.
4. When in a secured police facility.
5. When consuming alcohol at a licensed liquor establishment, except if a peace officer's employing agency authorizes the consumption of alcohol in the performance of the peace officer's duties.
6. In a location prohibited by federal law.
7. Pursuant to court order.
8. Pursuant to any state or federal law that makes the officer a prohibited possessor.
9. When in the judgment of the department head, or the department head's designee, the peace officer exhibits any impairment, including any physical or mental impairment that would cause concern for the well-being and safety of the officer, the officer's law enforcement agency, law enforcement agency employees or the community.
E. A presiding judge may establish rules or policies that are consistent with this section for the protection of the court.
F. This section does not create any civil liability for acting or failing to act.
G. For the purposes of this section:
1. "Firearm" has the same meaning prescribed in §13-105.
2. "Peace officer" has the same meaning prescribed in §1-215.
3. "Relieved of duty" means when a peace officer is no longer required to perform, either temporarily or permanently, the duties for which the officer was employed.
4. "Retired peace officer" means a person who has honorably served as a law enforcement officer in the United States for at least ten consecutive years and who possesses a photographic identification or a letter from a law enforcement agency that states the person has served for at least ten consecutive years as a law enforcement officer in the United States.
5. "Secured police facility" means a building or structure that is used primarily by a public agency and that is not accessible to the general public except by controlled access. <Gun "rights" enacted for police in 2007, HB2457, as amended>

TITLE 41 • STATE GOVERNMENT

41-860.02. State firearm
The Colt single action army revolver is the official state firearm.

41-1967. Child care resource and referral system
E. Child care home providers identified in subsection c, paragraph 2 of this section may be excluded or removed from the child care home provider registry and the child care resource and referral database if:
7. The provider fails to separately store firearms and ammunition under lock and key or combination lock.

41-4201. Arizona rangers
The Arizona rangers are an unpaid, noncommissioned civilian auxiliary that is available for the purpose of assisting and supporting law enforcement in this state. The Arizona rangers do not possess any law enforcement or investigative powers that are not provided or established in law for all citizens of this state. Law enforcement support and assistance services are provided on the request of, and under the direction, control and supervision of, established law enforcement officials or officers.

STATE CONSTITUTION, ARTICLE 16 • MILITIA

§1. Composition of militia
Section 1. The militia of the state of Arizona shall consist of all capable citizens of the state between the ages of eighteen and forty-five years, and of those between said ages who shall have declared their intention to become citizens of the United States, residing therein, subject to such exemptions as now exist, or as may hereafter be created, by the laws of the United States or of this state.

§2. Composition and designation of organized militia
Section 2. The organized militia shall be designated "The National Guard of Arizona," and shall consist of such organized military bodies as now exist under the laws of the territory of Arizona or as may hereafter be authorized by law.

§3. Conformity to federal regulations
Section 3. The organization, equipment, and discipline of the national guard shall conform as nearly as shall be practicable to the regulations for the government of the armies of the United States.

About Alan Korwin

Alan Korwin, author of six books and co-author of eight others, is a full-time freelance writer, consultant and businessman with a thirty-year track record. He is a founder and two-term past president of the Arizona Book Publishing Association, which has presented him with its Visionary Leadership award, named in his honor, the Korwin Award. He has received national awards for his publicity work as a member of the Society for Technical Communication, and is a past board member of the Phoenix, Arizona chapter of the Society of Professional Journalists.

Mr. Korwin wrote the business plan that raised $5 million in venture capital and launched the in-flight catalog *SkyMall*; he did the publicity for Pulitzer Prize cartoonist Steve Benson's fourth book; working with American Express, he wrote the strategic plan that defined their worldwide telecommunications strategy for the 1990s; and he had a hand in developing ASPED, Arizona's economic strategic plan. His writing appears nationally regularly.

Korwin turned his first book, *The Arizona Gun Owner's Guide*, into a self-published best-seller, now in its 26th edition. With his wife Cheryl he operates Bloomfield Press, which has grown into the largest publisher and distributor of gun-law books in the country. Built around ten books he has written on the subject, it includes the unabridged federal guides *Gun Laws of America* and *Supreme Court Gun Cases*, a line of more than 300 books, buttons and DVDs, and more than 1,000 radio and TV appearances. He was an invited guest at the U.S. Supreme Court for oral argument in *D.C. v. Heller*, which led to his 11th book, *The Heller Case: Gun Rights Affirmed*. His 12th book, on the limits of free speech, *Bomb Jokes at Airports*, was followed by *After You Shoot: Your gun's hot. The perp's not. Now what?* In 2014 he made national headlines, winning the First Amendment "Guns Save Lives" censorship case against the city of Phoenix.

Alan Korwin is originally from New York City, where his clients included IBM, AT&T, NYNEX and others, many with real names. He is a pretty good guitarist and singer, with a penchant for parody (his current band is The Cartridge Family). In 1986, finally married, he moved to the Valley of the Sun. It was a joyful and successful move.

Bloomfield Press has it all—
State-by-state gun-law guides
National gun-law guides
Tactics and strategies for personal safety

Books, DVDs and eBooks for:
Newcomers, Advanced Students, Instructors
Men, Women, Children, Political Activists

Call for our free full-color catalog
or just look or download it online

| California | Florida | Indiana | Kansas | Massachusetts | Michigan |
| #CA $24.95 | #FL $34.50 | #IN $26.95 | #KS $24.95 | #MA $24.50 | #MI $19.95 |

| Minnesota | Missouri 1 | Missouri 2 | Montana | Nevada | New Hampshire |
| #MN $24.95 | #MO $23.95 | #MOE $24.95 | #MT $12.95 | #NEV $8.95 | #NH $24.95 |

| New Mexico | New Jersey | New York | North Carolina | Ohio 1 | Ohio 2 |
| #NM $10.95 | #NJ $49.95 | #NY $38.95 | #NC $25.00 | #OH $19.95 | #OH2 $19.95 |

| Oregon | South Carolina | Tennessee | Utah | Vermont | Washington |
| #OR $12.95 | #SC $24.95 | #TN $14.95 | #UT $19.95 | #VT $15.00 | #WA $10.95 |

More than 300 items—call or visit online!

Published by
BLOOMFIELD PRESS